GETTING AHEAD

GETTING AHEAD

A Family's Journey

—— FROM ——

ITALIAN SERFDOM TO AMERICAN SUCCESS

DEAN "DINO" CORTOPASSI

BLACK HOLE PRESS

Black Hole Press
11292 North Alpine Road
Stockton, CA 95212

ISBN 978-0-9905092-0-2
Printed in Canada

First Edition

ACKNOWLEDGMENTS

ALTHOUGH MY NAME is on the cover, I would be greatly remiss to not acknowledge the significant contributions of several persons during the four-year gestation period of this book.

First and foremost is Bruce Henderson, who was originally engaged as a ghostwriter to help me in putting together multi-generational stories I wanted to recount. Bruce contributed greatly in the early going, interviewing me during many half-day sessions at San Tomo. The persistence of his follow up "rolling why" questioning throughout those many, many hours, stimulated my specific recollections in vivid "I said—he said" detail akin to replaying a movie reel! Absent Bruce's enthusiastic and persistent oral interviewing, that vivid recall would have remained locked inaccessibly in my deep memory.

I do enjoy recounting stories, and those taped interviews produced so much material we needed a professional service to convert oral tape to a voluminous amount of typed text. Additionally, Bruce interviewing partners and colleagues produced even more text. The combination was way too much, and it became clear that a whole lot of episode elimination/plus text condensing was necessary.

As that shrinking process progressed, I came to feel that Bruce was "not speaking in my voice," so I took over selecting the episodes and drafting the manuscript. Bruce, the latter notwithstanding, my warmest thanks for your dynamic early contributions, which provided an abundant episodic base from which to choose. I hope readers are as engaged as you were throughout the entire inter-viewing process.

Sandy Ervine has served as my Executive Assistant for more years than either of us wishes to acknowledge. In addition to her over-flowing plate of managing my calendar/correspondence and pub-lishing the San Tomo Digest; Sandy performed yeoman service in re-typing my manuscript drafts ad infinitum! (My perfectionist habit resulted in laborious editing/re-editing/re-re-editing, to get the "final-final" copy into my comfort zone.) Sandy's patience and encouragement—"It's really interesting Dino—keep going" were key to my eventually staggering over the finish line. Sandy, thank you for your ongoing encouragement, patience, and good work!

As we entered the home stretch, like California Chrome at the Belmont, I was definitely running out of gas! Pulling together photos from a very wide range of sources, and somehow creating manageable order out of pictorial chaos, Christine Wabakken and Ann Bell were indispensable. After their/my winnowing down pro-cess, they worked hand-in-hand with photographer Dick Belcher to convert disparate colors/disparate sizes/disparate textures, (from originals of many years) into the reproduced versions depicted herein. Since I intended that the text focus is mostly on business activity; the photo sections focus is mostly on family activities, which are in fact, the truest measure of life success. Christine and Ann, thank you for your organizational skills in getting us through the photo selection process.

Diane Gedymin served as publisher, which I belatedly came to learn, involved quite a number of editorial specialists, all of whom endeavored to "professionalize" the final product. Notwithstanding my own desire for perfection, the professionalizing got to the point where I threw up my hands; "Enough already! I'm tired and don't care if it reads or looks professional. Let's just get the damn thing printed!" Diane, thank you for bringing talented people to this project, and for accepting my need to calve this long-gestating elephant!

In the last 100 yards to the finish line, Ann Bell again rode to the rescue! Working closely with Art Director Pauline Neuwirth,

Ann managed the complex cross-currents of paper alternatives (pro's/con's); photo placement alternatives (pro's/con's); and related hurdles to producing the final product. Ann divides Executive Assistant responsibilities with Sandy, and is my "go-to" Manager of a wide range of special projects. Annie, I'm deeply grateful for your getting this project across the finish line. Mille Grazie!

Finally, thank you dear reader for overlooking any shortcomings of form or substance you may find. I tend to write the way I talk and this book represents my best efforts to truthfully describe our family's multi-generational trek from Italian serfdom to American Success. Thanks for your interest in our story, and feel free to express any feedback you wish to pass along.

Ciao, e tutte buone cose nel futuro!

DISTILLED WISDOM
(DINO'S FAVORITES)

Opportunities sometimes arrive disguised as insoluble problems.

Life is a banquet but many choose to starve.

Chance favors the prepared mind.

Get in position to get lucky.

Hunt where the ducks are.

Arithmetic is not an opinion.

Loyalty is a two-way street.

What gets measured gets done.

Look for the big end of the cow.

You can't make good wine from bad grapes.

Eat your veggies before reaching for dessert.

When in doubt, tell the truth—it's easier to remember.

Better a horse that needs the rein than one that needs the whip.

If you don't know the destination, any road
gets you there.

Don't make promises you can't keep.

Nothing sells like the truth.

Dumb it down to farmer level.

To prevent forest fires, look for wisps of smoke.

Tell me the time — not how to make a watch.

Good judgment comes from having experience;

experience comes from having bad judgment.

Great strategy and average tactics

beats average strategy and great tactics.

Customer loyalty is earned one at a time.

You can't sell from an empty wagon.

We're not for everyone.

When up to your ass in alligators, try to remember
the mission was draining the swamp!

CONTENTS

AS I STOOD at the podium, facing a glittering gala of 700 members and guests of the Horatio Alger Association gathered to honor the 2005 award recipients, I thought of my late father, Amerigo Cortopassi and was flooded with emotion. Like so many other Italians of his era, immigration to the United States meant escape from the lack of opportunity and a chance to achieve the American dream.

"In humbly accepting this award, please understand I stand here not as a self-made man, but rather as the proxy for key contributors to my life mosaic. Those key persons include immigrant parents who instilled the ethic of family honor, a strong focus on results, and their great love of America. Of course, the most key person in my mosaic is Joan, who in the course of our 47-year marriage was a steadfast partner through thick and thin, diligently strove to smooth my sharp edges, and is the mother of our four terrific children, Gino, Katie, Becky, and Dave."

I then asked Joan and our adult sons, daughters and their spouses to stand and share the spotlight.

Accompanying our family to Washington, D.C. were 30 relatives, friends and business colleagues, all of whom flew with us from California in three chartered Gulfstream jets. They, too, were contributors to the mosaic along the way, and I wanted to share this special occasion with them.

Named for the mid-19th century author of hundreds of rags-to-riches booklets, the Horatio Alger Association annually selects ten Americans for their own remarkable stories of overcoming adversity. Through its activities, the Association raises and distributes $5 million a year in need-based scholarships to high school seniors who have achieved scholastic success despite heart-wrenching family circumstances.

In my acceptance remarks I wanted to reach out to the attending National Scholars with comments useful to their own future careers. "Like my fellow inductees I encountered adversities early in life and throughout my career," I said. "In retrospect, the best part of facing those challenges came more from the satisfaction of *achieving*, rather than from the *achievement*." Those early adversities helped me understand that from time to time life presents us with opportunity which arrives cleverly disguised as an insoluble problem.

"That understanding led me to hang two framed quotations side-by-side on my office wall that I followed throughout my business career. The first is from Dr. Louis Pasteur, the great French researcher, who postulated: Chance Favors the Prepared Mind. The second is my personal interpretation of Pasteur's postulate: Get in Position to Get Lucky!

"Scholars, I believe a prepared mind arises from a life-long thirst for knowledge. Preparing the mind requires an insatiable desire to learn the why of things. Then when life presents a disguised opportunity, a prepared mind helps you see through the disguise and get lucky. I urge you to develop a life-long habit of seeking the why of things, which prepares your mind to recognize opportunity when others see only a problem."

When my father and his immigrant contemporaries arrived in America, their dreams were relatively simple—to Get Ahead. In their own words: *Fare progressi.* I was born in 1937, and as far back as I remember "getting ahead" was a goal my father's generation shared.

Most immigrants came to America to escape *la miseria*, the grinding poverty and limited possibilities of the old country. With no money, three grades of elementary education, and limited employable skills, their early years in America meant working hard at menial jobs, living frugally, and saving for the future. Their Getting Ahead dreams included being able to buy a home some day, or perhaps some land, to provide better education for their kids, and to gain family security.

In most cases the Italian-immigrant community rooted for each other's success. As a boy, I often heard my father and his friends speaking about someone who had secured a good job, or bought a house, or in some other way improved his lot in life. One of them would say, *"Vedi, Luigi fa progressi!"* (See, Luigi is getting ahead!), and all would nod approvingly.

My own story about Getting Ahead begins *before* my father arrived in San Joaquin County in December 1921 at age seventeen, *before* his marriage to my mother, Teresa Avansino in 1934, and *before* the young couple struggled through the worst years of the depression with Amerigo in farming partnership with fellow immigrants, and Teresa cooking for the partners and caring for me, their firstborn child.

It begins in the Tuscan hills above Lucca with a man named Serafino. He was my *bis-nonno* or great-grandfather, the first Cortopassi to take a giant step out of feudal serfdom by becoming a small landowner—in his time, a rare occurrence.

GETTING AHEAD

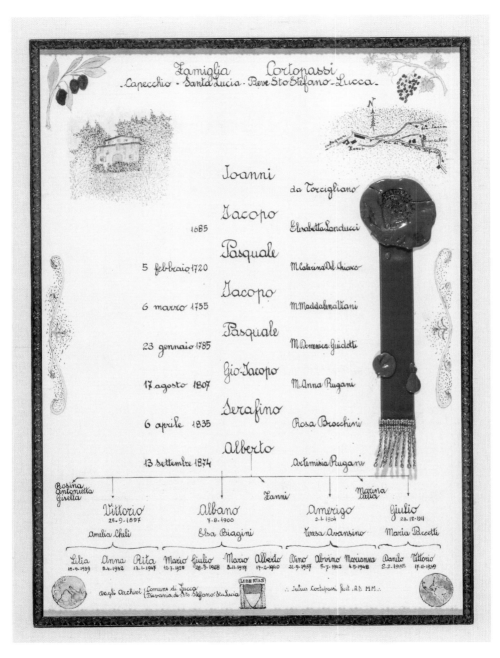

300 years of Cortopassis in one parish! This family tree researched and created by cousin Giulio Cortopassi, an architect in Lucca.

RECOGNIZING OPPORTUNITY

My great-grandfather, Serafino Cortopassi, as several generations of Cortopassis before him, worked one of the 23 small terraced farms nestled within a mountainous forested property above Lucca known as *Fattoria di Forci*. (See the genealogical chart researched by my cousin Giulio Cortopassi.) Forci had been owned by a series of noble families and its 23 tiny farms were worked by separate *contadino* (farmer) families under the feudal *Mezzadria* system. Mezzadria was the 50-50 sharecropping system whereby the *Padrone* (landowner) provided the farm and a few inputs purchased for cash from town, and the contadino family supplied 100 percent of the labor necessary to produce that farm's total output. Each of the farms had its own modest house and livestock quarters, and each had a unique name. Serafino and his family worked the Forci farm named Capecchio, which had been continuously occupied by several generations of Cortopassis, all on the Mezzadria system of tenure.

Forci's headquarters consisted of the Count/Padrone's grand villa and several large Fattoria buildings, including olive oil and wine-making facilities. Each tenant hauled his grapes and olives to the facilities to be made into wine and oil and received half of that production. Wheat was grown on the terraces between rows of grapes or olives, milk was made into cheese, and swine into cured meats,

Capecchio farmstead where Cortopassis were tenants for 250 years! Restored for summer rental by Baronessa Diamantina Scuola-Camerini, whose family owned Forci for the past 100 years.

all of which was equally split between the Padrone and the contadino. The only farm produce the contadinos kept all for themselves were free-ranging chickens and their eggs. What was left after the Padrone took his share provided little more than the family's food and clothing. As a result, *contadino* families found it very difficult to accumulate cash, or to escape sustenance level circumstances. In 19th Century Italy there was very little upward mobility!

Over time, the ambitious Serafino gained the responsibility (and very small extra stipend) of *Sotto-Fattore*—assistant to the *Fattore* (manager of the *Fattoria*) who in turn reported to the *Padrone*. However, Serafino and his family's main livelihood came from working Capecchio as contadini.

Shortly after the time of America's Civil War, Serafino and the *Fattore* visited an agricultural fair in the city of Lucca where they saw a new invention that fired Serafino's imagination. It was a rectangular wooden machine about three feet by four feet by five feet with a flywheel crank hand-powered by three men. The little machine was designed to thresh wheat and separate the kernels from the chaff.

In that era, contadino families harvested wheat as they had for generations. Mature wheat was cut at ground level with scythes, gathered into shocks, and stood with wheat heads upright to dry. After drying, the shocks were hauled from the farm terraces and spread loosely on a hard-packed central courtyard. A mule or cow hooked to a wooden roller was led round and round over the stalks to thresh the kernels loose. The straw was removed with pitchforks and hand-stacked for later use as livestock bedding. The wheat kernels and chaff left on the ground were swept into homemade flat baskets which women tossed in the air to let chaff blow away until only kernels remained in the basket. After this laborious process, half of the grain was delivered to the landlord and the other half put aside to be later ground into flour used to make the family's bread and pasta throughout the year.

As Serafino watched a demonstration of the little machine, which not only threshed the wheat but also separated the chaff from the kernels, he quickly saw it as a big technological breakthrough! Realizing the little machine could be hauled from farm to farm to do custom threshing, Serafino quickly saw the business opportunity. There was only one problem: he didn't have the cash to buy it.

On the way back from the fair, Serafino sounded out the Fattore about approaching the Padrone to loan him the money. With the Fattore's permission, Serafino presented his proposition to the Count. If he would lend him the money to buy the machine, as interest on the loan Serafino would thresh the wheat on all of Forci's farms free of charge until the debt was repaid. Because the Padrone's share of Forci's wheat crop would be of higher quality, it could be sold at higher prices.

"Fine," said the Count, "but how are you going to pay back the loan?"

Serafino explained that in addition to threshing wheat on all Forci properties, he would custom-thresh wheat for others as well, earning cash to pay off the loan. The Count admired Serafino's initiative and since it was a fair proposition, agreed to loan him the money.

I always had a great curiosity about Serafino, who I would have loved to have met, but he died before I was born. Over the years I asked many older relatives and their friends to tell me what they knew about Serafino, what he was like. Through these stories I came to feel I knew him myself, and I was struck by his vision in seeing the opportunity of the new technology and by his courage in taking on debt to back his belief.

Gradually I came to understand that Serafino was a man who planned ahead and then made his plans come true. In so doing he broke free from the economic bondage of the Mezzadria system and became the Cortopassi family's first entrepreneur.

Once Serafino had paid off his debt to the Count, he began accumulating cash which he invested in a second and then a third machine to expand his custom-threshing enterprise, demonstrating that he intuitively understood scale economics and leveraging the labor of others. As his cash flow increased, Serafino entered the landowner class by buying a tiny forested property above Forci named Macenere. So isolated it didn't have a road, everything Macenere produced had to be sledded downhill by mule, including trees sold for lumber and firewood sold for charcoal.

While continuing to support his expanding family with Capecchio's contadino income, the frugal Serafino then invested cash reserves in buying a nine-acre farm with better soil and relatively modern buildings. This farm was named Modena and produced olives, grapes, wheat, and the forage for three milk cows, all tended by a contadino family that paid a 50 percent crop-share to Serafino!

Later he bought two *campi* (a *campo* is a land measure dating from Roman times consisting of 2.2 acres) of alluvial soil adjacent to the Serchio River near the little village of Sant'Alessio.

In one remarkable lifetime Serafino, who died of an infection from a broken leg in 1923, vaulted his family from contadino serfdom into the landowner class.

I was to hear another story about Serafino, originally from two uncles, Zio Albano and Zio Giulio, which was subsequently reluctantly verified by my father. The tale was recounted as *"la leggenda di* Serafino," which I will retell as it was told to me.

While still a bachelor, Serafino was courting a young woman from a small village located one valley east of Forci and his parish of Pieve Santo Stefano. Down the mountain, across the valley, and up the next mountain Serafino would go to call upon this girl who came to believe that he intended to marry her.

One day, the girl was told by a friend, "I hear your boyfriend is getting married to someone from Pieve a Elice" (a parish on the west side of Forci). At first the girl refused to believe it but her friend said that the banns announcing the impending wedding had been posted at the Pieve Santo Stefano church. So the distraught girl got on her bicycle and traveled to see for herself. Sure enough, at the church she found the announcement of the upcoming marriage of Serafino Cortopassi to Rosa Brocchini of Pieve a Elice.

As the legend goes, the devastated young woman went looking for Serafino. Finding him at Capecchio, she allegedly placed a *maledizione* upon him saying, "Marry who you will but the voices of your children you will never hear!" (*Sposa chi ti pare pero le voce dei tuoi figli non li sentirai mai!*) With that she got back on the bike, rode away and was never heard from again.

1912—CAPECCHIO   *Serafino/Rosa Cortopassi with son Alberto's family. (Amerigo 3rd from the left in back row.)*

FAMIGLIA CORTOPASSI   -   fotografia del 1912-

1.	SERAFINO	nato	6/ 4/1835
2.	ROSA BROCCHINI (moglie)		10/11/1840
3.	GIOVANNI (Ciucci) (figlio di Serafino)		25/11/1876
4.	ALBERTO	"	13/ 9/1874
5.	ARTEMISIA RUGANI 5(moglie di Alberto)		27/ 9/1871
6.	ROSA (figlia di Alberto)		23/ 6/1894
7.	ANTONIETTA	"	23/ 6/1894
8.	GISELLA	"	4/11/1895
9.	VITTORIO	"	25/ 9/1897
10.	ALBANO	"	7/ 8/1900
11.	FANNI	"	22/ 4/1902
12.	AMERIGO	")	2/ 1/1904
13.	MARINA	"⌐	2/ 1/1906
14.	CLELIA	"	30/ 4/1908
15.	GIULIO	"	24/12/1911

Serafino did marry Rosa Brocchini, and they had three sons: my grandfather Alberto, and great-uncles Egisto and Giovanni. But here's the eerie part—*all three sons were born deaf-mutes and unable to hear or speak throughout their lives.* So Serafino never heard the voices of his children!

The three brothers were sent to a school for deaf-mutes in Siena where they learned sign language, reading, writing, arithmetic, and a trade. Egisto, the oldest, became a cabinet maker, married, and had children. As a relatively young man, he drowned one Sunday afternoon swimming in the Serchio River after a big meal. My grandfather, Alberto, learned to be a tailor and when he returned from Siena, began making men's suits for local contadini, as well as doing his share of farm work. Giovanni, the youngest, was trained as a draftsman but was emotionally unstable and lived with Alberto's family throughout his life. During WWII, returning from Macenere to Modena through the forest, he was jumped by a squad of German soldiers. Badly frightened by the experience, his mind retreated further into flights of fancy, and ultimately he was committed to an insane asylum near Lucca where I saw him during our 1947 trip to Italy.

Although he would never hear a sound nor utter a word, my grandfather Alberto was a capable man in many ways, not the least of which was siring and helping support a family of ten children after marrying my grandmother, Artemisia Rugani Cortopassi. Artemisia, who had learned sign language to communicate with Alberto, gravitated to head of business matters due to her husband's impairment. A strong personality, she was quite intelligent and capable in her own right. Of course, Alberto occasionally had strong opinions, which he voiced by making guttural sounds and signing furiously if he didn't like the way things were going. Mostly though he was a calm, dignified person.

I have many happy memories of Nonno Alberto and his beautiful cursive handwriting on onion-skin letters sent to America. In 1947, my parents, brother Alvin, and I journeyed to Italy and lived with the *Nonni* (grandparents) and their youngest son Zio Giulio and his wife Zia Maria at Modena. One year later Alberto died.

Born in 1904, my father Amerigo was the seventh of ten children and the third-born of Alberto and Artemisia's four sons. Following the end of the first World War the Italian economy was in shambles and opportunity non-existent. While the family was better off than their contadino contemporaries, Artemisia thought it best for Amerigo to immigrate to America.

Besides the widely-held Italian belief that America was the land of opportunity, Artemisia was motivated by anecdotal evidence from two Rugani nephews who had immigrated to California a decade earlier and become well-established farmers. The eldest of Artemisia's sons, Vittorio, had left for America in June 1921, and was working for the Ruganis on their farm near Stockton.

Five months after Vittorio's departure, Artemisia received a letter from nephew Giorgio Rugani advising that if she had any intention of sending another son to America, it should be sooner rather than later. The United States was in the process of passing a new immigration law which would effectively close the gates to southern European immigration by a strict quota system based on ethnic origin.

Artemisia showed the letter to Amerigo and explained that unless he departed at once when he turned 18 in January, 1922 he would be conscripted into Italy's mandatory military service, and by then America's immigration door would have slammed shut for Italians.

Amerigo asked her what he should do. Imagine the strong heart of this woman, who said, "*Sara meglio per te se vai in* America." (It will be better for you if you go to America.) Amerigo agreed and Artemisia immediately went to book passage, but Italians up and down the peninsula had bought all the steerage and cabin-class tickets on every ship. Using the family's financial horsepower, the undeterred Artemisia purchased a first-class ticket, and in December 1921 Amerigo boarded a steamer for America.

Amerigo's 1921 passport.

Italian Immigration to the United States
1870 -1941

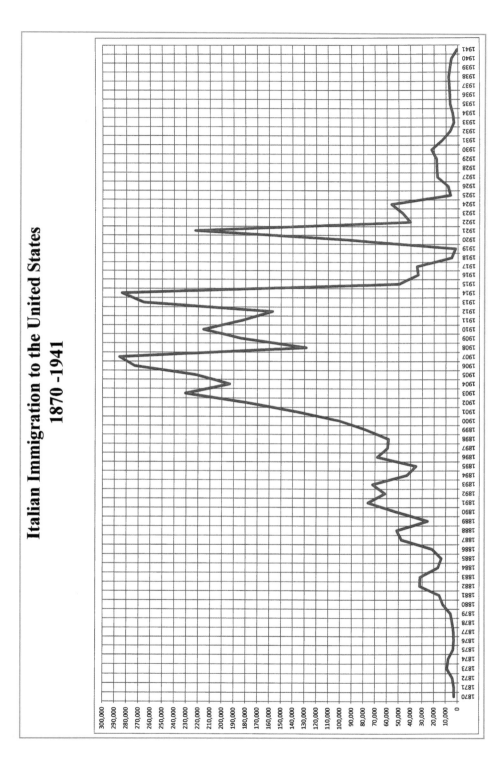

AMERIGO'S DREAM

One bright spring morning not long ago I pulled off Eight Mile Road onto a dirt driveway between two orchards near Linden, California, and drove into the yard of a faded farmhouse that needed painting. Out back was an old barn and a rundown former bunkhouse.

I do not own this property, but believe me this old farmstead would look a lot different if I did. I had driven in to have a look because it's what's left of the old Lucky Ranch where I was born and spent the first five years of my life. These days, more often than in years past, I find myself contemplating what it was like for my father getting started in this country nearly a century ago.

In the final month of his seventeenth year, and during a long seasick ocean voyage, Amerigo was befriended by a fellow Italian passenger returning to California. After de-boarding the ship in New York City, the duo got on a westbound train and four days later Amerigo arrived at the Stockton, California railroad station. He was met by his brother Vittorio who had immigrated five months earlier and two older Rugani cousins. Luigi ("Gigi") and Giorgio Rugani had immigrated from Lucca some ten years before, and had become successful farmers in the Morada area near Stockton. They served as sponsors of the two Cortopassi brothers, and provided them room and board plus the opportunity to earn some spending money doing manual labor. The following December the two Cortopassi brothers moved to the Pacific Coast near Davenport and joined some fellow *toscani* (Tuscans) in a 12-man partnership growing artichokes and Brussels sprouts on leased land.

The immigrant partnerships of that era consisted of a number of labor partners and one or two money partners joining forces to produce the labor-intensive 'chokes and sprouts in the cool, misty climate of Santa Cruz County. After deducting the landlord's crop share and the cash invested by the money partners, the remainder was divided up among the labor partners. Amerigo and Vittorio did that for a few years, but saw little possibility of Getting Ahead under those arrangements. They then returned to the Stockton area to join four other labor partners and four money partners—two of whom were the Rugani brothers—in buying 320 acres of fertile, undeveloped land.

It was this farmstead on Eight Mile Road where my father and Zio Vittorio came to live with four other bachelor labor partners; they contributed what we call today "sweat equity." The financing came from two produce shippers, an insurance man, and the two Rugani brothers. The agreed plan was to develop all 320 acres in fruit trees and start generating cash income without delay to pay off the land mortgage.

1923—SAN FRANCISCO *While working in Santa Cruz County, Amerigo posed for a picture to send back to his family.*

The first step was clearing the great number of oak trees on the property. Amerigo learned to work with dynamite to blow out large tree stumps. After clearing and burning, they worked day and night with two small tractors and drag scrapers to rough-level the land for irrigation. One year into this back-breaking work, two of the labor partners quit. Water wells were drilled, pumps installed, and annual crops of kidney beans were grown to generate a little income while the planting of cherry and peach orchards began.

After completing the development of 120 acres, the two shippers and insurance guy reneged on their financial commitment and refused to put up the money to continue development of the remaining 200 acres. Instead, they wanted to wait until the 120 acres began producing fruit, and then use that income to fund the rest of the development.

The Ruganis objected. "We promised these young men to put up the money to develop the whole ranch right away so they could earn ownership in exchange for their labor. If we stop developing now and wait for the orchards to bear, mortgage interest will pile up and these boys will never get ahead."

It soon became apparent that the only solution was to divide the partnership. Because the four labor partners wanted to continue, the Ruganis agreed to back them and suggested a traditional solution from the Old Country. "*Uno fa la parte—l'altro sciegle.*" (One divides the parts—the other chooses.) The three money men agreed and elected to be the dividers, so a lawyer drew up a contract binding both sides to the divide/choose process.

A few weeks later all hands met at the lawyer's office. The financial guys had divided the property into two parcels: the 120 acres that were developed, and the 200 acres still undeveloped. Reasoning that the under-capitalized labor partners would have to choose the 120 developed acres for its imminent cash flow, the dividers placed a very high price on it; they anticipated ending up with the undeveloped 200 acres, which they had priced at a very low value.

After huddling for a while, the Ruganis and the labor partners chose the undeveloped 200 acres. Flabbergasted and trapped by their own greed, the money men complained: "Wait a minute! We thought you would want the developed part."

The members of the Rugani group were unmoved: "You divided the parts and we chose." Matter closed.

The labor partners and Ruganis decided such an auspicious beginning deserved a special name so Lucky Ranch came into being. The work of clearing, leveling, and planting resumed with renewed gusto while the Ruganis courageously guaranteed bank loans to pay for development expenses. Growing kidney beans between the young tree rows provided a bit of cash flow to Lucky Ranch, and by 1929 it was well-known in the area as a comparatively large property owned by Italian immigrants with promising new orchards.

Turning my car around, I retraced my path on the dirt driveway back onto Eight Mile Road. As I passed an original section of cherry orchard, I pulled over. Gazing upon the 80-year-old cherry trees with huge thick trunks and gnarly limbs contorted by age, with misted eyes I envisioned my father, a strong young man who could outwork anyone, planting these trees with his partners a lifetime ago.

Like Lucky Ranch, many early orchards in the Stockton-Linden area were developed by Italian immigrants. Beginning at the turn of the century these men arrived in California knowing little other than farming because that's what contadini did for a living. Upon arrival, none of them knew English, and most had only a rudimentary three Rs education. But what they did possess was a green thumb for growing things.

Prior to immigrants' arrival, the main commercial crop in San Joaquin County was dry-land grains which, compared to fruits and vegetables, were relatively easy to grow: grain farmers harrowed barley or wheat seed into lightly-tilled soil in the fall, and when the winter rains came, the seeds sprouted and grew through the spring. Grain matured and was harvested in the summer, and crop yields were principally determined by Mother Nature.

Dry-land grain men preferred clay-type soils which hold more water to carry the crop to maturity. In the 1920s, a grain farmer might harvest 15-20 sacks of wheat per acre and sell them for $3 to $4 apiece, grossing between $40 to $80 per acre. To make any money, a grain man needed lots of acres, along with large-scale specialized machinery.

Many area landowners were pioneer families who settled the area after the 1849 gold rush. Prospectors who hadn't struck it rich came down from the hills and soon realized there was more gold in farming the great valley than in the Mother Lode streams where they had panned for gold. The principal crop planted on these vast valley acreages was dry-land grain, and the post-Gold Rush years through the mid-1880s were profitable for farmers exporting their wheat to Europe. Circa 1890, a global depression hit, and the price of wheat dropped to rock bottom and stayed there until the advent of World War I in 1915. As a result, the value of valley land declined, providing entry opportunity to green-thumb immigrants.

The primary crops for the Italian newcomers were fruit and vegetables which required much more labor to grow than grain, but had a higher dollar return per acre. In the days that grain growers were grossing $60 per acre, a fruit orchard could gross $400-$500 an acre.

The Italians looked for loamy soils that drained well, allowing tree roots to remain healthy. These soils were found on alluvial fans adjacent to rivers. Over the millennia, fast-flowing snow melt from the mountains carried soil particles in suspension to the valley floor until the flows fanned out and slowed, dropping the heavy sandy particles first, followed by loamy particles next. A sandy loam soil was excellent for growing the trees and vegetables that immigrants favored. Conversely, sandy loam was less desirable for grain farmers who preferred soils further out on the alluvial fan, where smaller soil particles—specifically, clay—eventually settled out of still waters.

That's why dry-land grain farmers tended to sell sandy loam soils to Italian and Japanese truck farmers and hold onto heavier clay soils to grow wheat. As a result, Italian immigrants ended up in concentrated communities located on or near loamy soils growing irrigated fruit and vegetable crops—the foundation upon which they built financial success. Even as their economic circumstances were improving, a major challenge lay ahead: The Great Depression.

In 1928 Lucky Ranch signed a long-term contract with Schuckle Cannery of San Jose at $35 per ton for what would be the partners' first crop of clingstone peaches, due for the first harvest in 1931. In developing their 200 acres, the partners had chosen to concentrate on both fresh-market and canning peaches because they were the fastest tree crop to generate income, coming into bearing in their third year. By contrast, cherries took six years to bear, and walnuts took eight years. Like peaches, wine grapes came into bearing in year three, but after Prohibition (1920-1932) finding a market for wine grapes was problematic.

In 1929 the stock market crash occurred and by 1931 the Great Depression had set in. With the nation's economy still worsening, by the summer of 1931 the cash price of canning peaches had dropped to $10 a ton, and Schuckle Cannery was desperate to renegotiate the Lucky Ranch contract. However, the Ruganis and their partners felt that a deal was a deal. Had the price of peaches gone above $35 a ton, they would have received no more than the contracted price, so why should they accept less because the price went the other direction? They refused to renegotiate their valid contract and started to deliver the 1931 first crop on schedule.

Schuckle Cannery set up a grading station on Lucky Ranch manned by a crop inspector who was a Schuckle employee—there was no third-party state inspection as there is today. The cannery inspector would grade the peaches for size and quality as they came in from the fields in lug boxes stacked on horse-drawn wagons.

I remember Amerigo recalling with pride the "bee-you-ti-ful" first crop of peaches from their young trees. He had driven the first wagon-load up to the grading station, then watched as the cannery's man inspected and rejected the peaches.

My father was shocked and asked why.

"They don't meet our specifications."

The second wagon-load met the same fate, and the next, and the next. For three days, the cannery inspector rejected each load of peaches Amerigo and his partners delivered to the grading station. With rejected peaches piling up on the ground, and fruit on the trees in danger of over-maturity, the cannery issued an ultimatum to Lucky Ranch: either renegotiate the contract price, or they would keep rejecting every load of the 1931 crop.

Having consulted with an attorney who reviewed the contract, the Ruganis reported that the cannery had the unilateral right to inspect and grade the peaches to any standard they chose, and failing that standard they could reject them. It was a bitter pill, but Lucky Ranch was forced to accept a renegotiated price of $17 per ton, half as much as their 1928 contract had specified.

For the rest of his life that bitter experience stuck in Amerigo's craw. He was always a man of his word who believed that a deal is a deal, and he resented what Schuckle had done to Lucky Ranch and other farmers.

In January 1934, 13 years after he came to America, 30-year-old Amerigo married Teresa Avansino, age 23. A first-generation Italian-American, she was the third child of Giacomo and Alice Avansino, who had individually immigrated to America in 1902 and 1906 from the Genova region of Italy.

Amerigo and Teresa's marriage began shortly after Lucky Ranch almost lost the farm to bank foreclosure. During the Depression there was a 25 percent unemployment rate and bread lines were everywhere. Farmers had no choice but to sell their produce at below-cost prices, and were facing disaster. What saved agriculture throughout the country was the election of Franklin D. Roosevelt in 1932.

Inaugurated in January 1933, FDR moved swiftly to bolster the nation's financial system which was teetering on collapse. The new president's first move was to declare a week-long bank holiday with all the nation's banks shut down by executive order. Prior to re-opening the banks, FDR initiated his "Fireside Chats" via radio starting the first one with, "We have nothing to fear but fear itself." Simultaneously, FDR empowered the Federal Reserve Bank to guarantee 100 percent of all bank deposits all across America. The combination stopped the panic, and when the banks reopened people gradually began re-depositing the dollars withdrawn prior to the bank holiday.

1934—LINDEN *Amerigo/Teresa's wedding with their entire bridal party, Delfina Cicerone (cousin) and Vittorio Cortopassi (brother).*

1951—AVANSINO CLAN AT FREGGIARO'S FOR HOLIDAYS.
*Nonni Giacomo/Alice Avansino, John/Ethyl, Jim/Ray Avansino, Vic/Alma, Eddy/
Nonna Pina Freggiaro, Amerigo/Teresa, Dino, Alvin, and Marianne.*

FDR followed up with the Farm Credit Act that rescued banks sinking under uncollectable farm mortgages. The Farm Credit Act offered to buy existing agricultural loans from banks at 100 percent of face value, which removed the need for banks to foreclose on those loans, and kept farms going all across the country. Saved from foreclosure, Lucky Ranch continued scraping by for six more years to the end of the Depression in 1940.

The dream of many immigrants of my father's generation was to make enough money so they could return to their families in Italy and live out their lives with some financial security, but that was not Amerigo's dream. He believed in and loved America, and embraced the future prospects for his own children in his adopted country. I grew up hearing him say hundreds of times, "God Bless America."

After working all day in the fields, he attended night school in preparation for becoming a U.S. citizen. Though learning to read English on his own was difficult, with my mother's help he did not find it drudgery at all; rather, it was a discipline he liked and undertook with real purpose. He learned about the three branches of government, the Constitution, the colonies, the Declaration of Independence, the Revolutionary War, and other topics that expanded his knowledge, his horizons, and his love for America. December 17, 1938 was a proud day for Amerigo when he was

1938—STOCKTON *Amerigo's Certificate of Citizenship, of which he was very proud!*

sworn in as a U.S. citizen in a courtroom filled with people from many lands.

Well into his golden years, my father could still recite the entire preamble of the Constitution from memory. He was proud of his Italian heritage, but to his dying day, Amerigo Cortopassi was proudest of being an American!

MY HEROES HAVE ALWAYS
BEEN FARMERS

L ike the farmer I was destined to become, I waited until after the summer harvest to be born on September 22, 1937 at Lucky Ranch. It would be a while before I appreciated that my first stroke of good luck was having Amerigo and Teresa as parents. For them there was nothing easy about those early years, but I would not trade the values lived and lessons learned for anything. Whenever I'm asked about the steps to success, I always start with: Choose good parents!

My father had a reputation as the hardest worker in the area. When it came to physical labor, no one could keep up with

1939—MICKE GROVE   *The 1939 Waterloo tug-of-war team.* BACK ROW: *Steve Sanguinetti (Coach), Louis Barosso, Marion Gogna, Joe Zolezzi, Fred Tozi, Louis Conti, Lloyd Pezzi (sponsor).* FRONT ROW: *Amerigo Cortopassi, Tonin Pezzi, John Avansino, John Garibaldi, Dave Sanguinetti. (Ten of the twelve men were farmers!)*

Amerigo Cortopassi. Only 5-foot-10 with a medium build, he was strong for his size, and took on every job with a high level of intensity—his partners nicknamed him "Bronco." Amerigo was very production-oriented; a taskmaster driven to maximizing his own and everyone else's efforts to get the most out of available resources. More so than most of his immigrant peers, Amerigo was a risk-taker, especially when it came to land acquisition. Like his grandfather Serafino, Amerigo was not afraid to take a chance when an opportunity presented itself, and he made up for a lack of formal education with sound business instincts.

My mother came at life from a different direction. Risk-averse, she always worried about my father overextending their finances whenever he took on new farm debt. Neither of my parents would have dreamed of taking on debt for personal purchases. When it came to personal expenses, their motto was pay cash or do without!

1929—STOCKTON   *18 year-old Teresa Avansino, "Miss Linden" of that year.*

Exceedingly well-organized, my mother was very process-oriented. She was a born perfectionist, always looking for the best way to do anything, and striving to be as efficient as possible.

When she reached the mandatory school age of 16, her father pulled her from the high school she loved and made her and her two siblings work full-time on the farm. Because she had more schooling than Amerigo, and because of her continuing self-education thereafter, he relied on Teresa for all of their business documents and bookkeeping. She possessed an intuitive intelligence, her thirst for knowledge was unquenchable, and she always pursued learning "the why" of things.

ABOVE: 1938—LUCKY RANCH   *What a depression era farmstead looked like.*

OPPOSITE: 1937—LUCKY RANCH   *Teresa/Dino in ranch house eating area.*

Whether the traits I inherited from my parents were genetic or ingrained through their examples I do not know. What is clear is that certain characteristics from both of them became part of my own makeup. While a number of those traits provided the foundation for business success, it is equally clear to me that their emphasis on Getting Ahead negatively affected the intensity of my personality.

After the 1939 harvest, my father sold his 25 percent share of the Lucky Ranch partnership, leased 160 acres of pasture land to develop into irrigable farm land, and moved his family into a rented house at Waterloo junction a few miles from the leased property.

The owner of the 160 acres was a man of Norwegian descent named Brandstad, whose home farm was across the road from Lucky Ranch. For many years my father had great respect for Mr.

1941—WATERLOO   *Amerigo, Dino, and 1936 Ford pickup.*

Brandstad because he was a well-educated man, and Amerigo always deferred to well-educated people because of his own limited schooling.

The deal with Brandstad was a six-year "Development Lease" wherein my father paid the costs of leveling the land for irrigation, installing a well and pump, and paying $10 per acre annual rent. It was a reasonable arrangement for both parties. After the necessary development work in the spring of 1940, Amerigo farmed the property to kidney beans as he subsequently did in 1941 and 1942.

Sometimes my father took me with him to the fields, especially when I wouldn't get in the way. Whenever he gave me a make-believe job to do—especially one that involved digging in the dirt—I just loved it. One day my mother took a snapshot of us standing in front of his 1936 Ford pickup. My father is leaning on a shovel, and I'm holding a small spade.

I wanted to be a farmer for as long as I can remember. I would play for hours in my sandbox with toy wooden tractors pulling toy discs which my father had made from scraps. I worked my sand farms like I saw he and my uncles work their farms. In those days young boys had comic-book cowboys and soldiers for heroes. I did too, but my main heroes were farmers. I looked up to my father, to his friends, to my uncles—farmers all—listening as they spoke of the weather, crops, market prices, equipment, and I remember how farming seemed so *manly*.

I started first grade a couple of weeks before my sixth birthday in a one-room, country school where a lone teacher taught first through eighth grades. Mrs. Orcutt managed this challenge by having the older students help the younger ones with reading and math, and by enforcing strict discipline.

1943—CALAVERAS SCHOOL *One-room country schoolhouse; 22 students— grades 1st through 8th; one teacher. (Dino seated right side.)*

The World War II years were profitable for American farmers because the prices for their crops skyrocketed. For example, just the cherry crop income Lucky Ranch earned in 1942 was equal to what my father had sold his 25 percent ownership share of the farm three years earlier! Any regrets Amerigo harbored about selling too early were made up for by the higher prices he was receiving for his beans. However with the jump in commodity prices, Mr. Brandstad began trying to raise Amerigo's rent on the 160 acres. (Out of respect, Amerigo always referred to him as "MISTER Brandstad.")

In his broken English, Amerigo protested, "*Mister* Brandstad, we make a deal. We have a *lista* (lease) for you farm, and la renta is $10 an acre."

If my father's crop failed or the price of beans dropped, he was required to pay the same amount of rent to Brandstad, so Amerigo didn't see why he should pay more rent just because the price of beans had gone up and he was making good money. After all, he had taken the financial risk of paying all the land development costs.

Sometime thereafter, Brandstad came to my father with a claim that Amerigo had broken the lease. "The lease requires you to level the whole ranch," he said. "There's a corner you didn't level."

In one corner of the 160-acre property, there were three acres so alkaline that not even grass would grow. As any farmer would have, my father had not even bothered to level or farm the three acres.

"The alkali corner?" Amerigo said. "Nottin' grows there!"

"It doesn't matter. The lease requires you to level all the land."

"Okay. I level it for you."

"No, now it's too late. Once the lease is broken, you can't fix it unless I agree."

That was pure baloney. The lease could have easily been remedied and Amerigo had been advised he could go to court to protect his Lessee rights. Given the higher war-time crop prices, it was of significant financial advantage for my dad to continue farming the

160 acres through the remaining term of the lease. For Amerigo, however, *this issue was larger than money.*

"*Mister* Brandstad, you giva me your word and I giva you my word!"

"The lease is the lease," Brandstad replied, looking for a way to void the agreement so he could impose a higher rent.

Amerigo was outraged and made a statement of principle. "*Mister* Brandstad, you a very rich man and you gotta lot of school. I not a rich man and I no gotta much school. But *Mister* Brandstad, my word is good and I'm a good man. Your word is no good and you a no-good *bastardo* so you take your ranch and stick it uppa yo ass."

With that, Amerigo walked away from the 160 acres he had developed and was entitled to profitably farm for another three years; he walked away from a man he had once put on a pedestal but never spoke to again in his lifetime. Amerigo was a man of principle.

Over the years, my father would sometimes repeat to me his broken-English speech to Brandstad as he tried to ingrain in me his philosophy of family honor. "Dino, remember, even if a man is not too smart, if his word is good, he's a good man. But if his word is no good, it don't matter how smart he is, he's a *no good son-of-a-bitch*! Don't do business with any man whose word is no good." It was truth revealed which in due course I would learn from experience that men's characters get tested when it's not easy to keep one's word.

The landlord's duplicitous conduct might have caused a lesser man to avoid future risks, but not Amerigo. He never wavered in his desire to Get Ahead and work hard to produce results. Shortly after walking away from the Brandstad lease, his brother-in-law and good friend, Vic Freggiaro, generously took Amerigo into a working partnership on *Barba* Vic's ("Barba" is uncle in the Genovese dialect) family farm during the remainder of the WWII years. (See the photo of Amerigo, Barba Vic, my cousin Eddy, and me on the Santa Cruz beach.)

1942—SANTA CRUZ *Cousin Eddy Freggiaro, Dino, Amerigo, and "Barba Vic" Freggiaro.*

After the war ended, Amerigo began looking for land to buy. In 1946 he and his brother Vittorio partnered with the Vignolo brothers to purchase a 1,300-acre peat-soil farm in the San Joaquin Delta. To be able to buy such a large tract of fertile land was more than any of them could have imagined doing. But the combination of a low purchase price, their combined savings, and with some bank debt, they pulled it off. The Vignolo's and Cortopassi's Getting Ahead moment was the subject of much talk and admiration within the local Italian community.

In 1945 my parents had to move out of the rented Waterloo junction house and built a modest home on a vacant lot next door to my Avansino grandparents on Pleasant Avenue. The house was in a working-class neighborhood in east Stockton, which we moved into shortly before my ninth birthday. In the meantime Amerigo had been looking for a farm to buy with the original plan being that my grandparents would move into the newer house whenever my parents bought a farm with a house on it and we moved back to the country. However, because the Vignolo-Cortopassi Delta farm was subject to flooding and unsuitable for housing, our family remained in the house next door to my grandparents where I lived until eventually going away to college.

1957—STOCKTON   *My maternal "Nonno/Nonna," Giacomo/Alice on their 50th anniversary at 936 Pleasant Avenue home.*

LEFT: 1907—OAKLAND   *The marriage of Giacomo Avansino and Alice Tabaco.*

BELOW: 1959—WATERLOO   *Surprise 25th anniversary party for Amerigo/Teresa in Vittorio/Amelia Cortopassi's basement party room.*

The end of the war did provide the opportunity for my father's long-postponed return to visit his family in Italy. After planting the Delta farm to barley in December 1946, Amerigo, Teresa, I, and my five-year-old younger brother Alvin, left for Italy in January 1947. My mother had signed me out of school for the spring semester and we planned to return in June for the summer grain harvest. This was my father's first trip back to the old country since coming to America 25 years earlier. He was eager to see his aging parents, as well as siblings and their families, and to introduce them to his wife and sons.

In January 1947 commercial air travel was still relatively novel transportation and especially so for the local Italian community. When my father announced our whole family was going to fly to Italy, friends and relatives were aghast. "That's dangerous," they said. "You'll all be killed." Undeterred, he had my mother buy four roundtrip tickets.

As it turned out, the flight *nearly did kill me*. San Francisco to New York via a United Airlines DC-4 required a fueling stop in Omaha. Besides being incredibly slow by modern standards, the lumbering DC-4 couldn't fly very high. We were in stormy January weather the entire way and I spent practically every waking moment succumbing to air sickness. Arriving at LaGuardia Airport after some 18 hours, we stayed the night in New York City.

I had barely recovered the next morning when we boarded one of the newest aircraft in the Trans-World Airlines fleet: a four-engine, tri-tail Constellation. The sleek and elegant "Connie" was slightly faster than the DC-4, but still couldn't climb above the rough weather that today's jetliners fly over at 40,000 feet. Lacking sufficient range to proceed directly across the Atlantic, the Connie flew a u-shaped route with refueling stops in Newfoundland, Labrador, Shannon, Ireland, and the Azores Islands, Portugal, before finally landing in Rome 30 hours after leaving New York. I have no idea how many pounds I had lost since leaving home, but *Italia* was the perfect place for a nine-year-old to regain his appetite!

Zio Albano and Zio Giulio were waiting for us at the Ciampino airport in Rome and it was a tearful reunion for my father with the two brothers he hadn't seen for 25 years. From that moment on my brother *"Alvino"* and I were embraced in the hugs of our extended family which consisted of our paternal grandparents, Nonno Alberto and Nonna Artemisia, 8 pairs of uncles and aunts, and 25 first cousins! During our five-month stay, I got to know and love my deaf-mute grandfather Alberto, and left with many happy memories of him. He died one year later. The visit to our family's roots continued to enrich my life through the warm relationships that were formed, and renewed during the many happy return trips Joan and I made to Italy in later years.

1947—CARIGNANO: LUCCA, ITALY *Amerigo's nine brothers/sisters/ spouses (Vittorio/Amelia in California), his parents (Alberto/Artemisia), his two sons (Dino/Alvin), and two nephews (Danilo/Vittorio).*

ABOVE: 1947—CARIGNANO   *Dino/Alvin hauling water with Zio Giulio's matched "Bruna Alpina" team.*

BELOW: 1947—CARIGNANO   *Wheat harvest at Cortopassi Farm. Zio Giulio, neighbors, Dino and Amerigo. (Nonno Alberto on straw stack.)*

MY PARENTS ALWAYS believed in the salutary benefits of work for children, a practice I would follow with our own children a generation later. Starting about age six, every day I gathered eggs from the chicken coop and made sure the rabbits were fed and had water. Periodically I had to clean out the rabbit pens, which I hated. The nature of my chores shifted when we moved to town and had fewer animals, but I still had regular chores which I was not paid for because they were considered household responsibilities.

In the summer of my tenth year, my father put me to work on the Vignolo and Cortopassi farm during the summer grain harvest. Amerigo explained that because this work was different than household chores I would be paid. Starting me off at 50 cents an hour, he encouraged me to save my earnings. I would ride my Schwinn to the Bank of America Wilson Way branch, depositing my wages in a savings account. Typical of my father's unending drive, that first job came about as a way for him to increase productivity.

My dad was in charge of the Vignolo and Cortopassi summer grain harvest and had hired a man named Ernie Perry to haul the harvested grain from the field to a commercial warehouse in Stockton. Fresh from wartime service in the U.S. Navy, Ernie had bought two ten-wheeler trucks—a 1937 Mack cab-over and a WWII military 6 X 6—to haul grain. When one truck was filled, he would drive it to Stockton, leaving the empty truck in the field. While Ernie was gone, each time its bin filled with grain the harvester, pulled by a crawler tractor, would "deadhead" travel to where the driverless truck was parked to unload. Frustrated by this lost time, Amerigo announced that I would learn to drive the truck in the field to wherever the harvester was located when its grain bin filled, thereby saving harvester deadhead time.

I was a pretty good-sized kid for my age, but even so it took a stretch to reach the truck pedals. And when I did get my feet to the gas and clutch, I had to look through the steering wheel to see where I was going.

Once Amerigo was satisfied that I wouldn't drive the truck into the drainage ditches adjoining each field, I was on my own. He made a signal flag from a piece of galvanized metal on a hinged rod, and would raise the signal whenever the harvester's bin approached full. I waited in the truck as the Cat pulled the harvester around the standing grain in a square pattern. When the flag went up, I would start the truck and drive over harvested stubble to the harvester. The tractor driver would get off the Cat and line me up so the truck's bed was centered under the harvester's unloading auger. After the harvester bin was emptied, the Cat and harvester would continue on and I'd stay where I was until the flag went up again and we repeated the process. When Ernie returned from town, he and I would switch trucks and repeat the cycle.

After a couple of weeks Amerigo figured I had learned to drive the truck well enough to unload the harvester bin "on the go." This involved driving the truck under the auger while keeping pace with the *moving harvester*! He would engage the auger and unload the bin while the harvester continued cutting grain, thereby gaining productivity.

Inside the sweltering cab, I choked on dust and grain particles and could barely see, especially when we were traveling downwind. I not only had to keep the truck aligned with the moving harvester, but also had to keep pace with its varying speed. If I went too slow, the harvester would pull ahead and augured grain would rain down on the cab of the truck. If I went too fast, augured grain would fall on the ground behind the truck.

After an all too brief break-in period Amerigo expected neither of those to happen and would get mad if any grain was spilled. To be sure, driving those big ten-wheelers and unloading on the go was a man's work, but the combination of my dad's coaching and my desire to please him resulted in getting the job done. And that's how I spent the next two summers, working the grain harvest on the Vignolo and Cortopassi farm.

When I was twelve, my father taught me to drive the Cat pulling the harvester while the Cat-skinner was on his lunch break. In those days harvester tractor drivers were known as "Cat skinners," a term derived from the "muleskinners" who expertly drove the mule teams that pulled grain harvesters in the old days. Through this lunchtime relief job I gained experience driving the Cat. But I sure wasn't as good as the regular skinner, Jim Christian, who we would pick up on Stockton's skid row each morning en route from our eastside home to the Delta. Jim was a very good Cat skinner, but he was also a wino. Periodically he would go on a bender and not show up for a day or two, greatly irritating Amerigo.

One morning when Jim wasn't waiting at the pick-up corner, my father drove around the block a few times before blowing his top and making clear with a string of curses that Jim Christian was history. In broken English and Italian he announced that he was through with winos: "Dino, from now on you gonna be the Cat skinner."

My father's job was to ride on the harvester as the "separator man," constantly watching the harvester and adjusting its settings as the grain conditions changed. In the pecking order of harvester crews, the separator man ranked at the top, closely followed by the Cat skinner with the truck tender a distant third.

The Cat skinner controlled the width of the header cut and the forward threshing speed. If the harvester was pulled too fast, grain would jam the cylinder and the harvester would throw its main flat belt. Everything would come to a standstill for 15 minutes to unplug the harvester and get the belt back on. If the harvester was pulled too slowly, threshing productivity dropped, which my father wouldn't stand for. In comparison with tractors doing tillage work, harvester Cat-skinning required much more skill.

Once again responding to my father's high expectations, I set out to fulfill my new assignment driving that Allis-Chalmers HD-7 Cat all day long. At first, limited arm strength made it difficult for me to pull the tractor's steering levers and to keep the header lined up on the grain cut. I had to put my feet up against the dashboard to gain the leverage to pull the levers. Then at each turn, the tractor had to be jack-knifed so the harvester would make a square 90-degree turn into the next side of the square.

Initially Amerigo cut me some slack, overlooking my less than optimum driving. Soon however, he was pushing me to improve. With his constant drive to maximize production, he would become irritated if I drove too slowly, or even worse drove too fast and plugged the harvester. For the first several weeks I certainly wasn't as good as Jim Christian. But then I started to grow into the job, and by season's end my father told me I was better than Jim, who we never saw again.

Working on the farm was how I spent the summers of my youth, as well as weekends and school breaks during planting seasons. I was always paid the going wage for whatever job I was doing and liked the work even though it caused me to miss out on some fun activities with my peers during vacations. Amerigo didn't give many attaboys and if I was messing up or not pulling my weight, I soon heard about it.

I remember once while I was still learning to be a Cat skinner, out of frustration with his criticism, I let slip a smart remark, "What do you expect from me? I'm just a kid."

He stared at me, then in Italian said sternly, "Listen, you're the boss's son. When you're the boss's son, you have to be better than the rest of the men. Not as good, better. You understand? Until you're better, I'm going to push you." And that was the standard he always held me to.

One Sunday Amerigo decided that we would harvest some seepage fields that were very weedy. Because the commercial warehouse in town was closed on Sunday, and we could only fill the two empty trucks, he decreed we would use Sundays for the slow grind of threshing weedy grain and fill up both the trucks ready to go to town first thing Monday morning.

The weeds were thick, and we crawled along as slow as I could make the tractor go, including riding the clutch. Inevitably a weed clump would jam the spike-toothed threshing cylinder inside the harvester, throwing the belt. To unplug the cylinder, it was my job to crawl inside the harvester "doghouse" to pull out the clump by hand while Amerigo stood outside with a crow bar and turned the cylinder backwards a little at a time.

When the cylinder was free, he would get the flat belt started back onto the pulley. After engaging the spring-loaded throttle from idle to wide open, the clutch would be slammed in, the flat belt would hopefully thread on and the cylinder would start clearing.

It was a sizzling summer day and inside the doghouse it was even hotter. Soaked with sweat and cramped in the narrow space, I started pulling out weed clumps as my father inched the cylinder backward. With a steel wall between us, we could not see each other.

Impatient as always, he yelled, "It feels loose so it's probably clean enough."

The cylinder was starting to free up, but I knew if I didn't clear all the clumps it would re-plug, re-throw the belt, and Amerigo would have a fit.

"Wait a minute," I hollered. "A little bit more."

Unfortunately he didn't hear me, and suddenly I heard the harvester engine go from idle to full roar and knew what was coming next. Amerigo had threaded the flat belt onto the pulley and was about to throw the clutch in hard, which would spin the spiked cylinder to full rpm. Although I started screaming, he couldn't hear me over the roar of the engine even though I was no more than three feet away. But that time he did two things he normally didn't do, which ever since has made me think I had a guardian angel looking out for me that day. First of all, instead of jamming the clutch hard, his usual practice, he engaged it slowly, causing the feeder chain and cylinder to start moving *slowly*.

On hands and knees in the doghouse and screaming my lungs out, I began backpedaling over the feeder chain as the spike-tooth cylinder began turning two feet in front of me. In another instant I was going to get fed head-first into the spinning spikes, which would have left little of me to put in the casket!

The second thing out of the ordinary Amerigo did that day was to lift the dust curtain and look into the doghouse. Horrified to see his son scrambling to stay out of the turning cylinder, he killed the engine and helped me crawl out of the doghouse.

Hugging each other and crying our eyes out, we sat on the harvester drawbar, shaking, sobbing and holding on to each other for a long, long time.

It had been a *very* close call—Amerigo had come within a whisker of losing his first-born son by his own hand—and we both got on our knees in the dirt and thanked God.

"Dino, the hell with these weedy fields," he told me. "We are never going to harvest on Sunday again." And we never did.

The year I turned fourteen, I was busy greasing the old harvester and overheard my dad and his partner Dave Vignolo talking nearby. To speed up the summer grain harvest, they had just purchased a new Massey-Harris self-propelled harvester and were discussing how to run both machines. Dave asked Amerigo who was going to operate the new harvester. "I think Dino can handle it," he said. "Let's put him on it."

My chest swelled because despite his demanding ways, my father was still my hero. He handed out few compliments to my face, yet here he was telling his partner that I could handle this new high-tech machine. It was a very proud moment of my young life.

During that first summer operating the self-propelled, I realized that productivity could be increased by harvesting back and forth in parallel passes rather than the way it had always been done: starting out at the field perimeter and harvesting in a square pattern on all four sides working toward the middle. The reason the old harvesters were pulled in the square pattern was because their reaping blades were on one side, which required the harvester and Cat to drive on the harvested stubble alongside the remaining grain. But the new self-propelled harvester had the reaping blades in front of its drive wheels and therefore had the option of cutting standing grain back and forth in parallel passes.

I carefully calculated the reduced turns and time saved if we changed from the square pattern to the back-and-forth pattern. Knowing Amerigo's resistance to change, I picked what I thought was a good time to bring up the new concept, showing him my diagram and simple calculations. He would have none of it.

"Everybody goes round and round the field," he exclaimed. "Are they stupid? Who do you think you are? American boy with big ideas?" For Amerigo, calling someone "American boy" was his most scathing insult. It was also used interchangeably with another insult, delivered in Italian: "*Avvocato delle ditte perse*" (lawyer of lost causes).

Later I approached Dave Vignolo who was always very kind to me and explained my calculations. He seemed persuaded by my reasoning, but didn't want to go against his partner. Dave said he would talk to Amerigo in the off-season and I finished that summer driving the new harvester in the old-style box pattern.

Next summer, as we prepared to start the grain harvest, my father told me I could use my new back-and-forth harvesting pattern. "It won't make any difference, but you go ahead and do it the way you want."

We never went back to the old square pattern, and as self-propelled harvesters became prevalent, neither did anyone else. For me this was an early example of thinking about *why* things are done the way they are—and if there is a better way—just the kind of questions my mother always asked herself. In this instance, the arrival of a new technology provided an opportunity to re-evaluate the conventional way of doing things, and make a change for the better.

I didn't know it then, but it was an early step in my long road to learning to think like a strategist.

COMING OF AGE

Children growing up in 1950s America often found themselves at odds with the lives their depression-era parents hoped for them, but none more so than the offspring of Italian immigrants.

In later years I came to recognize the origin of this tension as cultural. My father came to this country as a young man formed by Old World values. Although my mother was born here, for all practical purposes she, too, was an immigrant, given the strictly Old World household in which she grew up.

In Italy, young Italians did not aspire to achieve more than their parents, but rather to live in the same region, do the same work, share the same social standards—in short, to grow up similar to the preceding generation.

America, however, was not Italy, and the sons and daughters of immigrants were not like their parents. To remain in good graces at home we learned to respect our parents' old-world ways and to obey their rules, but outside the home, interacting with schoolmates and other non-Italian peers opened new vistas. Even though my parents loved and admired America, their culture reflected the old country. At home we were *very* Italian. Conversations at the dinner table were trilingual. My father would speak in Tuscan—"real" Italian, my mother would speak in her Genoese dialect, a distant derivative of Tuscan, or in English. After I entered first grade, I usually responded in English, although I spoke both Tuscan and Genoese.

I am chagrined to admit that when I started school and began visiting non-Italian kids' homes, I was sometimes embarrassed by the "Italian-ness" of my parents and of our home. In the 1940s being Italian was not very popular in the United States. During and after WWII there was some hostility toward Germans, Japanese, and Italians—the peoples and their products—and that changed slowly over time. I heard slurs like "Dirty Dago" many, many times and had occasional fistfights to defend being Italian.

Although everyone in the family called me Dino, in elementary school I began using Dean, my actual first name, because it sounded more American. But by the time I got to high school, "Dino" Martin was impressing young women with his "Cool Cat" image and romantic ballads. Seeing how well Italianess worked for Martin, in high school I returned to being "Dino"!

My schoolmates' parents were more permissive with their children than were mine. When I wanted to hang out with friends, I had to get my parent's permission, which not infrequently was denied, usually having to do with chores or other work they felt more useful of my time. Other than the time to play sports, I felt deprived seeing peers enjoy many more social opportunities to have fun.

There was another more painful tension in our household: my father's belief in "spare the rod and spoil the child." It is how he was raised in Italy; his parents liberally administered corporal punishment as I'm sure earlier generations of Cortopassi fathers had.

In my case, depending on my age and the offense I had committed, punishment could be delivered with swats on the hands, slaps on the face, or a leather belt on bare backsides. The last time my father tried to administer corporal punishment was at the beginning of my junior year in high school. I had an after-school job at a farm owned by a Nisei neighbor. One afternoon a friend and I cut school in the company of a couple of girls and hoped to make the most of our opportunity. With the girls in the car, I drove to my Japanese employer so I could explain the situation. "Taca" Tsutsui was a fun-loving veteran of WWII who had served in the 442nd Battalion of the U.S. Army. He laughed like hell and said, "Go have a good time."

That afternoon, Amerigo drove by the Tsutsui farm and realized I wasn't at work. Despite Taca telling him he had given me permission to try sowing some wild oats, my father's point of view was unyielding: *If you have a job, you show up.* It had to do with personal and family honor. In Amerigo's mind, I had dishonored myself and him.

I didn't come home until late that night, but the next day he charged me like an enraged bull and took a swing at my chin. I was pretty strong by then, and was able to grab his wrist, stopping his fist in midair. We stood nose-to-nose with muscles straining.

Red-faced and angry, my father stared at me.

"You are not going to hit me anymore," I said defiantly.

At that moment, realizing we had arrived at a threshold, he relaxed his arm and turned away. Thereafter, while he could still become angry, he never again tried to hit me.

In 1952, upon learning that his widowed mother was in ill health, Amerigo and I took our second trip to Italy. As we had in 1947, we left in early February, and returned in mid-June in time for the grain harvest. In planning the trip, my father explained that railroads and steamships were two modes of transportation that were not going to be around much longer and he wanted me to experience both. In Sacramento we boarded the California Zephyr with its vista-domed chair cars and Pullman sleepers, and after a 24-hour stopover in Chicago to visit an old friend, arrived in New York days later. The next morning we sailed from New York on the brand new Italian ocean liner, *Andrea Doria*—which four years later would be rammed by a Swedish ship in heavy fog, sinking with a loss of many lives.

This 1952 visit to Italy differed from our first one in 1947, no doubt in part because I was older and looking forward to meeting Italian girls. Also, my aged and failing Nonna Artemisia and Zio Giulio's family had moved from Modena—the terraced hillside farm where we had lived in 1947—to the little village of St. Alessio, a suburb of Lucca. Whereas before I had experienced farm life from another era, I now became part of village life in transition to a newer era.

Zio Giulio and Zia Maria had two boys: cousin Danilo, who was two years older than me, and Vittorio, who was two years younger. I mostly hung around with Danilo and his friends, including Vito who was 21 and the village barber. During the day while Danilo was at work, I would often sit in Vito's barbershop and listen to the customers' conversations—many of them of a political nature. The Communists were then the second largest political party in Italy. Upon learning I lived in California, the village mechanic, an outspoken Communist, would say: "Mao is going to come over from China and get you rich Americans." For the most part however, almost everyone—even complete strangers—were very friendly, especially when they learned I was an American. Although Mussolini-led Italy had joined the Axis against the Allies during World War II, most Italians looked upon Americans as their liberators.

In the nearby town of Ponte San Pietro was the home of Zio Albano, a butcher by trade. He had three sons: Giulio the eldest, an architect who had emigrated to Brazil; Mario who was my age, although already finished with school and busy learning his father's

CIRCA—2000 *Annual dinner at cousin Mario Cortopassi's house along with his brothers Giulio/Alberto, wives Lelia/Laura, and family friend Bonini.*

trade; and Alberto who was several years younger and a mama's boy. I frequently stayed at their house during our visit, and helped Zio Albano make salami and sausage at his butcher shop.

Amerigo came from a family of ten, so there were many visits to relatives' homes and countless big meals partaken. My father presented me to his siblings with pride. Being Amerigo Cortopassi's son, however, came with certain behavior responsibilities. He expected me to comport myself politely and honorably at all times, which in Italian is said to be *ben-educato* (respectful and well-mannered) and never, ever *mal-educato* (impolite). For Italians, ben-educato comportment reflected honor on the family.

Although at work or at home Amerigo could be quick tempered, in social settings he was always most gracious. Among his rules for his kids: whenever we went to someone's home and were offered cookies or a drink, at first we should decline. If asked again, we could accept the offering, but we must never take more than one cookie or go back for seconds. If we were dinner guests, we were expected to take modest portions of whatever was offered. As a boy in the presence of adults, whether they were relatives or not, I was expected to respond when spoken to, and otherwise just listen.

One clear impression of my childhood visits to Italy is the sense of family I felt with my relatives even before I got to know them. For as long as I remembered, letters from Italy would periodically arrive, even during the war. I can still picture the beautiful cursive writing of my Nonno Alberto—penned in Italian, of course. The missives filled us in on the lives and happenings of our extended family in Italy; chronicling births and deaths, and recounting colorful stories. Undoubtedly another reason for the welcome I felt in Italy: I had many more relatives there than in this country.

When we returned home I continued to work with my father on the farm during summer months and school holidays throughout my high school years. In spite of the 12-hour workdays, and the hard, dirty labor in climes ranging from hot and dusty to cold and rainy, I still wanted to be a farmer. I still wanted to emulate my childhood heroes. For my father however, the fact I wanted to become a farmer was a source of tension between us. Had we lived in Italy, he probably would have felt differently. But my becoming a farmer in America would symbolize a failed dream of making a better future for his children. Both of my parents wanted a better life for us kids and they couldn't see how that would come from farming. Both my parents had long preached: "Go to school, get a good job in town, live in a nice house." By a good job, they meant a "real job"—one that paid a salary, had financial security, and was a step up the social ladder. For their son, farming would not qualify as a higher calling. Working for the government, yes. Working in a bank, yes. Planting grain and beans, no.

Notwithstanding their desire for me to go to school, my parents could offer little advice about educational content. In fact, most of the kids in our blue-collar neighborhood were bound for a trade, not further education. During my junior/senior years in high school, I began to socialize more with kids who lived in the tony northwest side of Stockton, colloquially known as the "Oxford Circle" area. In those households, the majority of parents were college graduates, doctors, lawyers, bankers, engineers, and business owners.

Joan/Dino, and "cool" 1953 Ford.

Joan and ten French class girls' departure for Europe February 1954.

They planned for their children to go to college, and made sure their high school curriculum prepared them for that future. When it came to selecting college-prep courses like algebra, geometry, chemistry, languages, etc., these kids received good advice at home, as well as from school counselors preparing them for the collegiate route. By contrast, I was not exposed to such advice, partly because my parents didn't understand the educational system, partly because we lived in the working-class eastside, and partly because each time I told a counselor I wanted to be a farmer, it reinforced their directing me to a vocational curriculum. Counselors would sign me up for English, U.S. history and arithmetic math—basic requirements for high school graduation—and filled the rest of my schedule with shop courses.

At the beginning of my last semester in high school, I contracted a serious fever with complete body paralysis, leading our Irish M.D., Dr. Patrick McHugh, to diagnose either rheumatic fever or polio, which was then the big scare. Fortunately, it turned out to be the former, but after the paralysis subsided, the fever left the mitral valve of my heart significantly damaged. To allow for healing, Dr. McHugh prescribed *total bed rest for four months*. The school provided a tutor so I could study at home and graduate with my class.

During my convalescence, an older girl from across the street started visiting me most afternoons. On graduation day, I got off my sick bed to attend the Class of 1954's commencement ceremonies, take the across-the-street girl to the Seniors' Ball, and initiate a summertime romance.

With my damaged heart facing a long healing process, the doctor recommended I avoid strenuous activity and that's how I ended up going to junior college that fall and getting a part-time job as a nursery deliveryman—a job that gave me a close-up view of how those Oxford Circle folks lived. They were good customers for nursery products, which I delivered to their homes. I began noticing the fanciness of their houses, gardens, and lifestyles.

But by the middle of my second semester, I quit junior college. I was still living at home, and when I told my parents my decision they were very upset. It wasn't that I found the curriculum difficult, but rather that it hit me that I'd never catch up with the Oxford Circle kids. They were just too far ahead of me in so many different ways. In addition, most of my long-time Eastside friends were now working full-time jobs at good wages, which gave them plenty of spending money to date girls who had also not gone on to college. These guys had embarked on adulthood while I was still a JC student working part-time. I felt stuck in no man's land. I was neither a serious student nor a decent wage-earner. So I dropped out of school, found a full-time job, and forgot about catching up with the Oxford Circle bunch.

I hired on as a truck driver hauling grain, and later in the summer hauling tomatoes, receiving 25 percent of whatever my truck grossed. While the potential of making money hauling grain was limited, the tomato harvest presented me with the first opportunity to make what I considered big bucks. A driver could earn $35 hauling one load of tomatoes per day. But on days I could double up with two loads, I could make a whopping $70 a day! Most drivers were content to double-up occasionally, but I set out to find a way to do it *every day*, which was a challenge given all the driving, waiting, and unloading time that would entail.

My plan depended on being the first loaded truck out of the field every morning in order to arrive at the cannery when there was no line of waiting trucks and get unloaded by noon. Hurrying back to the field, I could get loaded a second time before the end of the day. However, by the time I arrived back at the cannery with my afternoon load, there would be a yard full of trucks lined up waiting to be unloaded which could take anywhere from 10 to 12 hours. Some drivers went home for the night and unloaded in the morning. Others would drag through the nighttime unloading and go home to sleep in the morning. Not me. My bedroom was under the trailer. I would swing down the steel army cot I had welded there and spread a sleeping bag on it. I gave the night gatekeeper five dollars to wake me just before my unloading number came up during the wee hours. After being unloaded, I would drive back to the tomato field—stopping only to pick up coffee and donuts to go—ensuring I would be the first truck in line to be loaded in the morning. If it was still dark when I arrived, I would drop the cot and catch another couple hours or so of shuteye.

This high-paced regimen did generate "big bucks" but did not provide adequate sleep or proper nutrition, and flew in the face of Dr. McHugh's sound advice to get lots of rest and avoid strenuous work. But I was a young man, eager to Get Ahead, and stayed with it until it all came crashing down midway through the tomato harvest.

It was a Sunday, and a rare day off from hauling tomatoes. Laying on the couch watching television, I suddenly realized something was very wrong. My heart started hurting, and seemed to be rebelling in the middle of my chest. I hollered to my mother, who was in the kitchen. She came running and I said, "Ma! Something's going wrong with my heart—call the doctor!" In those days doctors still made house calls.

By the time Dr. McHugh arrived, I was bathed in sweat in great pain, and convinced I was dying of a heart attack. He put the stethoscope to my chest. The stroke of a normal heart makes a double-thump sound. That day my heartbeat was making a thump-shhh sound! The rheumatic fever scar tissue in the mitral valve had torn loose, and my heart was leaking on every stroke. Off to the hospital I went for a battery of tests and EKGs.

The next day Dr. McHugh delivered the news. He explained that the hectic schedule I had been working caused the healing from my six months of bed rest to regress and I had suffered something akin to a "baby heart attack."

"Dino, there is only one cure," he said.

"What's that, Doc?"

"Lots of high-quality rest to allow complete healing of your heart valve this time. Absolutely no strenuous activity of any kind."

"Okay," I said, relegated to again having to take it easy for a few months. As tough as it would be to stay idle for so long, I had done it before.

"How long this time?" I asked.

Dr. McHugh looked at me sternly. "Two years."

Do nothing for two years?!

I had started working with my father at age 10, and loved it. I had recently turned eighteen, and still loved working. And I still wanted to be a farmer.

The doctor's verdict sounded like a death sentence.

MY PILLSBURY MBA

F or the first few months of my forced inactivity, I would sleep all morning and go play bocce ball most afternoons at the Waterloo Club with a group of elderly Italians, many of whom were retired. I was bored and feeling sorry for myself—instead of getting started in life, I was spending my days with men who were a lot nearer to the end of theirs.

During the Christmas holidays of 1956 my life took a turn for the better when Dean DeCarli came to visit me. I had met Dean when I started dating his daughter, Joan, during the fall semester of our senior year in high school. An attractive, intelligent brunette,

Joan had spent the spring semester of that year in Europe as an exchange student. By the time she returned that summer, I was dating the girl from across the street and we had gone our separate ways.

At the time of Dean's Christmas visit to me, Joan was in her second year at University of California Davis (UC Davis). Dean remembered my dream of being a farmer and had recently heard that I was "grounded" and unable to work. Because he was a graduate of UC Davis' two-year course, it occurred to him that the two-year program might work for me.

My initial response to Dean was to explain that I had not completed the prerequisites to attend a four-year college. He told me they were not necessary because this was a non-degree program—essentially an AA program—and offered to take me to Davis for a campus tour. Everything I saw there looked far more interesting than playing bocce at the Waterloo Club. The program seemed just the ticket to get through my doctor's two-year, no-work edict, and perhaps could be the prelude to my lifelong dream of becoming a farmer. So in February 1956 I enrolled at mid-year for the spring semester and moved to Davis, into a rented room adjacent to the campus.

My UC Davis experience turned out to be much more than I had anticipated and though the two-year program was being phased down, even that proved beneficial. With a shrunken two-year program curriculum—previously focused on practical problem solving on a working farm—we could fill out class schedules with four-year degree courses in the Ag Sciences. This unique blend of the practical and theoretical meshed with my own hands-on farm experience over the years. Courses like soil science, pomology, plant pathology, agronomy, entomology, and farm mathematics were very helpful to me later on.

My time at Davis narrowed the academic gap between myself and high school peers who had gone on to college right out of high school, plus it exposed me to the social aspects of being a college student. In short, I had loads of fun!

After dating a number of other girls during my first year at UC Davis, I reconnected with Joan, who had been angry at her father because she didn't want me to think she had sent him to recruit me to Davis. During my second year as a Cal Aggie we started "going steady" and were subsequently married in June 1958.

UC Davis Party 1956

ABOVE: **WINTER—1957**
Skiing with college friends, Milena Gregovitch and Ted Johnson.

RIGHT: **DECEMBER—1957**
Christmas formal.

OPPOSITE: *A radiant bride with parents Dean/Edna DeCarli.*

JUNE—1958   *Morris Chapel—University of the Pacific.*

Sam Toccoli/Gail DeCarli; Jim Avansino/Dolores DeCarli; Joan/Dino; Tony Mattioli/
Nancy McRae; Lorna Sanderson/Eddy Freggiaro; Bev Witbeck/Brett Romer.

Were it not for my high school rheumatic fever bout and the truck-driver baby heart attack—both of which I considered disasters at the time—I probably would not have gone to college. In all likelihood, I would not have shown up at UC Davis, and would have missed the chance to woo Joan DeCarli. The vagaries of fate are unknowable, but these "disasters" eventually convinced me that "bad luck" can become pivot points from which good outcomes flow!

Holding a Commercial Class A driver's license from my truck-driving days, I hired on with the UC Davis transportation department to drive busses on student field trips. Other pastimes included playing goalie on the water polo team, and becoming sports editor of the college newspaper. In addition to those normal student activities, I also majored in poker. I had started playing as a high school senior and worked on becoming more proficient during the UC Davis years. I hosted a weekly game in my off-campus room, cutting the pot to pay for sandwiches and refreshments, and also played for higher stakes in a downtown Davis card room, and K Street card rooms in Sacramento.

Although I didn't realize it at the time, poker was providing lessons that would subsequently prove useful in business. For example, if you play poker long enough, the odds of being dealt good cards and bad cards tend to even out. If you risk money playing bad cards, the odds are you're going to lose. Whereas risking money playing good cards, the odds favor winning. The key to winning poker is the *discipline of money management*, which means only playing in those hands when you *have the edge*. When you do have the edge, you increase the amount of the betting action causing the pots to be bigger. That's good money management even if a "bad beat" subsequently causes you to lose a particular hand where you're the statistical favorite. A bad beat is a Texas Hold 'em term for losing despite a winning hand/favorable odds when an opponent draws a long-shot last card. When you don't have the edge, you must do the hardest thing in poker: fold your cards and conserve your money to bet when you do have the edge.

Obviously, one needs to know the odds for and against drawing into certain hands and to be vigilant in reading other players' behavior. When players' behavior tip their hand's strength, it's called a "tell." Playing with professionals in Vegas, you aren't going to see any tells, which is a good reason for amateurs to not play in Vegas! Against less skilled competitors, however, being observant can lead to reading subtle tells of others at the table.

As for bluffing, the only game I've seen in which occasional bluffing can be a winning strategy is the previously mentioned Texas Hold 'em, a wild and wooly poker variant in which each player is dealt two cards face down and a total of five community cards are dealt face-up. Players can check, bet, raise, or fold after each deal. Personally, I see bluffing's principal value as advertising, since bluffs have a relatively low success rate. For me, the main reason to bluff is to encourage other players to call me on another hand where I've got the edge and have bet it strong. In my experience, consistent bluffers are consistent losers.

In 1957 the three partners of Vignolo and Cortopassi amicably split up their Wright Tract ownership, with my father accepting 350 acres and some cash as his one-third share. My hope had been to start farming on Wright Tract with my father after graduating from Davis in February 1958. However, Amerigo dashed those hopes by promptly leasing his land to a neighbor for 15 years! He did so seeking relief from the high-intensity work style he had always practiced, but also because he did not want me to go into farming as a way of life.

I saw my father's refusal to back me in farming as yet another great adversity in my life. Even though he valued having me work beside him in the fields, he acted to discourage me from following in those footsteps. As much as I was set on farming, he was just as certain it was the worst thing I could do, and he was not going to help me make that mistake.

Shortly before I finished up at Davis in February 1958, my father bought a rundown 30-acre farm planted to an old chestnut orchard. After a lifetime of work and a year of retirement, he bought the little 30-acre place to "keep from going crazy." Needing help with removing the giant old chestnut trees and preparing to replant the 30 acres to cherries, Amerigo hired me for $300 a month. This was only temporary work while I was supposed to be looking for a "real job."

Joan and I were engaged to be married in June and, as part of my pay, we planned to live in the small, old, salt box style house on the farm rent-free. The previous tenant had kept chickens in one upstairs bedroom, and the roof was so bad six pots were needed to catch rain leaks in the combination living-dining room. Needless to say, I undertook a lot of repair projects that spring, and after Joan and I married in June 1958, the patched-up house became our first home. For the next five years we lived in the salt-box where three of our four children were born.

ABOVE: *Joan and Queenie check out Dino/Amerigo laying floor tiles.*

LEFT: APRIL—1958   *Fixing up the old house on East Main Street. Dino/Joan/
Amerigo.*

SUMMER—1958   *Queenie, Dino, and Model A Ford irrigating pickup.*

While working clearing the chestnut orchard the spring/
summer of 1958, I kept checking out farmland that came on the
market. Unwilling to relinquish my hope of finding a farm to
purchase, something which would require Amerigo's financial
support, I often dragged him along with me. Predictably, he
found something wrong with every property, so much so that it

got to be a sore point between us. Not only did he repeatedly turn thumbs down, but he began nagging me nonstop about finding a real job. Finally he accused me of wanting to farm *because I couldn't get a real job.*

As luck had it, a few days later a high school friend, Phil Clark, came to have dinner with Joan and me. Phil was in a Master's program in Oregon and had taken a summer job at Pillsbury Grain Trading Company in Stockton. He mentioned that Pillsbury was looking for a full-time field man to buy grain from local farmers. Still simmering from Amerigo's jab that I couldn't get a real job, with Phil's help an interview was arranged.

In my first-ever full-time job interview, I earnestly explained that since I was a local farm boy of Italian stock—like many of the farmers whose grain I would be trying to buy—and also a UC Davis graduate, they should hire me. My interviewer and soon-to-be boss, Blair Erigero, nodded, and after a few minutes startled me by asking, "What are your pay expectations?"

Pay expectations? I hadn't thought about that, and the only reference point I had was the $300 a month I was earning helping to take out the chestnut orchard. So taking a deep breath I blurted out, "Three hundred and fifty a month."

Blair leaned back, smiled, and said, "Well, young man, you've got the job."

Right then I realized I should have asked for more. Blair, who became a key mentor to me, would later teach me that good traders seek to know the other guy's objectives before disclosing their own. After I had been on the job for a few months he voluntarily raised my salary to $450 a month.

My father was proud of me and I was pretty pleased, too. Initially, it was mostly about showing him that I could get a job. However, I soon realized there was much to learn about how markets work in theory and in practice, and how much Blair could teach me, and I stopped looking for land to buy. I had not given up my dream; far from it. I was still determined to farm someday, but I was learning important things in crisscrossing Stanislaus and

San Joaquin counties calling on farmers, and observing their land, crops, and farming techniques.

My first eye-opener was understanding that farming success could be achieved on *rented* land, which naturally requires less capital than farming *owned* land. Also was the belief I could learn to farm as well as or better than some of the farmers I called upon. Yes, that view was colored by youthful hubris; nonetheless, I concluded that I could compete with the average tenant farmer in finding land to rent and using modern techniques to profitably produce crops.

In the meantime I resolved to learn everything I could about markets while working for Blair. The mission of our office was to buy and sell grain on the cash market to earn trading profits. We also used futures to hedge our cash grain positions against price change risk. In the process, I became exposed to market fundamentals and nuances thereof.

Seeing my insatiable curiosity about the trading side of the business, Blair taught me as much as I could absorb about markets and how they functioned, taking me to the San Francisco Grain Exchange, and mentoring me on trading strategies and techniques. This included the mechanics of hedging from both the "long" and "short" side, and tuning in on market moods. "The market is reality, don't fight it Blair would say, don't fall in love with your position." He also shared his values about trading ethics and sounded like my father's twin: "Dino, a trader's word must be his bond—your word has to be 100 percent good all the time."

With his patient guidance I learned about risk management in the real world. Taking the time to answer countless why questions, Blair mentored me towards a market-oriented foundation from which to conduct business. I used concepts I learned from him repeatedly over subsequent decades in reaching significant decisions. In my view, the three years I worked at Pillsbury were as good as any MBA program, which is why I always referred to that experience as my "Pillsbury MBA."

Of course, there were occasional misfires along the way. A particular doozy is etched in my memory as "Winnipeg Rye," and its conclusion arrived just before Christmas 1959. Early that summer, Pillsbury's research department in Minneapolis began to recommend the "Sept/Dec Corn Spread" on the Chicago Board of Trade futures market. By then I knew a spread was being long in one contract month and short in another. The reason the September-December spread exists is September is basically an "old crop" month and December is a "new crop" month, and a seasonal change in harvest timing can widen or narrow the relative values of each month.

Minneapolis was recommending going long on the September corn future and shorting the December corn future at no less than a ten-cent per bushel price premium to the September. So, in the worst case of September corn declining vis-à-vis December corn, the spreader could simply take physical delivery of the long September corn, store it in a public warehouse, and deliver it against the December short contract, with the storage and interest cost being covered by the ten-cent differential locked into the original long-short spread.

However, as September approached if the differential widened to say 15 cents per bushel, we could unwind the spread (sell out the long September futures and buy in the short December futures) and profit by the five-cent per bushel the spread had widened.

Blair explained that seasoned grain people looked for various spreads to put on safely, thereby setting up the possibility of profit from relatively risk-free timing mismatches. Stimulated by Minneapolis' advice, he placed a substantial amount of our office's risk capital into the Sept/Dec corn spread.

Respecting Blair's acumen, I called Jim Auble, a friend who worked at a stock brokerage firm, opened a commodity account, and put some of my own money into the same Sept/Dec spread. Well as luck would have it, the Sept/Dec spread did widen considerably, our office earned a sizeable profit on the trade, and my profit equaled several months of my salary, which I thought was pretty damn cool!

Since it seemed easy to make money this way, I started watching the office teletype a lot closer, looking for other trades that Minneapolis was recommending which is how I became aware of rye futures in the Winnipeg (Canada) Grain Exchange. Over a period of weeks the Minneapolis analysts were increasingly bullish on going long December rye on the Winnipeg exchange. That seemed good enough to me so I telephoned Jim and invested my Sept/Dec corn spread profits into buying Winnipeg December rye futures. I didn't talk to Blair about this because our office didn't trade rye, and also I knew he wasn't concerned about trades in my own account.

What I didn't yet realize was that the Chicago Board of Trade (CBOT), then the world's largest commodity futures exchange, was a regulated market with huge daily volumes that made it very safe from market manipulation. By contrast, the Winnipeg Grain Exchange—at least when it came to rye futures—was another story.

Soon the price of my December rye futures began slipping, but the teletype messages from Minneapolis continued saying rye fundamentals looked very good. With that positive reinforcement I stayed with my December rye position. Unfortunately, the price kept going the wrong way, triggering my first ever margin call. Jim told me I needed to bring more money right away to cover margin requirements. When I asked him how much, his reply floored me.

"Three thousand."

"Three thousand dollars?!"

"Yes, and it has to be cash or a cashier's check. How soon can you bring it?"

For the year I had worked for Pillsbury, Joan and I had lived off my salary and saved most of her $450-a-month teaching salary. But she had stopped working shortly before Gino, our first child, was born in June 1959. Between savings from my high school days working in the Delta, and Joan's salary we had saved, we had $4,500 in our savings account. I went to the bank, got a $3,000 cashier's check, took it to the brokerage house and closed out my Winnipeg rye position. That was a good thing since December rye continued heading south like a flock of Canadian geese.

That night I had to break the news to Joan, explaining how the Winnipeg rye market had gone against me.

"What about the money you made before on the corn spread?"

"That's all gone, honey."

Then I got to the worst part. Telling my loving wife just three weeks before our first Christmas with our new baby that I had lost most of our savings made me feel lower than a snake's belly. I don't think I cried, but I sure felt like it. Joan thought about it for a while before commenting.

Finally she said, "Well, it's probably a good lesson. Dino you're a risk-taker and you're pretty good at it, but this is a good lesson for you. It's okay, I know you'll make it back in the future."

That moment confirmed that I had married the right woman!

The following day I told Blair what had happened. He couldn't believe it. "Winnipeg rye?" he said incredulously. "Jesus, any grain man worth his salt knows that old Harry Smith controls the rye futures market in Winnipeg and runs it up and down like a yo-yo to pick off amateurs."

As further proof to Blair's reaction, in the end the Minneapolis analysts' information proved to be correct. Ultimately, December rye went very high, but because it was a manipulated market, it had first gone very low to pick off suckers like me. In addition to not knowing about the market being manipulated, my biggest mistake had been to take on more risk than I had money to back up. Ironically, I already knew that from my poker days.

Poker players have a saying: "Guys who play with the grocery money are playing with *scared money*." A solid player can eventually beat a guy playing with the grocery money. With Winnipeg rye I was playing with the grocery money, at a level past the size of the stake I could afford to lose. I didn't go near commodities futures for years, but Winnipeg rye wouldn't be the last time I risked money on the markets. Joan was right on both counts: I did learn a good lesson, and I would make it back—and then some. But I never again played the markets with the grocery money.

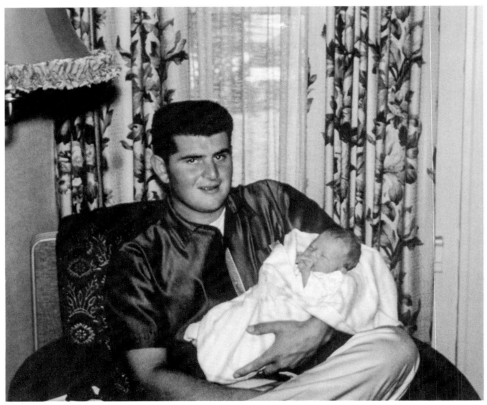

ABOVE: WINTER—1960   *Winter time Bridge with Jim and Mary Auble at East Main house.*

OPPOSITE TOP: JUNE—1959   *New mom and Gino.*

OPPOSITE BOTTOM: JUNE—1959   *New dad and Gino.*

DOUBLE-CROPPING OPENS
THE DOOR

As I called on farmers for Pillsbury I noticed that only a few of them were double-cropping. I wondered why more of them didn't grow two crops back-to-back in one year on the same land in order to generate more revenue and profit per acre per year. I soon discovered the answer. Most were tenant farming under crop-share rental agreement leases that paid the landowner a percentage of gross crop revenues—just like my great-grandfather Serafino before his breakthrough to land ownership. Double-cropping was a lot more work for the farmer, but under percentage-rent leases it didn't help him Get Ahead much since he ended up paying a share rent on both crops. Also, with the growing costs borne entirely by the tenant, he had 100 percent of the loss in the event of an early winter and a failure of the second crop. So most tenant farmers went with just one crop per season. I began to think a lot about finding a better way to compete for rented land.

Part-time farming was the first entry to my long-held dream. During my second year with Pillsbury, I went into partnership with my younger brother Alvin to rent 65 acres on which the landlord had harvested a first crop of barley. I negotiated a low cash rent for the second crop, borrowed a small crawler tractor from our father, rented a disc from an uncle, hired a neighbor with a big tractor to chisel up the ground, bought an old John Deere cultivating tractor for $500, and we planted a double crop of milo. Sixty-five rented acres wasn't much of a farming operation, but it was a start. That summer I worked eight hours a day for Pillsbury and eight hours a day on our milo crop.

Having evolved from trying to buy land to renting it I saw double-cropping as my start to building a farming business. For this to work we had to lease land on a *fixed cash rent* per acre instead of a crop-share basis. This set up a win-win situation for both parties. The landowner would get above-market cash rent, which we were willing to pay because of the added cash flow anticipated from double-cropping. The benefit was we did not have to share the extra gross revenue from the second crop with the landowner. Of course, our added risk was that early winter rains could damage the second crop.

In my third and final year at Pillsbury in 1960 I arranged with Blair to buy grain on commission rather than on salary, which gave me more hours during the farming season. We increased our rented holdings to two adjacent parcels, farming a total of 195 acres, bought more second-hand equipment, and double-cropped every acre to barley, followed by kidney beans.

As hoped, double-cropping rented land turned out to be a key part of Getting Ahead in farming. The *perceived risk* that many tenant farmers saw with planting a second crop was greater than the *actual*

ABOVE: FALL—1960   *Our first bean harvester.*

BELOW: EARLY—1960s   *Wintertime cash flow from buying used tractors in Kern County/ reselling them to neighbors.*

Around sixty at the time, Ernie greeted me warmly with a hand-shake and showed me to a chair next to his desk on the loan plat-form situated out in the open in the middle of the bank. As if he had all the time in the world, Ernie always spoke slowly, accentu-ating the syllables of certain words, such as my name.

"Well, Di--no. Tell me, what can I do for you?"

I was dressed nicely—slacks, sports shirt open at the neck, leather oxfords—but did not have on a coat or tie because that would have been over the top for a farmer. At Davis they had taught us how to apply for an agricultural loan, so I had prepared a budget of the crops we were going to grow the upcoming season, the costs for doing so, a capital budget for the additional used equipment needed, and a cash flow chart.

"Ernie," I said, "I came to borrow some money."

"Good. We're in that business."

"Let me show you my plans, budget, cash flow . . . " I eagerly reached into my stack of papers, and started pulling them out and placing them in front of him on his desk, pointing to columns of numbers and explaining.

I hadn't gone through half my papers yet when Ernie said very patiently, "Di--no, how much money do you need?"

I hadn't gotten to that part yet. "Well, I haven't showed you all this."

"Don't wor--ry about that. How much do you need?"

Gulping, I said, "Well, it's about twenty-five thousand dollars."

"Di--no, I've known you since you were a boy. I know your father and mother. You come from a good family. You're going to pay us back. You got the twenty-five thousand dollars. Draw it out as you need it."

I was stunned. I wasn't sure whether I should show the rest of my papers or quit while I was ahead. As if reading my mind, Ernie said, "Don't worry about the papers. You can leave them with me, but you have the money, Di--no."

That was one of many times I realized of all their gifts, the greatest legacy my parents gave me was an honorable family name.

By 1963 Cortopassi Farms had 600 acres rented and under production; most of the land on long-term leases and either double-cropped to barley and beans, or planted to cannery tomatoes.

Finally I was living my long-held dream!

Footnote: Since the age of 12 I've enjoyed hunting, and the camaraderie of fellow hunters. Here's a small sample thereof.

Duck hunting at Wright Tract: Tony Mattioli, Frank Raspo, George Terzakis, and Dino.

ABOVE: FALL—1962   *Buck hunting Merritt Mountain, Nevada with Jim Auble and Duke Leffler..*

OPPOSITE TOP: LATE—1960s   *Dino, Amerigo, Duke Leffler (Jim Auble taking picture) buck hunting Tuscarora, Nevada*

OPPOSITE BOTTOM: EARLY—1970s   *Buck hunting Grace, Idaho.*

ABOVE: JANUARY—1976 *Quail hunting at Mariposa Ranch—Fritz, Walt Hogan, Mark, and Dino.*

OPPOSITE TOP: SEPTEMBER—1977 *Dove hunting—Amerigo, Dino, and Cici.*

OPPOSITE BOTTOM: SUMMER—1978 *Canadian fishing trip. Dino/David; Fritz/ Mark Grupe; Curt/Joey Purden; and George Brown.*

CORTOPASSI FARMS

Soon after my brother Alvin was married in 1962, he and his bride Doris accepted my father's offer to move into a house on a 50-acre peach orchard that Amerigo owned near Modesto, and to take over farming the orchard from the existing tenant. We brought the peach farming into Cortopassi Farms. Our name had become Cortopassi Farms, but we were still a 50-50 partnership, with me farming row crops on 600 rented acres east of Stockton and Alvin farming the 50 acres of peaches near Modesto.

This arrangement lasted a couple of years until Alvin and Doris wanted to move back closer to home. Amerigo was not happy because he had parted with a long-time tenant to make room for Alvin, so he put the farm up for sale. I was not happy because I had enjoyed working on my own for two years and not having to deal with Alvin's complaints about farming "tiger-shit" ground. I knew Alvin was a smart guy but I didn't want to deal with his grumbling so I proposed splitting up the partnership. Amerigo was very upset with me, feeling that as the older brother I had a responsibility to stay in the partnership.

It was a very difficult time between my father and me, but knowing how different Alvin's and my personalities were, Joan urged me to stick to my decision and divide the partnership. In the interim, Alvin had lined up 100 acres of very good land in Linden with a nice house on it that he could rent from two retired brothers he had worked for during high school summers.

I told Alvin if he wanted to take over part of our rented acreage, we could work that out.

"I don't want to farm tiger-shit land," he said. "I want to farm good ground."

So we negotiated a price for me to buy him out of the Cortopassi Farms partnership. I financed the buyout with a bank and Alvin went on to farm in the Linden area for many years on his own.

Incorporating the existing name (Cortopassi Farms, Inc.) and carrying new debt Joan and I became sole owners of CFI. Its business strategy was based on intensively farming rented land, relying on bank loans to finance seasonal operations, and plowing profits back into buying more equipment to farm more rented land. Having inherited my father's non-stop drive to maximize productivity, and my mother's non-stop drive to maximize efficiency, it wasn't surprising that I chose to follow crop strategies requiring more labor and know-how, but which could produce more profit per acre than simpler crops.

Believing I was a comparatively good risk manager and developing more intensive farming practices than my competitors, CFI accepted more uncertainty than they did. These risks included growing what I called "headache crops" with high labor intensity and green-thumb requirements. I believed that finding headaches to solve was the key to Getting Ahead with limited capital. CFI took on row crops like canning tomatoes, fresh-market tomatoes, cucumbers, bell peppers, onions—all of which required lots of hand labor, tended to be weather sensitive, disease prone, and in some cases, carried significant market price risk.

SPRING—1968   *Onion direct-seeder, designed/built by CFI.*

MID—1960s   *Furrowing tomato beds.*

More than any single crop, growing canning tomatoes would prove to be the springboard to CFI's capital growth during the mid-1960s, a time of dynamic change, which was as revolutionary for California agriculture as it was culturally and politically.

Beginning back in 1961, Robert Gianecchini had been my primary mentor in learning how to overcome canning tomato headaches. Year after year, when the state average yield was 17 to 18 tons of tomatoes per acre, Robert would consistently produce 25 tons or more per acre. That record was due to skill, not luck, and I wanted to learn how he did it.

Robert, an American-born son of immigrant parents, was about ten years older than me, a soft-spoken, humble guy, and a somewhat reluctant mentor. Not wanting to disrespect my father's role, in the beginning he would say, "Talk to your father; he knows a lot about tomatoes."

"You're right Bob, he does, and I do listen to him," I would say, "but you've got tomato growing really dialed in and I'd appreciate your advice in learning how to do that."

Over time and little by little, Robert opened up. "Well, with my tomatoes I try to do this . . ." and "If it was me, I'd do it this way . . ." He was always in tune with his crop and had a tomato-growing green thumb.

I listened to Robert's every word and watched what he did. Occasionally I would ask him to come look at my fields. He would hop into my pickup and off we'd go to walk the rows. Invariably Robert would say, "You've done a good job, but next time you might try . . ." We developed a close relationship and I always thought of Bob as the best grower of the old tomato varieties—now called Heirloom tomatoes—I ever knew.

The varieties farmed in the early 1960s were botanically classified as "indeterminate" because the vine could theoretically live forever. An indeterminate plant continues sequentially blooming and producing fruit until frost or something else kills the plant. I once saw a 27-year-old tomato plant in a seed breeder's greenhouse! With these varieties, the key to success was manipulating vine growth to set an abundant crop that could be hand-picked in no more than three field pickings. There were numerous tilling, fertilization, and irrigation strategies that facilitated setting a good crop, and my tomato mentor knew most of them.

In those days, hand-picking canning tomatoes was necessary to selectively pick the "first set" at its maturity while leaving the vines in good shape to ripen subsequent sets. It was a careful balancing act to not only set a tomato crop, but to also grow vines of a vigor capable of producing above average tonnage. Farmers who consistently produced in the 25-plus tons per acre range were considered "aces" in the tomato-growing fraternity, and thanks to Robert's mentoring, I eventually became one of them.

Adding to the green-thumb challenges of growing indeterminate tomato varieties (which took longer to mature than subsequent mechanical-harvest varieties) was the perennial risk of September/October rains. Within that weather risk, however, profit opportunities dwelled! I embraced the green-thumb challenges inherent with tomatoes and other headache crops, and in fact, regarded risk management as CFI's core strategy.

THE GAME CHANGER

The Great Tomato Revolution started at UC Davis, where Dr. Jack Hanna and his researchers developed a tomato vine that would only live for a determinate period of time—it would bloom once, set once, ripen fruit all at once, and then die. The purpose of breeding determinate varieties was to accommodate a once-over mechanical harvest, rather than the multiple hand-pickings required by the long-lived indeterminate varieties.

As soon as UC Davis released their first Type-145 varieties in 1963, I began experimenting to learn how to grow them. Type-145 tomatoes required an entirely different approach to fertilization and irrigation than the existing indeterminate varieties. I was young enough, and maybe foolhardy enough, to see the burgeoning opportunity of mechanized harvest of canning tomatoes. By contrast, many old-time tomato growers who rejected or were slow to accept these new developments missed the chance to catch a wave of technology that forever changed the canning tomato industry.

I was still learning how to grow the Type-145 varieties when the first mechanical tomato harvesters came to market. Blackwelder, Inc., an equipment manufacturing company based in Rio Vista, California, built 75 machines under UC Davis's patent, and pre-sold them to farmers in the spring of 1964.

BELOW: SUMMER—1964 *Our first tomato harvester. Dino, Gino, Bob Reich, and Magdalena Vargas.*

OPPOSITE TOP: SPRING—1965 *The first ever combination incorporator/bed-shaper/tomato planter. (Designed/built by Dino.)*

OPPOSITE BOTTOM: SUMMER—1968 *Designed/built by Dino.*

The Sacramento Union
Thursday, January 30, 1969

New Machine Eases Work In Tomato Vine Training

RIO VISTA — The Blackwelder Manufacturing Co. here has introduced a new tomato vine trainer.

According to Ernest F. Blackwelder, president of the tomato harvester manufacturing firm, the new implement is ground-driven and designed to be mounted on the front tool bar of any high-clearance tractor or cultivator.

The idea was developed by Dean Cortopassi, a Stockton area grower, to be used all season long in conjunction with normal field maintenance on beds or flat plantings.

The implement tucks vine ends horizontally into the main growth area. It can be adjusted to any bed spacing or flatbed row spacing.

The results of using the implement, besides "substantially increasing recovery" of tomatoes — up to 10 tons per acre — are:

Furrows cleared for uniform irrigation; uniform maturity encouraged; better weed control; mold loss reduced; larger fruit development promoted; winds do not blow vines over; fruit kept on beds clear of harvester wheels.

Other advantages: reduction of sunscald and sunburn; more uniform distribution of fertilizer; cultivation made easier; wider row spacing on beds for more uniform and additional fruit set; and cleaner harvest.

Newly developed tomato vine trainer

DEAN CORTOPASSI watches the performance of vine training units on a high clearance tractor. The front wheels of the tractor are barely visible in the tangled vines, which is a sharp contrast to the row at the left, already retrained back on the beds.

FALL—1967   *CFI's third tomato harvester—a Button Johnson.*

The development of the first surge of tomato harvesters was spurred by then President Kennedy's friendship with Cesar Chavez who was attempting to unionize farm labor in California. Beginning in 1962 Willard Wirtz, Kennedy's Secretary of Labor, began threatening to terminate the Mexican National Farm Labor Program (a.k.a. the Bracero Program), which since 1942 had provided Mexican nationals temporary work permits to work in U.S. agriculture, primarily in California. Washington's threat of a Bracero Program shut-down caused many traditional tomato farmers whose crops were harvested entirely by Mexican nationals to reduce or eliminate acreage.

What other growers were seeing as a giant problem, I was seeing as a giant opportunity. So in 1963, as other growers were cutting back, Cortopassi Farms increased its tomato acreage. I was betting the Kennedy administration was running a bluff, and at the eleventh hour would release Braceros for the 1963 fall harvest—which is what happened!

Increasing tomato acreage was the first leg of our 1963 bet, and the second leg was a hunch that canning tomatoes would be short and canners would keep bidding higher prices as harvest approached. So we "rode them open," meaning unlike the majority of other tomato growers we did not contract to presell our crop at planting time—and gleefully watched prices climb steadily all the way to harvest. The year of 1963 was Cortopassi Farm's first big hit and it was a bell-ringer!

After President Kennedy's assassination, the Johnson administration kept Secretary of Labor Wirtz, who talked even tougher and canners were really hungry for tomatoes, offering planting-time 1964 contracts at double the price they had offered the previous spring.

Convinced that this was another opportunity, I persuaded CFI's bank to finance another acreage increase and the money to buy one of the first 75 tomato harvesters ever built. The harvesters, costing some $27,000 each, were all contracted for before any were built and they were delivered just prior to harvest in the fall of 1964. CFI owned one machine outright and in July purchased 50 percent of a second one in partnership with a neighbor, John Kautz.

I was betting large on the Type-145 tomatoes, on mechanical harvesting, and on increased acreage. As was my practice when concluding I had the edge, I increased the size of the bet.

That first year of mechanical harvesting the new varieties involved a painful learning curve. But once again at the eleventh hour, Labor Secretary Wirtz blinked and allowed in Braceros who picked most of that year's crop for us. As we had done in 1963, I sold CFI's tomatoes at harvest at a very high price. Over the ensuing three years I kept increasing the size of our tomato operation, buying more harvesters, planting more acres, and riding them open until just prior to harvest.

The inherent dynamics of being a large-scale pioneer in the tomato-mechanization Game Change fit right in to my risk management strategy, and CFI was reasonably well-hedged all along the early-adoption curve. Fortunately, after the 1967 harvest I sensed it was time to take some chips off the table! So in early 1968 I pre-contracted CFI's entire canning tomato acreage which had grown to be sizeable. By the end of 1967 tomato mechanical harvesting had become fully adopted and I believed the 1968 crop would be over-supplied. Sure enough, that year's canning tomato over-production was so large that by the following spring, canners dropped the 1969 contract price in half.

During the dramatic shift from hand-picking the indeterminate varieties to mechanically harvesting the Type-145 varieties, the number of tomato growers plummeted. In 1962 there were 5,400 growers of California canning tomatoes and seven years later only 700 tomato growers who remained were producing double the 1962 tonnage. The tomato-mechanization Game Change was about rapidly adopting a new paradigm, and for CFI it was the A-ticket to rapid build-up of baseline capital.

In the beginning my dream was to become an established farmer within my peer group. However, I came to realize that achieving large scale was the key to maximum efficiency and productivity. How large? Bigger, always bigger. For those of us willing to take on the risks and the headaches, this was an exciting new era in agribusiness. However, for the risk-averse, the 1960s/1970s were unsettling times and the beginning of their disappearance.

Having been around small family farms my entire youth, I appreciated the depth of green-thumb knowledge in people like my father and his immigrant contemporaries. They were true sons of the soil who achieved financial independence in America despite their relatively small farms. They achieved success during an era when labor-intensity in agriculture was relatively high and hard work could still pay off the mortgage. But as labor-intensity shifted to capital-intensity, keeping up with technological change required greater scale to amortize greater capital investments.

Raised in the earlier era of California farming I had grown up wanting to emulate the immigrant generation and their green-thumb successes. Although I was an early adopter of leading-edge Ag technology, I was not charging into it blindly.

Business schools graph an "adoption curve" that juxtaposes the percentage that a new technology has been adopted (vertical axis), against the length of time (horizontal axis) it takes for that new technology to become 100 percent adopted. This curve can be divided into four phases: pre-adoptive; early-adoptive; adoptive; fully adopted.

Generally speaking, the greatest profit opportunities flowing from technological change occur in the early-adoptive and adoptive phases. However, in order to scale up in the early adoptive phase, one needs to *bear the losses inherent in the pre-adoptive phase.* Said another way, to be a profitable innovator one must be financially strong enough to fund pre-adoptive losses even if the new technology turns out to be a dud. And of course, successful innovators need to be right more times than they are wrong.

Even when the accepted way of doing things remained viable, like my mother, I was always looking for a better alternative. The key was to stay abreast of new developments, and test the promising ones quickly to see if they worked. I was always looking for a competitive edge because "finding an edge" was the key to sustainable growth.

During CFI's early years, Emiliano Vargas and Gene Wallom became key managers, dear personal friends, and eventually loyal stockholders. Emiliano Vargas was Cortopassi Brothers' first permanent employee, starting out as an irrigator and tractor driver. Emi was a skinny little guy with a big appetite for work and a loyal heart. When he joined us in 1961, he and his wife Magdalena (Maggie) had two small children, Ricardo (Ricky) and Consuelo (Connie), and the little family lived in a two-room wooden cabin we provided. Today, Emi has passed on but Maggie lives in a lovely country home, enjoying three generations of her family, and Ricky is a senior manager and a stockholder of Stanislaus Food Products.

During his many years at CFI, Emi became totally in charge of the company's labor force and a trusted advisor. In the turmoil of the Cesar Chavez years, under Emi's watchful guidance, CFI never had any strikes or labor confrontations. Initially a self-described "Mojado" from Mexico, Emi got U. S. citizenship, watched his five children—save one who died young—succeed in life, and became a highly-respected member of the Mexican-American community.

Gene Wallom came to CFI in 1967 from a prior job with a farm machinery dealer. Of sturdy Norwegian stock, Gene was an incredible worker with a can-do attitude and warm personality that despite his not speaking Spanish, came to endear him to CFI's Mexican work force. Once Gene had proved himself to Emi's satisfaction, the two became tighter than brothers. Gene's principal responsibilities included everything related to farm production except labor management which Emi handled. The bond between Gene and I was strong through good years and bad. Though we have both formally retired, up until last year Gene and I remained partners in some Ag lands. When he and Karen were not in Arizona for the winter, Gene shared some management responsibility for a 750-acre wildlife habitat that I developed in the San Joaquin Delta.

My business career has been enriched by quite a number of rewarding partnerships with people I became very close to. Of all those relationships, Emiliano Vargas and Gene Wallom rank right up at the top of my fond memories.

Dino says he has attempted to increase profitability by emphasizing and expanding in high gross-dollar crops, where technology is rewarded (or he hopes it will be rewarded). The springboard to his success has been processing tomatoes. It has not been an easy road, with shrinking margins and lower market prices.

The loss of hand labor in tomatoes was offset by full mechanization, but the labor problem still plagues Dino, just as it does every vegetable grower. Hand labor is still needed for such crops as cucumbers.

Dino has an inventive mind. As just one example, when a neighboring rancher's small tract of land was isolated by an irrigation canal, Dino bought it. Then instead of building an expensive bridge, he bought an old railroad car, placed it across the channel, took off the sides and had a cheap bridge.

Investments have been made in a farm chemicals supply company, in marketing type cooperatives, even a pickled specialty business which features the packing of pickled cucumbers, onions, peppers, and various pickled specialties. Dino will tell you that things aren't going as well as they should on his ranch, but there are a lot of people who haven't done as much in a lifetime as he has in the past 11 years.

Dino and his ranch manager, Gene Wallom, are astride one of their double-row tomato beds which Dino engineered for mechanical once-over picking. Dean's boy Geno checks in buckets of cucumbers as workers bring them into the bulk boxes. At bottom, is the Cortopassi office, nerve center of the ranch.

SUMMER—1969   *CFI's first Hart-Carter tomato harvesters. Ranch manager Gene Wallom and tomato harvest crew.*

OPPOSITE TOP: **MID—1970s DESIGNED/BUILT BY CFI.** *Putting a tractor on stilts to work two rows of vineyard per pass.*

OPPOSITE BOTTOM: *"She's ready to go to work"—John Mettler, Vineyard Manager.*

NEWS OF THE VALLEY

McClatchy Newspapers Service

THE FRESNO BEE   Monday, February 2, 1970   1-B

STATE'S BEST — Dean A. Cortopassi of Stockton, center, who was selected California's Outstanding Young Farmer during the California Jaycees awards banquet in Porterville over the weekend, and runnersup in the contest display plaques honoring their selections. From left are Ronald Metzler of Del Rey, first runnerup; Warren Carter of McFarland, second runnerup; Cortopassi; Richard Braden of Hughson, third runnerup, and Robert Cooper of El Nido, fourth runnerup.

TOP FARMER DEAN CORTOPASSI WITH WIFE AND FAMILY
Children Gino, David, Katie, and Becky (from left)

MANAGING FEAR

In 1970, along with three fellow recipients I had received the Outstanding Young Farmer (OYF) award from the U.S. Jaycees, a national leadership training and civic organization. While enjoying the honor and the national fraternity of past winners, I never let myself get too far from the concern that at CFI's scale of operation, a couple of back-to-back bad years could ding us up pretty badly. That kind of self-talk was never too far from my mind.

Over the years I've come to believe that fear of failure is a significant constant with most successful entrepreneurs. In my view, a fearless risk-taker is a stupid risk-taker. The idea is not to be

OYF Awards Congress Barnes/Oregon; Schivers/Illinois; Maxwells/Indiana; Cortopassis/ California.

fearless, but rather to face the risk and feel the fear as a prelude to managing both! However, during the winter of 1969-70 things got so bad, managing my fear of CFI going in the tank got close to the brink! Here's why.

While 1963 to 1968 had been profitable high-growth years for CFI, 1969 through 1972 were just the opposite. A nationwide oversupply of corn, soybeans, and wheat resulted in very low prices for grains and also for CFI's specialty processing crops whose prices keyed off of grain prices. The three-year industry-wide downturn, and a major hole to CFI revenues caused by a processor's breach of contract (see the Libby, McNeill & Libby saga in the next chapter) brought to mind an old Italian saying, *Richezza Mobile—Miseria Stabile* (Wealth is fleeting—Poverty a constant). Farm prices had gone so low that it was almost impossible for tenant farmers to present bank budgets for seasonal operating loans that didn't show red ink, and CFI got caught in that same bind.

In January 1970, Dino Georgi, the new Wilson Way Branch Manager, delivered me the ominous verdict that based on the 1970 crop budget CFI had submitted: "The bank cannot approve this loan."

What?! Realizing an appeal to Georgi was useless, I asked what higher authority I could talk to. He told me the Fresno Agri-Center was the location of the next officer in the chain of command, but added, "That regional officer has already turned down CFI's loan."

Knowing Georgi to be a by-the-book banker who preferred saying "no" to saying "yes," I guessed his comment meant he had already rained on CFI's parade at the regional level.

Nonetheless, I made the appointment in Fresno, and a few days later sat across from the regional guy to make my pitch. In the interim I had some sleepless nights knowing if CFI didn't get the 1970 operating loan the company was in deep doo-doo! During the preceding good years I had plowed CFI's substantial profits back into business expansion. Without bank financing for the upcoming farming season, CFI would have to drastically cut operations across the board, selling farm equipment and giving up land leases laboriously crafted and improved. CFI's large-scale farming model was most efficient at balanced utilization of leased land, machinery, and other assets. To dramatically downsize operations for lack of bank financing would be a huge setback to Getting Ahead!

I started my pitch to the regional officer: "CFI doesn't currently owe anyone else any money. I've always paid off past borrowings from the bank and have made quite a bit of money for both of us over the years. In the current Ag price downturn and because of the Libby contract breach, CFI is caught in a liquidity crunch but it owns lots of good assets. Given CFI's track record, I think B of A should make this loan. I know the budget doesn't look good, but I promise to make it work."

The banker asked a few skeptical questions making clear the bank was concerned about loan collateral.

Finally I looked him straight in the eye and said, "Look, you have the best collateral in the world and that is my word that I will pay you back no matter what happens."

He continued looking at me and then his pinched expression that had seemed to be a permanent fixture softened. "You know what Dino, I believe you will pay us back. So even though your budget doesn't pencil any margin of safety for the bank, I'm going to go out on a limb and okay CFI's loan. Borrowers like you whose word was our collateral, is what built this bank!"

A wave of relief washed through my body. We shook hands on the deal and I walked out of there floating on air.

I had chartered a single-engine Cessna to fly me to Fresno for this make-or-break meeting, but I was so high I could have flown home without the plane.

However, the next day my euphoria was dispelled when I walked into the Wilson Way branch. Manager Georgi grudgingly confirmed that the Fresno Regional Manager had okayed CFI's loan, but there was a new caveat.

"We will have to have your father's co-signature on CFI's note," Georgi said.

"What? Where did *that* come from?!"

"Fresno Agri-Center."

After futile efforts to persuade Georgi that wasn't part of the deal, I left the branch and called my savior in Fresno. Repeating what Georgi had told me, I reminded him we had shaken hands on a deal without any mention of a co-signer.

"Yes, we did. But when I relayed my loan approval to Georgi, he requested we add that loan condition so I agreed he could make that a loan requirement."

That damn "Mr. No" Georgi had managed to screw me in the end! If there was any other way out of the predicament, I would have taken it. But in the current environment walking into another bank I hadn't done business with before in the current environment was not a viable option. So, *very reluctantly*, I went to ask my father for his co-signature.

Although I had achieved post-breakup success and Alvin was doing fine with his separate farming interests, Amerigo had continued to hold me responsible for the partnership break-up. Talk about dishing out humble pie! My father let me have it in both Italian and fractured English, reiterating all the reasons I should have stayed in partnership with Alvin. Often more comfortable delivering criticism than compliments, Amerigo was scathing and disparaging in a very long harangue. After he had vented anger carried since the partnership's dissolution, I told him without his guarantee the bank might not fund CFI's loan. His response was, "I'll think about it." After letting me dangle for a couple of days—and unleashing another venting— he went ahead and co-signed CFI's loan.

Postscript: CFI struggled through the down-cycle and in June 1972, the USSR bought all of America's surplus grain, prices exploded upward, and CFI's shoe was on the other foot with B of A. My ultimatum to them was: "Cancel Amerigo's co-signature and get Mr. Georgi permanently out of CFI's loan approval process or I'm going elsewhere."

They met both conditions of my ultimatum and I never had to deal with "Mr. No" again. In fact the bank realized Georgi was not a good credit man and shunted him off into an administrative position where he remained until his retirement.

AS THE WORM TURNS—
THE LIBBY SAGA

O n top of depressed farm prices, the main reason that 1970 found CFI in a financial squeeze was the David vs. Goliath legal battle I had undertaken against one of the country's largest food processors—Chicago-based Libby, McNeill & Libby.

The story started in February 1969 when Libby found itself short of summer inventory for its line of frozen green beans. Their local field man had solicited CFI to grow 200 acres of early green beans for June harvest. Green beans for freezing had become a profitable crop for San Joaquin County farmers because they took only 90 days from seed to harvest. Most green bean contracts in San Joaquin County with various freezers were for 40 to 80 acres, so the possibility of a 200-acre Libby contract was attractive. However, as an experienced grower of dry beans, I knew that beans planted in the cool climate of March for June harvest would result in relatively low yields. Therefore, as an incentive to grow the early beans, I told Libby CFI would need a contract to double-crop the 200 acres back-to-back with late beans planted in June for September harvest. Together, the two bean crops represented a profitable opportunity for CFI. As I would later find out, Libby only wanted the spring-planted beans, but to induce me to grow the June beans they agreed to contract the second crop.

The early-bean crop was harvested on schedule in June, but when I received the paperwork as to how Libby had graded and priced my beans I was taken aback. In frozen green beans, the smaller size pods are paid at a higher price than larger, less desirable pods. That year Libby was paying growers $60 a ton for the larger pods, and $200 per ton for the smaller pods. An unexpectedly high percentage of CFI's June harvest was graded as the larger, lower-value beans. This did not jibe with what I had seen in the field. The result was that the average price CFI received was considerably lower than it should have been. Also, Libby had assigned some stiff deductions for dirt; in fact, several times higher than was the case with other processors.

I spoke to Bill Sheffield, the local Libby field man and a good guy, about my concerns, and Bill set up a meeting for me to meet with Dan Danielson, his boss from the Sunnyvale plant, during his next visit to Libby's Stockton office.

Danielson started off with, "So I hear you're not happy with your grades?"

"Well Mr. Danielson, to tell you the truth, I'm not. I got some pretty stiff grades on size and heavy deductions for dirt."

"Cortopassi, do you know how the grading is done at the plant?"

"No, I do not."

Holding up a yellow wood pencil, Danielson jutted his Teutonic jaw forward and said, "With this."

I looked at the pencil, not sure what it represented. Was he talking about comparing the beans to the size of the pencil?

"We call it pencil grading, Mr. Cortopassi. That means I use a pencil like this one to assign the size percentages and the dirt deductions."

I was shocked. Danielson was openly admitting that Libby arbitrarily assigned the bean grades. Farmers often talked amongst themselves about processors engaging in underhanded grading practices to save themselves money—and *cost* farmers money—but I had never heard a processor admit it!

Danielson continued: "So, stop your bitching. Because your grades could get worse," and he wagged the pencil slowly back and forth for effect.

Although fuming inside I had to keep control because without third-party inspection, there wasn't a thing I could do about Danielson's pencil grades—and I had 200 acres of September beans to go.

"Got it," I said, standing to leave. "Thanks for the meeting."

Okay, Libby had given CFI a whipping on the early beans, but I knew we could make up for it with our late beans, where I had figured the real money would come from all along. By then CFI had become a very good bean grower, and I was confident of bringing in a bumper September crop.

As we approached the late-bean harvest of September 1969 I was pleased by what I saw in the bean fields. The plants were healthy and carried a bountiful bean crop of beautiful quality. In order to harvest the beans over several weeks the fields had been planted in five staggered phases of 40 acres each.

But as the September beans neared maturity Libby delayed harvesting and demanded we irrigate the first field one more time. Although Libby had a contractual right to control the last irrigation, I protested that doing so would cause rot to develop on the beans. I urged them to start harvesting immediately, but Libby held its ground and forced CFI to irrigate.

When Libby's crew finally showed up to start harvesting the first 40 acres, they oddly harvested only one truckload and took it to their Sunnyvale plant. The next morning the field man informed me the plant had rejected not only that one load but the entire 40-acre field for *water rot*! Remembering the "pencil grading" threat, I knew I was being screwed!

After discussing the situation with our attorney Chris Greene, who was an old high school friend, we immediately notified Libby in writing that since they had delayed the harvest and then forced the last irrigation, the water rot was their problem and CFI expected to be paid for that 40 acres of beans.

At that point Libby became really devious. The following day they harvested another single truckload of beans from the same field, hauled it to their plant, and then rejected that load and the whole field because they had found one worm! Now, rejecting 25 tons of beans for *one worm* was ridiculous, but in their arrogance Libby asserted their contract's boilerplate language gave them "zero tolerance" rights, and they could reject the entire field upon the discovery of a single worm.

At this point Chris and I knew we were in for a legal fight.

To establish a base of comparability, I requested that the County Agricultural Department scientifically survey every company's contracted green-bean fields throughout San Joaquin County to establish a baseline for "normal" worm counts. The results were revealing: CFI had the most worm-free fields in the entire county. Yet, while my beans were being rejected by Libby, every other freezer company was accepting their contracted beans from local growers with absolutely no mention of worms?

Through September and into October, CFI's entire 200 acres of late beans—one 40-acre field after another—continued to be rejected for worms by Libby based on their spurious zero-tolerance claim.

By the late 1960s most processing crops in California were covered by state-mandated third-party state inspections to prevent processors from arbitrarily downgrading or rejecting farmers' contracted production. But in a carryover from the old days, green beans were not covered by the state mandate, which meant if CFI was to have contractual justice its only option was going to court.

At that point, there was no doubt in my mind that I had been set up by Libby's Sunnyvale management. Their intent all along had been to get CFI to grow the early beans which they badly needed, and then using spurious grounds to reject the late beans which they never wanted.

Having been cheated on the early crop grades and receiving no revenue from the late crop, CFI was taking a major financial hit. Along with the depressed prices of CFI's other crops, I wondered if Libby green beans would be the straw that broke CFI's back. As noted in the preceding chapter, CFI couldn't pay off its B of A 1969 operating loan, and the upcoming 1970 loan hadn't yet been approved.

Chris Greene and I girded ourselves for battle and in January 1970 filed a lawsuit against Libby. However, knowing CFI had been cheated and proving it in court were two different matters. Adding to our challenge was the fact that Libby was represented by one of the largest law firms in San Francisco.

Right away Libby's lawyers sought and received a transfer to U.S. Federal Court in Sacramento, which Libby was entitled to as a multi-state corporation. This necessitated our having to hire a second attorney licensed to practice in federal court to work with Chris and me on the case. Since CFI couldn't afford to retain a large firm, we shopped in the Sacramento area for an affordable practitioner. The older guy we found, Tom Martin, turned out to be not very well organized, nor a skilled interrogator, and had a bit of a drinking problem. So much for our legal dream team! Attorney Martin didn't seem to immediately grasp why we were suing Libby, nor did he think we had much of a case. He hired a former FBI forensic accountant to conduct a review, who also concluded we didn't have a case.

By sheer force of will—while somehow managing to pay the legal expenses (the lawyer fees were deferred on a "contingency basis")—Chris and I kept the case moving forward during three years of "discovery" and endless stalling tactics by Libby's lawyers. In order to win we would have to prove our case based on Libby's own records and their employees' testimony. Chris and I stayed up many nights writing out the questions to be asked during depositions of various Libby employees. Several times during this multi-year war of attrition we considered giving up the fight.

Fortunately each time our morale had ebbed, Libby's big-city lawyers would unleash another round of verbal abuse directed at Chris or me, often on the record during one of the 54 witness depositions in the case. They treated us like small-town hicks who didn't know a legal motion from a pile of manure.

"Mr. Greene," one of them would intone, "if you knew how stupid that question is, you would be embarrassed to have asked it."

These recurring jolts of emotional fuel renewed our resolve to beat the arrogant SOBs.

We slowly began to make progress in gathering the evidence we needed to prove Libby's fraudulent behavior. One of our biggest breakthroughs came a few months before the trial started when Chris, Tom, and I were finally allowed to inspect Libby's Sunnyvale plant. We showed up with a photographer and a videographer in tow. Also present were two Libby lawyers and assorted plant personnel.

Before we entered the plant, I had whispered to both of my lawyers to cool it and let me ask the questions as I understood mechanical processes better than they did. I was particularly interested in the bean sizing process, given what Danielson had said about pencil grading in June of 1969. In his sworn deposition Danielson had denied ever making that statement, and he was not the only Libby employee to lie under oath.

With the photographers in tow, we began tracking the process from the time a load of green beans arrived at the plant. When we got to the location where the beans were physically separated by size, I studied the bank of mechanical size-graders which looked like large squirrel cages. The beans were graded from sizes 1 to 6, with 6 being the largest.

After continued study of the sizers and the plant Supervisor's answers to my questions, I suddenly realized the machines were configured so that bean sizes 5 and 6 ($60 a ton) *could only go to the*

French-cut freezing line, and bean sizes 1-2-3-4 ($200/ton) *could only go to the premium-grade freezing line*!

With an increasing heartbeat but maintaining a poker face, I asked how many 5s and 6s might accidentally slip into the 1-2-3-4 line.

"Not very many; these machines are real accurate."

"Percentage-wise?" I asked.

The guy shrugged. "Maybe five percent."

"So all the size 5s and 6s end up in French-cut line and all the 1s through 4s end up in whole beans line?" At that point the light bulb was flashing in my brain, but keeping a poker face I calmly directed the video guy to take close-ups of the machines and the supervisor together while repeating my questions so his answers were audible on the tape. Neither Libby's lawyers, plant personnel, or my own lawyers realized I had just found the smoking gun! A couple of hours later, finally alone with Chris and Tom in the car, I explained my epiphany. We knew that "pencil grades" of the growers' bean deliveries were arbitrary, but the actual bean sizing machines were not *arbitrary*!

Excitedly I explained that the plant's daily production records of pounds of whole beans and pounds of French-cut beans would show exactly how many *actual pounds* of small beans ($200 a ton) and *actual pounds* of big beans ($60 a ton) there really were. We could then compare the daily weight of each of those actual size classes to the daily weights of pencil grade sizes Libby used in calculating grower payments. I knew there would be big weight discrepancies. So using Libby's own production records, we could prove they were cheating growers with pencil grades.

"You think there'll be a difference?" Chris asked.

"I *know* there's a difference! It'll be huge! The bastards are thieves!"

Finally the light went on for Chris and he grew excited, too, but Tom didn't get it until much later when we compared the plant production records to the growers' grades and it was just as I had predicted.

Earlier in the case as we had worked our way through the witnesses we wanted to depose one name stuck out. Marty Moore was an agricultural expert that Libby had sent to meet with me back in February 1969 before I agreed to grow beans for them. A little guy with coke-bottle prescription glasses, he was a real Wally Cox type. I had liked Marty right away, and we had a pleasant conversation one afternoon in my office.

Marty no longer worked for Libby, and we had been unable to find his current whereabouts. Not knowing whether Libby had any intention of calling him as a witness—perhaps they were holding him back as a last-minute surprise—we very much wanted to talk to Marty and find out what he would testify to if he was put on the stand. Through friends I finally managed to locate his wife living in Arizona, and via telephone she told me that Marty was working in Puerto Rico for Aguirre Central, one of the largest sugar companies in the world.

After discussing Marty with Chris and Tom, it was decided I was the best choice to go to Puerto Rico to look for him. It made sense that I go because I had met and conversed with Marty previously, and with my Spanish fluency I could find my way around Puerto Rico looking for him.

Before I left, Tom Martin handed me an ordinary-looking Samsonite briefcase outfitted for clandestine recordings, complete with a reel-to-reel tape recorder inside and a hidden microphone in the handle. Tom said, "If you can find him, get him to talk with this recorder on."

Feeling like James Bond, upon arrival in San Juan I took a cab to my hotel, checked my bags, and then left to find Marty if I could. Grabbing another cab, I went to the Aguirre Central main office— a huge complex where after asking many questions of many people (all in Spanish), I finally found someone who said they heard there was a white Americano working at the company's sugar plantation on the other side of Puerto Rico, near the city of Ponce. Promising my cabbie a very large amount of cash, I persuaded him to take me over the mountains to the opposite coast of the island, a five-hour drive on narrow, winding, two-lane roads.

Arriving at the Aguirre plantation set in undulating jungle topography, I found a medium-sized company town. At the Aguirre offices, I learned that, yes, a Mr. Marty Moore worked there and he was out checking fields driving a blue VW station wagon. After a couple of hour's wait we spotted the car and followed it to a parking spot in front of the post office in the center of town. I got out and was leaning against the blue VW when Marty came out with his mail. Being blind as a bat, Marty got within a few feet before he recognized me.

"Dino!" he said incredulously. "What the hell are you doing here?"

Not being James Bond, the only thing I could think of was, "Hi Marty, I'm just passing through."

"Yeah, right, just passing through. I heard you're in a lawsuit against Libby. Look, I don't want to testify. I don't want to be involved. I have a new job and I don't want anything to do with Libby."

"I understand, Marty. It's not a problem. I'm here now and I'm going to spend a few days relaxing. Do you know a place where I can bunk?"

Although he was still worried about why I was there, Marty was glad for the chance to visit with somebody from home, and invited me to stay with him in a big Hawaiian-style house used by the company for visiting Aguirre dignitaries. As I said, I liked Marty. Nice guy.

In all, it was a four-day marathon that consisted of eating, drinking, and partying with Marty's new Puerto Rican friends. On the evening of day three, as we sat in the house's second-story veranda for a round of gin-and-tonics, I told Marty that I didn't need him as a witness at trial, but there were a few facts I was trying to get straight that he could help me with. After 72 hours of boozy male bonding, Marty trusted me and agreed to talk about Libby as long he wasn't called as a witness. I promised that my side wouldn't call him. I took out a notepad, and said I'd like to start a statement that I would ask him to sign when we finished. While he was refilling our second round of gin and tonics, I flipped on my James Bond briefcase recorder.

I shared with Marty how Libby had treated me when it came time to harvest my late beans, first rejecting them for rot and then claiming zero-tolerance on worms.

"I was afraid of something like that," he said, shaking his head.

"Why do you say that, Marty?"

"I figured they'd find a way out. Sunnyvale only needed the early beans. They had contracts that year for more late beans than they could use."

We now had, from someone inside Libby, their motive for fraud. After we covered a number of issues, Marty signed the statement I wrote out, we went to Ponce for a farewell dinner, and I left for California the next day.

When I got back, I turned on the recorder to play the tape for Tom and Chris, but found it had only recorded the first part of the conversation and the rest was blank. So much for my short-lived career as James Bond!

Keeping my word, we never called Marty as a witness and Libby didn't either, mainly because they couldn't find him. But if they had, we would have been ready with his signed statement.

The six-week trial began in November 1971, and after a Christmas break, ended in January 1972. Every day of the proceedings my father sat behind me in the first row of the courtroom gallery. He felt my fight was also his fight of 40 years earlier when Schuckle Cannery arbitrarily rejected the Lucky Ranch peaches.

Fellow farmers from San Joaquin County were also in attendance virtually every day of the trial taking turns between work at home and driving to Sacramento. For these compatriots being at the trial was a show of solidarity. None of them had ever seen a farmer taking on a company the size of Libby in court. For all the times they had been screwed over by a processor, my fight was theirs as well.

We called to the stand a Libby employee who drew sample boxes from each truckload of green beans. The Libby lawyers had been slow to catch on to the significance of this Dust Bowl emigrant's testimony, which started off matter-of-factly. Then Tom Martin, who had great courtroom presence, concluded his questioning with a bang.

"Sir, let me be sure I understand your testimony. Libby actually instructed you to weigh all the dirt *from five sample boxes* and record that as the weight of dirt *from just one sample box?*"

"Yes, sir, that's the way they told me to do it, and that's what I did."

Boom. The damaging testimony struck the courtroom like a thunderbolt. Among the jurors, eyebrows shot up and heads wagged at the admission that Libby had cheated growers by *quintupling the dirt deduction from the growers' crop receipts.*

One lie down, and an even bigger one ahead!

Then it was time to show the jury how Libby had cheated growers with pencil graded bean sizing. I re-took the witness stand. We had already introduced into evidence all the grower grade certificates Libby had sent to its bean growers during 1969 as well as the plant's production records for every day of that season. The grade certificates purported to show the sizing breakdown of each load of a grower's beans; the $200 per ton smaller ones versus the $60 per ton larger ones.

For example, if a grower's green beans were size-graded as 66 percent small and 33 percent large, he would have $200 a ton coming for 66 percent of his beans and $60 a ton for the other 33 percent of his beans. In that case, the combined price he would have received for that load would be $151.80 per ton. The evidence we were about to put on, however, would reveal that the grower grade certificates generated by Libby's pencil grades were totally phony, and did not reflect the true size and therefore the true dollar value of growers' beans that Libby processed in 1969.

Tom Martin asked, "Mr. Cortopassi, have you used the growers' certificates marked into evidence to compute the total pounds of each bean size that Libby reported to growers?"

"Yes, sir, I have."

"Do you have those totals with you?"

"Yes, sir, I do."

"Please write those totals on the blackboard for the jury."

I went to the large blackboard standing on casters in the center of the courtroom. I'm not sure how many people were paying attention about then; it seemed as if Tom Martin had asked me to conduct a rote numerical exercise. Even the Libby lawyers looked a bit bored.

Standing at the blackboard, I pulled from my pocket a roll of adding-machine tape containing a long column of numbers—in those days adding machines were still in vogue. Holding the top end, I let the roll drop and it unwound along the polished hardwood floor for several feet. I confess this dramatic courtroom moment was something I had planned.

Tom Martin said, "Mr. Cortopassi, will you explain your calculations to the jury."

I made two columns on the board under the headings: "$200 a ton," and "$60 a ton." Referring to the totals on the tape, I wrote in the appropriate column the total daily weight of small beans and large beans reported to growers on each day's deliveries to the Sunnyvale plant. When I finished, the blackboard was half-filled.

"Mr. Cortopassi, have you used the Libby daily production records marked into evidence to compute the total pounds of small beans and large beans that Libby *actually processed* each day at its Sunnyvale plant?"

Heads suddenly came up at the Libby defense table.

"Yes, I have."

"Please write those totals on the board."

I reached into another pocket, and let a second roll of tape unspool on the floor, this time to tittering from the jury and gallery.

Using the same two bean sizing columns, I began filling in the other side with the actual pounds of daily production records. The difference between the bean sizing Libby reported to the growers versus the bean sizing of beans they actually received and processed was *huge*, just as I knew it would be that day at the plant when the light bulb had flashed on in my head.

At that point, the Libby lawyers began objecting, asking to approach the bench, and basically going crazy as the judge overruled every one of their objections and allowed all of my testimony to stand.

The blackboard comparison of Libby's own numbers—the grower grade certificates which Libby used to underpay growers, and plant production records of actual bean sizes—indelibly stamped Libby as a dishonorable company more than words alone could ever have done. Libby stood exposed to a jury as a fraudulent cheat. At that precise moment, the judge, jury, and even casual courtroom spectators understood the heart of our fraud case against Libby.

Years later, a trial lawyer would tell me that the best way to ensure courtroom victory is to catch the other side lying. Once a litigant is caught in one lie, juries believe that litigant has lied about everything else. The multiple lies we had caught Libby in convinced the jury the company had fraudulently rejected CFI's fall bean crop. It became clear that Libby did not want the fall crop and undertook a course to break the contract through whatever means necessary.

The jury returned a verdict in CFI's favor for both real and punitive damages. At our celebration party that night at Sacramento's famous Chinese restaurant, Frank Fats, even the trial judge stopped by to have a drink with the joyous crowd of family, friends, and lawyers.

But a few weeks later we were back in court before the same judge because Libby was appealing both the actual damages and punitive damages. Looking down from the bench at the Libby lawyers, the judge said sternly, "Mr. Cortopassi proved his case with respect to his contractual damages. *You pay him those actual damages now.*"

That was about $300,000, which made Cortopassi Farms whole for the loss of our 1969 bean crop and covered some of the legal expenses. My lawyers' contingency fees would come from the punitive damages.

Libby's lawyers raised the objection that punitive damages could not be awarded on the jury's verdict of "negligent misrepresentation." There turned out to be a tricky gotcha in the jury instructions drafted by Libby's lawyers and accepted by my weary two-man legal team at 10 p.m. the night before jury deliberations began. The instructions were shrewdly crafted in such a way that to award punitive damages, the jury needed to find Libby guilty of "*intentional* misrepresentation."

We found out later that a lone jury member, a retired Air Force sergeant, had held out for negligent misrepresentation, even though all the other jurors wanted to find Libby guilty of intentional misrepresentation. Thinking it made no difference, the majority agreed to negligent misrepresentation and unanimously awarded one million dollars of punitive damages. Libby lawyers now claimed that punitive damages could not be awarded for negligent misrepresentation.

The judge made it clear he was unhappy about the jury instructions mix-up because he felt CFI was entitled to punitive damages. "I'm instructing both sides to find me case law on this question," he said. "If there's any case law that says even one dollar of punitive damages can be awarded on negligent misrepresentation, then I am going to let the entire one million dollar award stand. I do not believe that amount is excessive given the proof at the trial. Conversely, if as a matter of law an award for punitive damages cannot be made on a finding of negligent misrepresentation, then I will have to strike the punitive damages. Come back in one month."

When we returned to court a month later, both sides had conducted extensive research but neither had found existing case law for their position. After hearing oral arguments, the judge announced that the case was concluded regarding the contract that had been broken by Libby and the actual contract damages awarded to me. But here was the kicker: the judge then ordered a new trial on the issue of intentional fraud and punitive damages. As confident as my lawyers were that we'd win the next round, I was disheartened at the prospect of a second trial.

As we talked outside the courtroom, Tom Martin said, "Pretty smart judge."

"How so?"

"The judge knows there's no way Libby's lawyers will allow this back to trial on intentional fraud and punitive damages. The judge knows that with all the damning evidence we put on in the first trial Libby has to try to settle the case."

Our phones didn't immediately ring with a settlement offer, so Chris and I flew to Chicago to take the deposition of Libby's president, David Guerrant, who had been a basketball star at University of Kansas. In the conference room where we met, Guerrant still looked good for ten rebounds a game, towering several inches above my 6-foot-3 height.

Chris and I sat on one side of a long conference table, and Guerrant on the other with the Libby lawyers.

Chris asked some opening questions, very basic in nature, and to each question Lloyd McCormick, Libby's lead lawyer, said, "I instruct the witness not to answer."

After this went on for about 20 minutes Chris asked, "Are you going to instruct him not to answer every question?"

"Yes, I am."

"Okay," said Chris, closing up his file. "I guess we'll have to appear in front of a law-and-motion judge here in Cook County and ask that this witness be compelled to answer."

After the court reporter folded up her dictation machine and left the room, Guerrant looked at me and said, "Can we talk off the record?"

"Sure, I said. "But you and me only—no lawyers."

Lloyd McCormick turned red and started sputtering, saying he wouldn't allow his client to be in talks without legal representation.

Real innocent like Chris said, "Gee, Mr. McCormick, I don't have any problem letting my client talk without me present. What are you afraid of?"

Clearly wanting to cool McCormick down, Guerrant said he needed to talk with his attorneys and asked where we were going to be for the next hour.

I said, "Having lunch at the restaurant on top of the Sears Tower."

"Fine. Will you take my call if I phone you there?"

"Yes, I will."

Sure enough, as Chris and I ate lunch high above Chicago's skyline, a white-jacketed waiter came to our table with a telephone he plugged into a socket at our booth, just like in the old movies. It was Guerrant, and he said, "I would like to meet with you alone in my office at your convenience."

Playing it cool I answered, "Okay, but we won't be through with lunch for another hour."

"Fine, I'll be here whenever you get here."

After I joined Guerrant in his big corner office in the Libby building overlooking Michigan Avenue our private discussion quickly turned to money. Bear in mind that at this point CFI was still struggling with low crop prices, and I wanted to get back to farming rather than going through another trial to win punitive damages. So when Guerrant offered $250,000, I thought about it and then made a decision. "No, Mr. Guerrant, I won't accept anything less than $375,000."

After several minutes of back and forth, neither of us were budging from our number. Finally, I stood and said, "Thank you, but I guess we're going to have to see you in court."

Guerrant came around his desk, we shook hands, and I started to leave.

I had my hand on the doorknob when he said, "Mr. Cortopassi, isn't there some way we can get this thing settled?"

Right at that instant my poker instincts told me this was the time to remain silent.

Then Guerrant said, "How about we split the difference?"

I swear I could feel electricity coming from the doorknob into my hand as I tuned into every sense in my body. Finally I said, "No, Mr. Guerrant, I won't split the difference, but I will flip you for your number or mine."

"Flip me for it?! You mean flip a coin?! How could I explain that to my board of directors?"

"I don't think you have to since it's just you and me in here."

"Are you saying that's the only way you'll settle this case?"

"Yes. It's the only way. If you win it's your $250,000 number. If I win it's my $375,000 number, and no, I won't split the difference."

He thought for a bit and I remained at the door with my hand on the knob. Finally he said, "Okay, let's flip."

Returning to his desk I dug a quarter out of my pocket. "Do you want to flip it or to call it?"

He checked both sides of the coin. "I'll flip. You call it in the air."

The coin sailed off his coiled thumb, heading for the opposite side of the room. The big guy had flung it like a jump ball.

As the coin flew I called, "Tails!"

The quarter hit the far wall and fell to the thick carpet.

We both rushed over and looked down.

The eagle with spread wings stared up at us. Tails it was!

Guerrant picked up the coin and handed it back to me.

"Mr. Cortopassi, you're a lucky man. Your number it is."

"No, Mr. Guerrant, I'm an honest man. And you lost because your Sunnyvale employees were dishonest."

"Maybe you're right," Guerrant said. "They were certainly stupid."

We shook hands and I never saw him again.

After the bean saga ended neighbor Foster Fleutsch presented Dino with a memento of the victory.

Later, I would think a lot about what happened that day. Had we gone back to court, I believed we would have knocked them in the creek and won big punitive damages. But after almost three years of legal battle, I asked myself if it was worth another year. Both Chris and I were fatigued with the case, and there were many other things that needed my attention. And the electricity I felt coming through that doorknob was not to be discounted. At that pivotal moment when I offered to flip a coin for the $125,000 difference, every sense in my body was telling me I would win, the long march would be over, and my attorneys could collect their well-earned share of the settlement.

I also thought about David Guerrant. Not too long after our settlement, Libby merged with Nestle, the world's largest food company, and Guerrant became president of the Nestle Company USA. I would be willing to bet he never told the Libby board of directors about the coin flip!

More important to me than the amount of punitive damages was the fact that we had won the court case, proving that Libby cheated me and other growers. I would long picture my father during our victory party at Frank Fats. He was so emotional and so happy, more than I had ever seen him be in public. And it had nothing at all to do with the amount of money. It had to do with how Schuckle had screwed him and his Lucky Ranch partners 40 years before.

At one point, he came over and hugged me in front of the entire gathering. "You beat 'em, Dino. You beat those sons of bitches! And you beat 'em for me, too. Good for you!"

We farmers, you see, stick together.

MARKET DECAY

T he prosperous, nine-year era I dubbed "The Halcyon Days of Agriculture" began in July 1972 with the USSR grain purchases and lasted until 1980 when Federal Reserve Chairman Paul Volcker broke inflation's back with 20 percent interest rates.

Beginning around 1970, USSR central planners were trying to increase the protein content of their people's diet with dairy, swine, and poultry, all of which required more feed grains. But the combination of Soviet farmer disincentives and weather variability kept thwarting the central plan. The extreme winter of 1971-72 damaged 1972 USSR grain prospects and magnified their problem of dwindling reserves.

Facing politically destabilizing food shortages, Soviet buyers negotiated secret purchase contracts with the three largest U.S. grain companies for virtually all the grain reserves then in storage under the government loan program. The USSR's stealthy contracting filled their 1972 needs at low prices, leading the press to label it "The Great Soviet Grain Heist"—a comparison to "The Great Train Robbery."

Subsequent to the July 1972 announcement that U.S. grain surpluses were gone, commodity prices on the Chicago Board of Trade skyrocketed. Over the following six months, soybeans, corn, wheat, and cotton registered doubling to tripling prices. By early 1973 the U.S. Department of Agriculture had rescinded feed grain acreage controls and was urging farmers "to plant fence-row to fence-row."

Since grains are the easiest crops to grow in California, sky-high grain prices caused specialty crop prices like canning tomatoes to also double in price. To be sure, farm inputs were also costing more. Still, farmers—especially those with large-scale operations— thrived, as did CFI.

Even during these heady times some wholesale buyers of fresh produce in East Coast markets (also called Receivers) continued the long-standing practice of "Croaking the Grower" whenever their local market prices softened compared to shipping point. Croaking meant inventing quality problems with the shipment in order to gain a price reduction from the shipper. In the summer of 1974 that happened involving CFI's crop of dry onions.

During the June harvest, CFI onions were being shipped to various terminal markets (Chicago, Philly, New York, Boston, etc.) by our longtime onion shipper, Mort Brown Company of Stockton. Mort had sold and shipped two railcars of CFI onions to Arrow Packing Company, one of many Receivers in the Boston market.

Having suffered unwarranted onion price "adjustments" in past years, at the outset of the 1974 season I had told Mort and his son, Rick, "No more Receiver adjustments unless I approve them."

A couple of weeks later Rick met me at CFI's onion field in the morning saying, "We've got a problem in Boston."

CFI onions ready to be shipped to Eastern markets.

"What kind of problem?"

"The Receiver says our onions have black mold under the outer skin."

"Rick, there's been no rain. We haven't even had any dew. How the hell can there be mold?"

"Yeah, I know. But this guy from Arrow Packing says the onions are so bad *they won't even unload them from the railcars.*"

We had shipped the same onions to several other terminal markets so I asked Rick if there had been any other reports of mold.

"None at all."

It was clear this looked like a classic case of what farmers sarcastically call "market decay," a term to describe an alleged quality defect whenever Receiver market prices have declined below agreed-upon FOB price plus freight costs. In those instances some Receivers would "croak" the grower by claiming the produce arrived in poor condition and negotiating a reduction to the agreed upon FOB price. By 1974 CFI had shipped plenty of fresh produce (e.g., onions, cherries, bell peppers) and periodically experienced market decay adjustments. So I knew how the fresh produce game was sometimes played, but never liked it. That's why in 1974 I resolved to not let that happen without seeing the allegedly defective product with my own eyes.

Like Amerigo, I strongly believed a deal is a deal and I didn't take kindly to being croaked, and this moldy onions claim sounded phony. From past experience I knew the Receiver would call the next day and muscle Mort for price adjustment because they would have a USDA grade certificate—inspector corruption was common in those days—showing moldy onions sitting in railcars 3,000 miles away.

"Rick, I'm going home to change clothes and book a red-eye to Boston. You can come with me or I will go alone." A short time later Rick and I were on our way to San Francisco to catch the red-eye to Boston. While we were enroute Mort arranged for his Boston agent to meet us at the airport and drive us to Arrow.

The agent picked us up at Logan Airport and brought us to the Boston terminal market mid-morning. The sprawling produce complex was a maze of rail spurs, buildings, and truck docks leased to Receiver tenants. Everywhere I looked, a wide variety of produce was being unloaded from railcars and long-haul trucks for sorting and retail bagging by Receivers. Arrow's operation was a good-sized one with crews of workers busily unloading and repacking produce.

We had come to see CFI's onions which Arrow's owner, a Sicilian guy named Sal Cipriano, had told Mort Brown the morning before were so moldy he wouldn't unload them from the railcar. We were pointed toward a row of glass-fronted offices that looked out onto the main floor. A worker took Rick's business card into the main office cubicle and handed it to a swarthy-complexioned guy sitting at his desk. The guy looked up and was obviously startled as Rick and I were pointed out.

He didn't come out right away, so I started looking around. Nearby were several pallets of onions in 50-pound mesh sacks in Mort Brown labels. "Rick, did you ship any onions here besides mine?"

"No, only yours."

"Well, those are your sacks. So I guess these are my onions."

We went over to where the Mort Brown sacks were being emptied onto a conveyor sorting table. I picked up a few onions, looked them over, took out my pocketknife and removed the outer skin. There wasn't the slightest spot of mold on any of them. The onions were as perfect as the day we had sacked them in CFI's fields. About then, this Cipriano guy came out of his office and joined us.

Rick politely introduced us, then said, "Mr. Cipriano, these look like our onions. Yesterday you told my dad you weren't going to unload them because of mold."

"Yeah, that's what I said to your dad, but I felt sorry for you guys so I decided to start running them and see what we could salvage to help you out."

I hadn't spoken yet, but if dirty looks could kill, Cipriano was a dead man!

"You just started running our onions this morning?" Rick asked.

"Just started. The rest are still in the railcars."

I couldn't take it any longer. "Wait a goddamn minute, Cipriano." My voice was booming, my face felt flushed, and my neck veins were bulging. "These are my onions, and you aren't doing me any goddamn favors trying to clean them up because there isn't a goddamned thing wrong with them! I've been watching this line. I want you to show me right now where there is any mold on these onions."

Cipriano glanced at the onions going past us on the line. "Well, this might be a good spot in the lot. They look pretty decent."

"Pretty decent? They're goddamn *perfect!*"

"But we had mold in the railcars," he claimed. "No question."

"Bullshit! I want to see my onions that are still in the railcars."

"I'll have to check with the floor boss to see where they are."

When Cipriano returned, he spoke to Rick, not me. "I didn't know this when I talked to your father yesterday, but it seems like we went ahead and started running your onions. These are the last of them—there's none left in the railcars."

The Arrow boss had called Mort Brown yesterday, flat-out lied about the onions being too moldy to unload, after they had already been unloaded, repackaged, and shipped to supermarkets. Had we not shown up unexpectedly, Cipriano would have called Mort that same morning and offered a low-ball price for my "moldy" onions.

I exploded. "You lying son of a bitch!" was the start of a tirade in which I called him every expletive that came to mind. By the time I went through my extensive repertoire, I was done with talking.

"I didn't come here to listen to your bullshit Cipriano. Step off this dock and into the street with me. We're gonna find out about moldy onions and lying assholes like you."

Cipriano was shorter than me, but stocky with powerful shoulders and arms. He looked tough and streetwise. Several of his men came up and stood on either side of him, no doubt ready to back him up.

"You guys stay out of this!" I barked. "This is between me and this son of a bitch!"

"No, no," Cipriano protested. "There's no problem."

"No problem? What are you paying for my onions?"

"I don't want no trouble. I'll pay the agreed FOB price."

"Okay. You do that, but both of us know if I hadn't showed up here this morning you would have screwed me. So it will be a cold day in hell before any of my onions ever come to you again." With that, we left and flew back to California.

I learned in later years that Mort Brown was never able to sell any more produce to Arrow from any Mort Brown growers. I guess

Cipriano didn't want the risk of one of Brown's crazy growers showing up one day and taking exception to being croaked!

By the way, today the great majority of Receivers like Arrow are no longer in business, nor are terminal markets so prevalent in big cities as they once were. Those Receiver/Repackagers became redundant after the development of controlled-atmosphere techniques for the transport of fresh produce in consumer-ready retail bags which are now shipped from point-of-origin.

ON THE HOME FRONT

Joan and I had been quite busy during our early years together. We had never talked about how many children we wanted. I think we both just figured nature would run its course. That turned out to be a fast and fertile track as our four children were born during our first six years of marriage. Giving up her teaching job after our firstborn thereafter Joan had her hands full at home. At one point we had two kids in diapers at the same time!

Joan and I always expected our kids to do a variety of chores around the house and yard. However, she was frequently frustrated by the kids not completing the chores assigned to them.

Each received a weekly allowance based on their age, but household chores were a different matter. Our view was, "You have to do chores for the privilege of living and eating here." As that message became increasingly ineffective, I decided to try a market-based approach.

Joan and I came up with a written list of daily/weekly chores and then sat down with the kids. We explained that they could decide how many minutes they thought each chore should take with "task minutes" being the equivalent of market prices. Some chores were daily—like doing the dishes—and others were weekly, like mowing the lawn. Explaining that after they had agreed on the task minutes for each chore, they would divide up the work by "bidding" for a specific chore, until each of them were responsible for an equal amount of task minutes. We let the youngest, David, go first, and then each child in turn bid for a chore. Eventually, all the chores were bid except for doing the supper dishes. I announced that whoever was short of their one-quarter share of total minutes had to take the dishes chore.

"Wait a minute, Dad, then I'll have more minutes than anyone else."

"Okay, then try trading one of your other chores to someone who is short of minutes," I said. "That's the way the free market works."

But no one would willingly bid to do the dishes. We went through a few more bidding sessions, each time increasing the task minutes value for doing the dishes, but to no avail. They all hated doing dishes so much we couldn't get the task minutes high enough to draw willing bidders. Finally, I had to admit the free market system didn't work for everything!

"Okay, here's what we're going to do," I said. "We'll have two teams, with the two boys on one team, and the two girls on the other. Each team will switch off weekly doing the dishes." I wasn't quite ready to forsake the free market, mind you, but I sure had been taught an economics lesson by the younger generation of Cortopassis.

IN THE SUMMER of 1970 we decided to rent a motorhome and take our kids—then ranging in age from 5 to 11 years of age—to see other regions of the country.

With summer a busy time for a farmer, I confess that first family road trip took Joan's perseverance for me to agree to be away for two weeks. Due to working on the farm every summer, one of the things I had missed in my own childhood was seeing much of the United States. By contrast, Joan's parents had taken their three daughters on summer trips every year. Agreeing that our children should have more opportunities to see the country than I had, we started what became a summer tradition, making annual motorhome trips through many of the lower 48 states, as well as Alaska and Mexico.

Following my becoming president of the Outstanding Young Farmers (OYF) fraternity, Joan and I planned a six-week family trip to visit OYF friends through a wide swath of America. In June 1975, as soon as the kids were out of school, we flew to Oklahoma and picked up a Newell 36-foot motorhome equipped with a Caterpillar V-8 rear engine and Allison six-speed power-shift transmission. It was a beautiful rig, reminiscent of my college bus driving job.

We drove through Arkansas, Mississippi, Alabama, Georgia, and the Carolinas, then Tennessee and Virginia, visiting OYF families all along the way. We toured most of New England before heading westward across Pennsylvania, Ohio, Indiana, and Illinois, then into the prairie states of Iowa and Nebraska, and through Montana, Wyoming, and Colorado on our way home.

Our usual practice was to pull into an OYF family farm, park for the night in their yard, and enjoy our hosts' down-home cooking and farmer hospitality. While our kids socialized with host-family kids, and wives compared notes on their husbands' deficiencies, I talked agribusiness with fellow OYFers.

Over the course of the trip, enjoying the family and our many sightseeing stops, I also ruminated about what might be the next big thing in California agriculture, which unfortunately turned out to be a big mistake.

RIGHT: AUGUST—1960
Joan and Katie at grandma's house.

BELOW: AUGUST—1960
Hello sweetie.

OPPOSITE PAGE:
MID—1960s *Skiing in Sun Valley with Phyllis and Fritz Grupe.*

MID—1960s *Lawnmower races with Grupe kids and our foursome at Alpine Road house.*

LATE—1960s   *Delta waterskiing with David and Becky.*

ABOVE:
MID—1970s
After church Sunday breakfast.

RIGHT:
JUNE—1998
Family portrait. Dino/Joan's 40th anniversary.

OPPOSITE:
CIRCA—1980
Family portrait.

Over the years Joan made sure grandkids got to know their roots. "Nonna" with Natalie Cortopassi and Cort Carlson at Capecchio.

BERENDA BLUES

The biggest error of my farming career came as a result of hubris—when the ball keeps bouncing your way it's easy to start believing you're bullet-proof! How could something like that happen to a person known for analytic objectivity and seeking an edge before laying down a bet?

Although the farming profitability of the Halcyon Days (1972-1980) certainly contributed to my over-confidence, when I look back after 35 years I think the words of George Bernard Shaw offer a key insight: "The moment we want to believe something, we suddenly see all arguments for it, and are blind to those against it."

As the family traveled through the western portion of the Midwest on that 1975 motorhome trip, we began seeing farms utilizing center-pivot irrigation systems. Center-pivots are a form of overhead irrigation sprinklers mounted on a pipe carried on wheeled towers, pivoting around a well at its center point. Requiring minimal labor, the automated system worked well in augmenting rainfall on the extensive farms prevalent in Nebraska, Kansas, and Colorado. In California, farms tended to be smaller, and we still employed hand-labor to set siphon pipes or hand-move sprinkler lines.

Near the end of that motorhome trip we passed a corn field on the eastern slope of the Rockies where I glimpsed what I came to believe might be the future of California irrigation. The field was irrigated by a center-pivot with a retractable arm to irrigate the corners.

Intrigued, I pulled off the road and found the farmer who the field belonged to. We talked farmer-to-farmer, and I learned these retractable arm systems were manufactured in Nebraska by a firm looking to expand its distribution west of the Rockies.

During the remainder of the drive home, I began to strategize the prospect of bringing the new "Square Circle" automated system to California where I thought it could work especially with the increasing farm-labor turmoil being brought on by Cesar Chavez and his United Farm Workers Union. I also pictured using the Square Circle system on permanent Beds. By the time our motorhome trip ended, I had convinced myself that the Square Circle system could be an innovative technology in California agriculture.

Contacting Valley Irrigation Company in Nebraska I invited their senior management to California for a meeting. We negotiated an exclusive dealership for a new company to sell their retractable arm systems in all of California north of the Tehachapis. In 1975 we formed Automated Farm Systems (AFS) and installed Murray Edwards, a bright Harvard B-School MBA as its president. Murray had grown up in Texas agribusiness and graduated from Texas A&M prior to going on to Harvard. To provide AFS a demonstration model, Jade Farms—a second partnership with my brother Alvin—purchased four irrigation machines to set up on its 1,700-acre Delta Property on Brack Tract.

AFS sales started off slowly; one system here and one there. California farmers, unaccustomed to pivot irrigation, were resistant. Consistent with my other mistakes, we kept barging ahead. That our center-pivot machines worked so well on Jade Farm's semi-peat soils made me recall the clusters of green circles I'd seen from jetliners over western Nebraska, and I was tempted to do a similar project in California.

When I learned about a 4,000-acre property southeast of Chowchilla for sale that temptation grew stronger. Berenda Ranch consisted of 2,500 furrow-irrigated acres and 1,500 acres of rolling, non-irrigated pasture land. I toured the property in the springtime when the owner-operator was working up the 2,500 irrigated acres and the sandy clay soil looked beautiful! Equally attractive was available water from an underground aquifer accessible via drilling deep wells. The owner wanted to retire, and relative to Halcyon Days crop values the purchase price seemed reasonable.

Like a girl viewed from afar, the more I reflected on Berenda's attributes for a center-pivot Square Circle project, the more my desire was fanned. As luck would have it, early that summer my dear friend and occasional business partner, Fritz Grupe and I hosted our fathers and two sons on a fly-in Alaskan fishing trip. Naturally enough, during evening cocktails Fritz and I began chatting about my vision of the Berenda project.

Fritz had grown up in the Linden area but our lifelong friendship began during our time at UC Davis. Despite his ongoing passion for the cattle business, after college Fritz had sensibly figured out that real estate would provide better opportunities for him and his new bride Phyllis. During our years as young parents, Fritz, Phyllis, Joan, I, and our kids spent lots of time together.

After first working as a real estate salesman, Fritz moved into suburban community development which built the capital base

ABOVE: *Our new Cesna 210 ferried me back and forth between CFI HDQ and "Berenda International"!*

OPPOSITE: *Bob Graham and I brought our bankers (Gene Root and Al Borelli) to Berenda.*

of what became the Grupe Company. A historical footnote: Each Grupe community was always meticulously planned and executed. As a result, those communities became known for enduring quality superior to comparable-era competitors, and remain so today.

By the late 1970s the Grupe Company was earning very significant profits, attuned to tax shelter, and as we talked, Fritz became attracted by the Berenda concept. An attraction no doubt influenced by my own "love is blind" enthusiasm and by Fritz's trust in my business judgment.

Soon after we returned from Alaska, a Grupe/CFI Berenda deal was structured. Land acquisition cost was financed by mortgage debt. (During the Halcyon Days banks were actively competing for farm loans.) Development costs were financed by Grupe Company from its own cash flow. AFS provided wells/pumps/square circles at its fully-loaded cost, and CFI provided land development operations at its out-of-pocket cost. All land and improvements were to be owned by Grupe Company in fee title and leased to CFI for five years on a cash-rent basis.

Whenever the property was sold and mortgage debt repaid, CFI would receive 50 percent of the capital gains profit above Grupe Company's total cash investment.

As shown in the accompanying pictures, Berenda's development turned out to be fraught with adverse winter weather and unforeseen problems—which resulted in significantly higher costs than I had originally projected. But the worst unforeseen problem had not yet appeared.

ABOVE: *Project development included drilling and "developing" wells.*

LEFT: *Trenching and installing many miles of pipelines, . . .*

BELOW: *. . . assembling and erecting 26 center-pivot sprinklers, . . .*

TOP: . . . *deep-ripping 1500 acres of rolling, virgin prairie,* . . .

BOTTOM: . . . *with CFI's fleet of triple-linked "caterpillars."*

Unfortunately, the heavens opened that first winter and the virgin prairie returned to its natural state!

The first year's crops stuck with CFI's proven baseline strategy of double-cropping wheat to beans. The wheat harvest turned out as planned but the subsequent bean double-crop hit a brick wall. It turned out that while Berenda's soil worked up nicely in spring tillage as I had seen on the initial property tour, after the soil was irrigated, dried, and re-irrigated, the surface began to seal up and irrigation water began running off instead of soaking in. Moreover, as the center-pivots revolved the wet-dry sealing problem steadily worsened—concurrent with my anxiety. How was I going to get us out of a trap I should have foreseen?!

By the time we harvested the beans and corn, yields were very low and my spirits even lower. But fortuitously, my career-long habit of experimentation offered a possible solution. Under one-half of one 150-acre center pivot, we had planted a milo (sorghum) double-crop directly into the wheat stubble without any tillage. The other half of that same center pivot we had tilled conventionally prior to planting the milo.

As the summer irrigations progressed, the two halves of that single center-pivot responded much differently. The 75 acres conventionally tilled prior to planting steadily worsened with stunted plants in the dry high spots and drowned plants in the wet low spots. In dramatic contrast the no-till 75 acres were lush and uniform; a lovely, undulating green carpet with no water runoff! How could this be? The two halves received the same seed, same fertilization, and same amount of water.

Getting down on hands and knees in the no-till field I discovered the answer. After the wheat roots from the first crop shriveled and disappeared, they left millions of tiny vertical passageways—think of capillaries—reaching downward from the soil surface. Those vertical passageways created by wheat roots allowed irrigation water to infiltrate the soil profile. That 75-acre no-till experiment showed us the way out of the Berenda soil-sealing trap and in subsequent years CFI grew bountiful double-crops of no-till beans using one-of-a-kind planting and harvesting equipment we designed and built.

ABOVE: *Eventually, the sun came out again and the 26 center-pivots became operational.*

BELOW: *The previously farmed fields (2500 acres) worked up beautifully and planted to kidney beans . . .*

ABOVE: *. . . which emerged beautifully as far as the eye could see, . . .*

BELOW: *. . . whetting my appetite for the bumper crop in the making!*

OPPOSITE: CIRCA—1980 *The entire CFI management team—Murphy's California.*

Thinking of what would have happened but for the no-till experiment made me shudder for years afterwards.

Even so, the "Berenda Blues" were not over. They reappeared in the fourth year of our tenure with ongoing calamitous rains that ruined virtually all of that season's crops. A year before, the Grupe Company had elected to put the property up for sale. At the time I was crushed by the decision—having come to terms with so many of her flaws I was still emotionally invested in Berenda.

Given the weather disaster of year four, Grupe's decision to sell the property turned out to be fortunate. Although CFI's 50 percent share of the capital gains was less than its year-four farming losses, it was helpful in reducing the heavy load CFI faced in the Bank of America workout.

In subsequent years Fritz and I went on to partner other deals, and to this day we exchange advice and remain very dear friends. Looking back on the Berenda story, I am both regretful and grateful. The regret is for the five years of all-in energy it took to get Fritz and CFI out of the quagmire my blind hubris had gotten us into. At the same time I'm grateful for the inner strength to have overcome the Berenda Blues *responsibly* and with *honor*, the twin goalposts of my life.

Whenever I am asked about mistakes I've made in my career, the AFS/Square Circle/Berenda experience is always included in that long list. It was a big mistake to convince myself automated irrigation was going to be the next big thing in California row crops, and it was an even bigger mistake to keep trying to make a circle fit into recto-linear fields. Despite Murray's excellent leadership AFS investors lost all their capital and even worse, fighting that battle caused us to miss other opportunities arising during the Halcyon Days era.

Ultimately, Murray returned to his Texas roots and began a very successful entrepreneurial career. He and his wife Kathy raised a wonderful family, became pillars of the community, and later in life Murray began writing very good short stories and two books.

WHILE WE'RE ON the subject of mistakes, my fixation with permanent beds for annual row crops turned out to be a big loser too. In open field planting, tractor tires ride in the irrigation furrows. With permanent beds, tires ride in the irrigation furrows, and the beds remain the same year-to-year. This isn't an issue in the Midwest because it rains so much, and farmers are focused on growing grain, not row crops.

Despite all the specialized equipment CFI developed, the necessities of small-seed crops like tomatoes, bell peppers, onions, etc. ultimately proved to be incompatible with our approach to permanent beds. The drip irrigation systems invented by the Israelis made this kind of planting practical, and today most of Stanislaus Foods tomato growers use permanent beds.

Another error was Jade Farm's own invention which we named "The BA-150"—a twin-bed tomato harvester. That, too, started from my outside-the-box mind, which my brother Alvin, who had natural engineering aptitudes, also embraced. We showed the prototype at the world-famous Tulare Farm Show, where a few tomato growers seemed interested. However, we couldn't find a manufacturer that wanted to build the BA-150 on a production basis.

Because Jade had put so much money into the Sherman-tank prototype, we occasionally used it, but truthfully it was not as effective as the single-row self-propelled harvesters that continue to this day.

Failures like these did not stop me from exploring new ideas; far from it. All my life I tried to think outside the box in a variety of ways. While being an innovator sometimes results in big paydays, "leading from the front" is painful when the innovation doesn't pan out.

On those occasions I would remind myself that many westward pioneers ended up with an ass-full of arrows rather than pockets full of gold. Periodically, my backside looked like a pincushion, but it was pain I was willing to endure because getting onto a winner early in the adoption curve yielded big payoffs that made up for the painful losers many times over.

GUITAR STRINGS

I had always been thirsty for new knowledge and going beyond conventional wisdom seemed to be part of my DNA. But after a number of successful years building up CFI, I began feeling constrained by the strategic limitations of farming.

The great majority of farmers produce fungible crops which are sold at undifferentiated prices from those produced down the road or in the next county. I could strive to increase crop yields or reduce per-unit production costs or expand CFI's scale—all of which I had done—but farming didn't include value-added differentiation.

A grower of fungible crops is stuck in passivity, waiting on outside forces to determine the market price he will receive. CFI could have a lot of money at risk to produce 100,000 sacks of onions, and if the market went up three dollars per sack that year, it would earn an extra $300,000. That's wonderful, but the extra profit was externally driven by the market rather than by internal strategy, and developing/implementing superior strategy was what wound my clock!

CFI had done well because I recognized some opportunities disguised as problems, and because I was willing to take on risks that other farmers shrank from. Acting on those opportunities and putting the pedal to the metal had been mostly good calls. For example, double-cropping winter grain to summer beans had been a strategic victory, albeit not terribly exciting. Akin to Woody Hayes' football at Ohio State University—which a sportswriter characterized as "three yards and a cloud of dust." Woody's strategy won OSU lots of games, but where was the pizzazz? I wasn't satisfied to keep winning with "three yards and a cloud of dust"!

It wasn't so much that I wanted more profits, although profitability is always a measure of success. Rather, my ambition became to engage in businesses with broader strategic latitude, and where the key to success relied more on great strategy than on great tactics. To put it another way: I was growing bored with playing only two strings of my guitar.

About that time I happened to be in a small local cooperative with a dozen members who grew cucumbers for the pickle market. The guy who had organized the co-op was John Kautz, the neighbor who I had first talked into buying 50 percent of my second tomato harvester back in the early 1960s. The co-op was a first-stage handler re-selling the members' fresh cucumber production to pickle processors who finished our cukes' journey into the pickle section in supermarkets. Unsatisfied with the thin first-stage margins, the members directed John and me to look for an opportunity for the co-op to forward-integrate into pickle processing.

MID—1960s *Dinner party at Harrah's Tahoe. John/Gail Kautz; Frank/Pauline Gianecchini; Dino/Joan; Ernie Perry, and date.*

In the course of our search, we discovered a small private company in Los Angeles that might be available. Their brand was "California Gift," and they had a line of pickled items—peppers, cauliflower, olives, etc., but not pickles per se—which they sold to supermarket chains. When we brought the Cal-Gift opportunity back to the other co-op members, they backed away from forward integration. John and I decided this was an opportunity we didn't want to pass up, so we asked the co-op members if they objected to the two of us buying the company on our own.

They didn't mind and John and I did just that, putting together a deal in December 1968 for a small company we named Cal-Gift Inc. (CGI). At the time of our acquisition it had annual sales of a little over $1 million, which we promptly set about to grow.

In those days the supermarket landscape looked much different than today. Back then there were many more supermarket chains of ten, twenty, thirty stores. These smaller chains depended on wholesale grocers to supply most of their items while the largest chains had just begun self-distributing to their stores through their own warehouse systems.

Midway through the ten years that we owned Cal-Gift, Bob Graham joined me as CFO and 10 percent partner in all of our private companies. I had met Bob at one of our annual Harvard Agribusiness Seminars I attended and we had hit it off. At the time Bob was a partner in a CPA firm in San Jose and their agribusiness expert. Bob brought professionalism to our financial affairs and sound advice I came to rely on during the 12 years of our partnership, until his early retirement from business and full commitment to his non-profit endeavors. Bob was a man of great integrity, a most supportive partner, and we became very close friends. Despite some tough times we sweated through, Bob left our companies a wealthy man.

During the California Gift decade we grew company sales significantly. However, this was also the era of intense supermarket consolidation, rather like a series of Pacman video games come to life, with one supermarket chain gobbling up another to become larger in ever expanding consolidations.

As this was taking place, the larger chains were gaining competitive advantage through rapid expansion of their own central warehouses and direct-to-store deliveries with their own truck fleets. Using the leverage of concentrated buying power, the larger chains began digging ever-deeper into the pockets of manufacturers via a legal shakedown called "slotting allowances." These allowances were payments to supermarket headquarters for just *the opportunity* to get manufacturers' products into the chain's central warehouse. Lacking the purchasing power muscle that larger chains were able to exert on manufacturers, independent grocery wholesalers were going out of business one by one.

About three-quarters of the way through this grocery marketplace transition (circa 1975), I reached the conclusion that being a small manufacturer selling into the supermarket channel was not a good place to be strategically. John Kautz and I were still 45-45 percent partners, with Bob Graham owning the remaining 10 percent, but as president of the company I began to look for the opportunity to sell Cal-Gift which, with John and Bob in agreement, we eventually did.

Did we make much money in that first value-added food processing business? No, not really, but the best thing that came out of it was ten years of hands-on experience in the real world of building and merchandising a branded product line. I had started out relatively unsophisticated in "value-added" strategy ten years earlier, but along the way learned some verities that would come in handy in the next food processing venture.

In the meantime, CFI had been farming on an ever-larger scale, and because of Halcyon Era crop prices was doing very well. Farming was in my genes, and I knew I would love it for the rest of my life. But a decade at the helm of Cal-Gift—during which I had the opportunity to pluck a couple more guitar strings—convinced me that competing in the value-added arena was where I wanted to be.

The next step in that direction would provide all the challenges beyond the farm gate that I could ever have imagined, including the chance to play on all six strings of the guitar!

.

A SLEEPY LITTLE COMPANY

With the outbreak of World War II, U.S. canned tomato imports from Italy—the principal source for delis/corner grocery stores in big-city "Little Italys"—came to a screeching halt. In response to that abrupt supply void, a half dozen new California canners began operations in 1942. Most of the founders were of Italian descent with Italian surnames, but during WWII being Italian was unpopular for individuals and for businesses. Accordingly, all of those 1942 startups were named for places rather than for their founders' names!

One of the 1942 new canners was founded by the Quartaroli family in Modesto, the county seat of Stanislaus County, which they named Stanislaus Food Products (SFP). The principal share-holders were Ralph Quartaroli, his wife Edna, Ralph's brother Lee, and their immigrant father, known to all as "Pop." Pop had been a production man in a San Jose cannery during the Depression so he was put in charge of the new company's canning operations. Lee was in charge of the mechanics, and Ralph who had been a "Field Broker," contracting tomatoes from growers and supplying them to several existing canneries handled tomato sourcing and product sales. Ralph's contacts provided the little startup direct access to local growers, plus he was a terrific salesman who had represented pre-war canners to the Italian trade in eastern big cities.

With limited capital the Quartarolis started small, making do with used equipment and hand-to-mouth supplies. After the Pearl Harbor attack in December 1941, FDR had put the country on a war footing, so many strategic materials were unavailable for civilian use. The Quartarolis improvised with patchwork canning lines set up in a rented corrugated-siding shed, and steam gener-ated from an old rented locomotive parked on an adjacent siding.

With all the canned goods SFP produced pre-contracted and pre-paid by anxious eastern buyers, they made it through the first season profitably and continued expanding capacity. In subsequent years SFP added freestone peaches and asparagus to their opera-tions, but tomatoes were always the main driver.

When the war ended, some Americans feared the country would slip back into another Depression. However, pent-up consumer demand and returning GIs combined to create prosperous times for many businesses, including SFP.

Ralph was something of a playboy and had divorced Edna and remarried during the 1950s. In 1960, Ralph, then 48 and SFP's president, was piloting his airplane on the way to Las Vegas with a girlfriend when he flew into the side of a mountain. After buying out Ralph's second wife, Edna and her daughter Susan took over full ownership of the company but they needed someone who knew the business to run it. Edna convinced Frank Piciullo—a widower and SFP's long-time Midwest broker—to move to Modesto and take over as president. A couple of years later, after a competitor tried to hire Frank away, Edna said, "To keep my president, I had to marry him!"

During the 1960s, a majority of SFP's pack was still in retail-size cans destined for mom-and-pop grocery stores in metro areas. But Frank foresaw that the emerging supermarket segment would gain dominance and continue to drive down prices packers would receive selling into the retail channel. Accordingly, he began steering SFP toward the expanding food service segment—pizzerias and Italian restaurants (P&I)—which purchased their tomato needs in one-gallon cans from independent distributors.

As the popularity of pizza and pasta continued to grow beyond ethnic neighborhoods, SFP's cadre of Italian-American distributors continued to need more tomato products, further fueling SFP's shift to the food service channel. The bonds of loyalty between SFP and its distributor customers were further strengthened by doing business "the Italian way" with a handshake rather than by contract.

Old World values were paramount to Frank Piciullo, a man I would come to regard as my most important mentor next to my father. Like Amerigo, Frank believed a man's word and personal honor were non-negotiable. When Frank said our word is our bond, he didn't just talk the talk but walked the walk. As a result, when I arrived on the scene in 1978 holding the same values, Frank and I hit it off from the beginning.

Frank held other non-negotiable views that had become part of SFP's uniqueness. Product quality had to be superior to competitors and SFP followed a one-price policy to all of its customers. Larger distributors, accustomed to receiving volume discounts from manufacturers, were told that SFP sold at the same price to everyone regardless of size. Whether they ordered 1,000 or 10,000 cases a year, one price to all.

Under Frank's direction, the company had established a comfortable food service niche at a plateau of 2.5 million cases of canned tomatoes sold annually. Frank and Edna agreed this was good enough for them; they were making a nice profit and living a comfortable life. Edna's daughter Susan was married but her husband had no interest in taking over the business and SFP had no succession plan. After Edna developed cancer in 1977, they decided to sell SFP for which Frank set a purchase price of $13 million. At the time sales were $25 million and after-tax profit was $1.25 million.

Two potential buyers had shown interest in SFP. The first couldn't get the financing for the deal and had to pass. TVG, a growers' co-op, seriously considered buying SFP. (Fortunately, co-op politics caused TVG to pass!) Its seven-member board included John Kautz and two other tomato growers; all three were urging TVG to buy SFP. But the four other board members—one peach grower, one olive grower, and two pear growers—didn't want the co-op to invest more capital in canning tomatoes! Aiding the naysayers was TVG's CFO who was opining that SFP's $13 million price tag was too high. As a result (and to my great relief!), TVG's Board voted 4-3 to turn down the purchase of SFP.

This was yet another example of co-op directors thinking like commodity producers rather than value adders. I had long believed that most farmers were smart on their farms, but left common sense at the farm gate whenever they went to a co-op meeting! Co-op directors' overriding concern *invariably focused on using the co-op to sell the crops they grew* rather than focusing on added value profitability as would a forward-looking shareholder. I remain convinced that this one systemic flaw was the principal reason almost all U.S. farmer co-ops ultimately went broke. Their cooperative structure kept the enterprise starved for equity capital, overloaded with debt, and always loathe to invest in value-added for the long-term.

We had already decided to sell Cal-Gift because I didn't like the trends in the retail channel. From what I could determine, the SFP asking price was indeed a little high for the private-label company it was. But I saw it as a sound foundation from which to build on, whereas John Kautz, influenced by TVG's CFO, saw the $13 million price as a deal-breaker. After he tried to get a price reduction from Frank (and came close to blowing the deal) John said no more abut the price being too high! We did pre-agree that if a deal could be put together, I would be in charge of running the company, which would entail a lifestyle change for me, reducing my CFI involvement and focusing on SFP.

I make no claim of having any special insight that we could grow SFP into the very large enterprise it became. I did, however, have both personal and strategic reasons for buying it. Personally, I really liked the idea of getting into tomato canning. I had been a tomato grower all my farming career and at that point CFI was a large operation and locally I was considered an "ace" tomato grower. Over the previous 18 years I had sold tomatoes to a dozen different canneries and had been a member of two tomato processing co-ops. So personally, becoming a canner was stimulating.

My strategic reasons included: the price of the SFP transaction *was manageable*; its small size represented a base we could build on; and SFP wasn't spread out in separate locations. It had one cannery located in Modesto, only 30 miles down Highway 99 from where I lived. Of great strategic importance to me was that most SFP products were sold into the food service channel through independent distributors supplying independent P & I restaurants. (I had a bellyful of the arrogant supermarket channel!) Finally, I recognized SFP as a quality company with a solid reputation, not only for its products but for the "stand-up" manner it conducted business. I had been raised with these same core values and they meant a lot to me right from the get-go.

During that summer of 1978 I visited with Frank Piciullo many times. Gradually we developed a comfort level with each other. As Frank would later say, he became convinced that I wouldn't screw up the business he had been instrumental in shaping. As for me, from the start I felt this straight-talking, old-school veteran would be a valuable mentor. I let Frank know that if John and I could put together the deal to buy SFP, I wanted him to stay on as president to teach me the ropes.

To buy SFP would require paying $3 million down and signing a $10 million low-interest note carried by Edna and her daughter Susan, as the two of them owned all of the company's stock. In those days, U.S. income tax policy was insane with interest collected on debt defined as "unearned income" and subject to 90 percent income tax! So, Frank had reasoned that the note interest rate was not as important to the sellers as getting the full $13 million asking price. As the guy who would be running the operation, I wanted to raise a total of $6 million cash, so after making the $3 million down payment we would have an extra $3 million to do the next deal, or heaven forbid, as a contingency fund in case SFP hit an earnings pothole.

With Bob Graham's help we structured a holding company concept named Suzy Bel Inc., and John and I put up $3 million cash to buy 50 percent of Suzy Bel's stock. We cut Bob Graham in for 5 percent and named him Suzy Bel's CFO. Were it not for my desire to raise the extra $3 million to hold in Suzy Bel's coffers, John and I could have acquired 100 percent of SFP with our $3 million cash. As it turned out, the total $6 million cash was raised through the sale of 30 shares of Suzy Bel stock with a $200,000 par value, purchased 50 percent by Dino/John, and the remaining 50 percent by 17 farming entities.

During the early 1970s I had become totally convinced of the structural flaw in the co-op business model and had been preaching a new "Third Way" model for farmers to invest in processing. By 1978 I had a burning desire to prove that Third Way to farmer friends and the Ag community, so Suzy Bel's structure was built on that model.

Each investor buying Suzy Bel stock also received a seven-year term contract to sell tomatoes to SFP. By separating company ownership from tomato delivery rights, Suzy Bel's structure allowed shareholders to sell their shares while holding onto their grower's contract—"keep on farmin'." Or sell their term contract and hold onto their shares—"stop farmin'/build stock value." Either way profit-oriented management was driving the processing company.

The Third Way model sought to make Suzy Bel shareholders comfortable re-investing profits for long-term value, rather than distributing them and starving long-term investment as farming co-ops inevitably did. We sold all 30 Suzy Bel shares and closed the deal to buy SFP in September 1978.

I was now at the helm of a sleepy little company I intended to wake up. We had not gone through the strenuous process of buying SFP to follow in the footsteps of the previous owners, content to idle along while earning a tidy yearly profit. At the same time I didn't want to throw the baby out with the bathwater by risking SFP's loyal business base. Above all, we needed to avoid an exodus of employees who knew how to run the place before learning everything I needed to know about the tomato canning business.

For starters, there was Frank Piciullo, who had agreed to stay on as SFP's president. A strong "hub-and-spokes" manager Frank ran the company from the top down, and was accustomed to giving orders not taking them. I would later hear that many people were dubious he and I could last one year together given the hoary metaphor of "two roosters in one barnyard." There was some merit in that description of our alpha-male personalities. Frank was a guy who could get hot quickly if you tried to boss him, and the same had been said of me. I resolved to keep him happy which meant being appropriately respectful. What the doubters didn't realize was that I understood Frank because I was Amerigo Cortopassi's son. Working beside my hair-trigger father years ago had prepared me to find ways of getting past potential issues where Frank fundamentally disagreed with a direction I wanted to take.

My respectful approach would be: "Frank, what do you think we ought to do about XYZ?" To which he would typically respond: "Well, my boy, it all depends on where you want to go." That would give me an opening to explain the "where" that I wanted to go to. If Frank didn't think that was a good destination, he would say so. But he wasn't anybody's fool and understood I was Suzy Bel's leader. So after forcefully registering his doubts, Frank would say,

"Okay Dino, if that's where you want to go, then let's figure out the best way to get there."

Notwithstanding the doubters, things worked out very well between Frank and me. Not only did he remain as SFP's president for the critical early years, but as a valued mentor I kept him on the Senior Management Committee (SMC) in a respected advisory role for years after. Frank had not gone to college but was very street savvy; not in the sense of tough-guy savvy, but in that he intuitively understood human nature. Phrases like "strategic planning" were foreign to him yet he intuitively understood the essence of strategy. For example, in an early discussion about my desire to start adding new SFP distributors, I asked Frank how we should decide who to take on and who we should avoid.

"Like this," Frank answered. "If a guy comes to you tomorrow and wants to buy our products, it's because he needs us. But before you decide whether to sell him, ask yourself this question: 'In three or four years, will he still need us more than we need him?' If you think he will, then take him on as a customer. But if you think we will end up needing him more than he needs us, forget it! You don't want those kinds of customers. Don't let yourself get in the position where one customer can damage your business. Keep your sales base spread out, strong, and build a fort around it."

This was long before Warren Buffett became famous for favoring businesses circled by moats!

Frank had a kind of business wisdom that even today doesn't exist in very many corporate suites. I recall one discussion about SFP's policy of selling each of our products at the same price to every distributor regardless of their annual volume. Nobody else did it then, and virtually nobody else does it today. In the beginning, Frank admitted to hearing lots of comments like, "Are you *crazy?*" I wanted to know if he had ever compromised on this rule to make a big sale? Virtually all food manufacturers would have of course.

"No," he said. "Whenever anyone asked me for a special deal I tell 'em this is our price and we don't do deals."

"Frank, how would you handle it if a really big distributor—good for maybe 100,000 cases a year—would offer to do business if you gave him a price concession?"

He smiled. "I'd say, 'My friend, I appreciate your interest in buying our company's goods. But why don't you do us both a favor and go make my competitor broke!'"

Frank's sense of humor and Chicago syntax always brought a smile to my face, but I also absorbed the wisdom embedded in his street talk. Over subsequent decades, I would use that exact line innumerable times when "Big-D" distributors tried flexing their muscles to get a lower price from us, and each time I thought of Frank. Succeeding at company growth while following the same-price-to-all strategy required many gut-check moments.

After a new customer would finally accept that same-price-to all was the *only* way SFP did business, they eventually stopped asking for special deals. Our unique same-price policy leveled the playing field for distributors of all sizes. Relatively small distributors competing on the street with Big-D appreciated being able to buy our goods at the same price as their behemoth competitors. Since loyalty in both life and business is a two-way street, over the years these independent distributors rewarded us with unswerving loyalty and helped us maintain reliability of supply to loyal restaurateurs when Big-Ds tried to push their own private labels. And since independent distributors would always need us more than we needed them, they provided the solid foundation upon which we could grow a solid business.

In the beginning my learning curve was steep, but I was motivated and a quick study. My early lessons were in production. It was important to learn and internalize the processing techniques and protocols that produced superior quality and value to our customers.

SFP output fell into two generic categories we referred to in-house as "Products" and "Tomatoes." "Products" are sauces of differing thickness, both seasoned and unseasoned, that are cooked *outside the can* before they are canned. Whereas "Tomatoes" are those items wherein raw tomato pulp is *cooked inside the can*, which partly explains SFP's natural flavor—I'm not going to share all our secrets!

I became fanatic about cooking both "Products" and "Tomatoes" for the shortest possible time at the lowest possible temperature. At SFP we live by the mantra: "Time and temperature are the enemy of fresh tomato flavor." This statement is not marketing baloney—impairment of natural tomato flavor occurs as a function of certain heat-induced chemical reactions.

Starting with fresh ripe tomatoes, sauces are thickened in large sealed vessels under vacuum which causes water vaporization to occur at a lower temperature than the usual 212 degrees Fahrenheit. After years of experience with specialized vacuum devices, at SFP we draw water out of ground tomatoes at 150 degrees greatly reducing the amount of heat as the sauce thickens. This—along with other trade secrets—gives SFP products a *demonstrably superior* fresh flavor.

Processing tomatoes at higher temperatures creates unpleasant compounds, among them pyrroles—from the Greek *pyros* meaning fire; and furfurals—heterocyclic aldehydes. These byproducts of excess heat infuse natural tomato flavors with an undesirable "cooked" taste.

The prevailing method of producing shelf-stable tomato products is to "remanufacture" them from bulk tomato paste. All the big brands in the retail channel—Heinz, Ragu, Prego, Classico, etc.—are remanufactured from 31 percent tomato paste re-mixed with water. The higher temperature/time needed to concentrate fresh tomatoes to paste—akin to "tomato tar"—creates off-flavor pyrroles and furfurals. As a result heavy seasonings are required to mask the "cooked tomato" taste. The two-step remanufacturing process costs much less to produce than fresh packed products. Because the retail grocery channel is a price war zone, pasta sauce manufacturers are forced to use the least expensive option.

During the mid-1980s, concern about remanufactured tomato sauces in the restaurant channel caused us to launch a major effort at FDA to require remanufactured products to be labeled "Made from Concentrate." Although our facts were indisputably correct, the politically powerful retail brand guys derailed most of our FDA efforts. Undeterred, we began a major educational effort in the food service channel, including the trademarked legend, *"Always* Packed From Fresh Tomatoes, *Never* From Concentrate" which was embossed on every can of our products, and prominent in every ad and every paper communication we originated. Over time, the constancy of that messaging helped restaurateurs become aware of *why* our products taste fresher.

When Suzy Bel bought SFP in 1978, there were 36 fresh-pack tomato canneries in California. Today there are only four left, proving that remanufactured sauces were indeed the threat we saw coming. Both then and now, SFP remained targeted on those restaurateurs oriented to maximizing their food quality rather than oriented to cheapest price, and that strategy has served us well.

From the first day I walked in the door, SFP was producing better products for discerning restaurateurs; that part of the Pizza and Italian (P&I) segment who knew the difference between Stanislaus quality and all the rest, *and* were willing to pay for it. I knew the products were good, and that was a major reason I wanted to buy the company. From the beginning however, my mission was to move our products from good to great which meant finding ways— evolution not revolution—to wake up this sleepy, little company.

Production procedures of those early years did result in comparatively better products, but I aspired to increase the degree of quality superiority and can-to-can consistency. To accomplish those goals, "mostly" practices would have to become "strictly" protocols and the company's culture had to be modified. Starting in the plant, we needed to move our personnel away from the union seniority mentality typically found in processing plants, and towards a team mind-set dedicated to winning the World Series every year. The man I chose to lead that in-plant evolution was not only up to the task, but also became a valued partner and friend. His name is Bob Ilse and how we got together is yet another story covered in a later chapter.

RAISING THE BAR AT SFP

F rom the beginning I felt SFP provided a small but solid foundation upon which to build a significant branded business. What I didn't realize was how many transforming changes in distribution and sales would be needed to move the company in the direction I wanted us to go. To avoid throwing the baby out with the bathwater, changes were introduced very gradually. Curbing impatience, I constantly reminded myself: evolution not revolution.

Of 1978s total 2.4 million cases sold, virtually all went into the food service channel, with about 75 percent under distributor "Private Labels." That meant the restaurateurs opening those cases didn't even know SFP existed, much less feel connected to the company. Going forward it was clear to me that future growth should be focused on our own brands by holding private-label sales static/not taking on any new private-label customers. This was an early fork in the SFP road that Frank Piciullo and I were on opposite sides of.

Frank had always viewed the distributors who bought our products as "the customer," and he was indifferent whether our products were sold under distributors' private labels or SFP labels. The relationships and loyalties he valued were between SFP and distributor not with the restaurateurs. As a result, Frank was initially very resistant to my intention of shifting focus to our own brands.

In those days most independent distributors preferred selling restaurateurs their own private label for two reasons: they could assert their own label was better than competing labels; and they could usually buy private-label products cheaper than manufacturers' brands. This was not the case at SFP where whether the item was shipped under distributor label or our own brand, the price was identical.

In marked contrast to Frank's view, I believed the *"Real* Customer" was the restaurateur who used the product, not the distributor. In order to communicate with the Real Customer, I intended to airmail brand messaging *over the heads of distributors and directly to restaurateurs.*

Because I believed end-users were the real decision makers, we needed to build branded case sales, and for that to happen we needed to limit future private-label sales to existing distributors and not accept any new private-label customers. Otherwise, our brokers would take the path of least resistance and continue pushing private label.

Taking my time, with patient, respectful persuasion, Frank eventually came to reluctantly accept I had not spearheaded the purchase of SFP to have it remain a private-label business. The strategic importance of our taking that branded fork in the road became starkly evident over ensuing years as most private-label fresh packers were squeezed out of business. Repositioning SFP on a branded basis proved to be the absolute key to surviving industry consolidation.

Beginning around 1980, another major strategic change was to broaden SFP's geographic footprint. When we bought Stanislaus, 90 percent of its case sales went to only five metro areas—New York, Boston, Chicago, Los Angeles, Detroit—with the other 10 percent dribbling to Baltimore, Pittsburg, and Miami. When I asked Frank why we didn't sell in other areas he would say, "Because there's nobody there." What he meant was other metro areas didn't have a high concentration of "Italian trade" specialty distributors which he always saw as SFP's customers.

To avoid riling up Frank—and Walt Schmidli, SFP's then Sales Manager—I would pour oil on troubled waters: "It's true that the company depends on those five core markets, and I don't want to interfere with you and Walt continuing what we're doing in those key areas."

Eventually, however, I got around to explaining my plan to start working with a newly-hired salesman, Louis Medeiros, in adding new geographic markets.

Smiling thinly Frank would say, "Okay my boy, but it will be like taking a trip to outer space *because there's nobody there!*"

Nonetheless, Louis and I set to work expanding SFP's footprint with me joining him on broker selection trips. Over the next two years we added 17 new geographic metro areas. In many instances we selected brokers who had some connections to the few "Italian Trade" specialty distributors in that market. A typical Specialty Distributor stocks 700 to 1200 stock-keeping units (SKUs), including pizza and Italian menu basics like pasta, flour, cheese, pepperoni, and, of course, tomato sauce. By comparison, a Broad-line Distributor services restaurants of all types and stocks 8,000 to 10,000 SKUs.

In choosing new markets we looked for a reasonable population of P&I restaurants, believing that our demonstrable product superiority could make gradual inroads into that segment. We were not interested in selling to mega-chains who invariably beat up potential suppliers on pricing and end up buying lesser quality ingredients.

Sensing that independent Italian restaurants competed on the basis of their food quality, I was hoping we would find some that would value high-quality ingredients. That fundamental belief was the foundation of SFP's heretical, branded strategy: build a following among P&I independents and force distributors to follow! I knew it would take lots of belly-to-belly selling to get our brands into P&I end users who had never seen them before. Accordingly we chose brokers who we believed would be willing to sell on the street and then began training them to go out and convert end users to our brands.

In the food-service channel most manufacturers used a "push" selling strategy rather than the "pull" marketing strategy SFP was launching. In those days branded tomato processors relied on "pushing" their products through distributors via promotional price reductions to incent distributors to "push" the promoted products through to end users. In reality most of those promo dollars ended up in the distributor's pocket!

In marked contrast to big-guy branded competitors (e.g., Hunts, Heinz, Contadina, etc.) I believed a "pull marketing" strategy would eventually result in end users insisting on our products, thereby *"pulling"* them through their distributor. In short, I intended to invest SFP's promotional dollars in communicating with restaurateurs. I called it "air-mailing the message" over distributors' heads.

***

AT THE OUTSET of SFP's first marketing efforts, being a member of the Young Presidents Organization (YPO) greatly assisted my learning curve. YPO was a national entity whose stated mission was "Making Better Presidents Through Education and Idea Exchange." As it did for most members, YPO provided me great benefits, not the least of which is the depth of enduring YPO friendships that have spanned 35-plus years.

In 1975, three years before buying SFP, I had gone through the fairly rigorous YPO admission process. At that time, the objective criteria of membership was to be CEO of a company with no less than 50 employees and $5 million in sales, but the subjective criteria was most determinative. For starters, an existing YPO member had to put your name in nomination and a local chapter member had to sponsor you.

I had first met Jerry Murphy, CEO of a Los Angeles-based olive company, at the annual Harvard Agribusiness Seminar and got to know him better during the early 1970s. Jerry nominated me for membership to YPO National, which turned the nomination over to the Northern California chapter.

Walt Hogan, the NorCal member who came to interview me, owned a steel fabrication company based in nearby Escalon. He was a salty, rough-and-tumble type guy, and our first meeting reflected the directness of Walt's personality—not surprisingly, Walt and I would end up becoming good friends.

By the end of our lunch, Walt said, "Dino, I believe you should be in YPO; it's a great outfit with a tough screening process, but if you're game, I'll be your sponsor."

The rest of the process included a second lunch interview with another chapter member who either concurred with the sponsor or did not.

After passing the second screening, Joan and I received an invitation to attend a NorCal chapter meeting. At the meeting I was asked to stand up and say a little something about the business and about our family. YPO has always been very family-oriented. Joan and I knew we were being discreetly evaluated so I made it through the cocktails/dinner without once donning a lamp shade, and was eventually invited to membership.

During my twelve years in YPO—everyone has to leave at age 50—Joan and I formed many enduring and treasured friendships. From a career perspective, the mental stimulation of idea exchange with peer presidents was a valuable boost for a farm boy on the road to town.

As I became more involved with YPO, one of the first individuals I sponsored for membership was Joseph Gallo. Sometime after we bought Stanislaus, Joe arranged a social occasion for me to meet his father, the legendary Ernest Gallo. Joe and his wife Ofelia, invited Joan and me to dinner at their home on the banks of the Tuolumne River east of Modesto. Joe's parents, Ernest and Amelia were dinner guests as were Frank and Edna Piciullo, who were social friends of the elder Gallos. As night fell, the tule fog formed and the trip from Stockton took longer than planned, especially when I missed the driveway turnoff! So Joan and I arrived late, an inauspicious way to begin with Ernest Gallo, a man with a reputation of not suffering fools gladly.

During dinner, in what I would later recognize as a Gallo trait, Ernest started putting a series of questions to me about my business background. After politely answering a number as best I could, I asked Ernest a question of my own. Instead of answering Ernest responded by asking me yet another question and so it went. Shortly after coffee and dessert, Ernest and Amelia departed.

It was a somewhat unsatisfying introduction to a man I looked upon as a marketing savant and who I'd hoped to gain as a mentor. I kicked myself for arriving late, thinking that may have precipitated the one-sided interrogation. So, sometime later I asked Frank to set up a lunch with Ernest in Modesto. The date arrived and Frank and I joined Ernest and Julio at their favorite table in the Cote D'Or restaurant, and yes we arrived on time.

To my disappointment the same one-sided Q&A unfolded over lunch, with Ernest responding with a question whenever I posed a question to him.

Toward the end of the meal I decided to roll the dice when Ernest again responded to my question with one of his own. Shaking my head, "Ernest, I will be happy to answer your question as soon as you respond to mine. I'm much more interested in hearing your thoughts than in giving you mine."

He stiffened and impassively looked me in the eyes.

Holding his gaze, I was thinking, "Jesus Christ, I've insulted Ernest Gallo! How could I have been so stupid to have confronted him like that? Dummy!"

After what seemed a long time but probably wasn't, his expression softened a bit, and with a faint smile Ernest said, "All right."

For the rest of that lunch, and during a number of subsequent lunches, Ernest would occasionally share some of his keen insights into human nature that is the underpinning of great marketing. I absorbed it all like a sponge. Getting Ernest to respond was never easy, but it was always worth it! What I was most interested in was his business philosophy and marketing instincts. I saw him as a unique resource and when he did open up a little, I listened to his cogent observations with rapt attention!

ATTRACTING WINNERS TO THE TEAM

THROUGHOUT MY BUSINESS career, I was fortunate to attract high-energy managers with a strong work ethic and their own desire to Get Ahead—bringing to mind my father's broken-English Italian aphorisms: "Better a horse that has to be reined than one that needs the whip," and "A good man is never overpaid, but a bad one is never cheap enough."

Over the years, key players proved themselves and became partners in the various enterprises we were engaged in. I have always strongly believed in the concept of partnership and wanted each of those key players to "own a piece of the rock."

My beliefs were—and remain—that managers who are vital cogs in privately-owned businesses, feel better and therefore *perform better* when they hold an ownership stake. Partnering with senior managers was a fundamental belief I embraced early in my career. The ownership purchase conditions were simple and have never changed: "Buy in at book value—sell out at book value." I provided 100 percent financing by letting these management partners sign a note and pay off the stock loan out of company distributions if/when these occurred. When someone left the company, either voluntarily or involuntarily, his or her shares were automatically redeemed at the then book value.

Over a 40-year span, not one piece-of-the-rock manager failed to appreciate the ownership opportunity, nor was there ever a legal dispute over share redemptions. I'm pleased to say that virtually all departed partners left with smiles on their faces and plenty of jingle in their jeans!

One of our senior management winners at SFP was Bill Butler, who came aboard in 1979. He was a very bright guy who had graduated from UC Davis and then earned an MBA at UC Berkeley. An excellent high school and college athlete, Bill still plays full-court basketball in his sixties. His first SFP assignment was a real challenge.

Frank had run the company with his own common-sense gyroscope: only five reports arrived on his desk each day; every six months an outside CPA would come in to do the books; and a financial statement was prepared annually. Bob Graham and I wanted more measurements, including quarterly financials. Bill Butler's first job was to pull together information needed to upgrade the quality and frequency of the company's financial reporting. Oh, and as we explained, he had to do so without ruffling Frank's feathers, even though from the outset Frank considered Bill to be a "Suzy Bel spy" and had domiciled his desk in a windowless storeroom.

As the always unflappable Bill would later observe, "Gaining Frank's confidence was an interesting challenge."

Over succeeding years, Bill's multiple capabilities resulted in his taking on evermore important responsibilities and becoming an SFP shareholder following the 1986 LBO. Today, Bill's title is Executive Vice President and he is Tom Cortopassi's strong right arm at SFP.

BUY A CANNERY—FIND A LEADER!

On SFP's production side, the leadership I sought eventually came from Bob Ilse. Bob had put himself through college working summers in a San Jose cannery, and in the ensuing decades had climbed through the plant management ranks of two farmer co-ops—Lindsay Olive Growers and California Canners and Growers (Cal-Can).

In July 1982, Suzy Bel Inc. made its second acquisition: an older, smaller tomato cannery in Gilroy, California, which we bought at the Cal-Can bankruptcy auction.

Needing someone to run our new Gilroy enterprise, I hired Bob Ilse who could hit the ground running. Bob had been in charge of all seven Cal-Can plants, knew the Gilroy plant well and who, despite some co-op political baggage, struck me as having leadership qualities.

Over time, Bob demonstrated the ability to herd unionized cannery workers in the directions he wanted them to go, and proved to be an able field general in our multiple battles with teamster unions. But after an entire career working for co-ops infused with grower politics, Bob's short suit was entrepreneurial thinking, which I made my job to remedy over ensuing years.

After Bob had managed Gilroy for two years, Suzy Bel's third acquisition was a peach-canning plant in Sacramento which had gone through one previous bankruptcy and was on the brink of a second. Needing him on an everyday basis to oversee both Gilroy and the Sacramento plant (Sierra Packers), I persuaded Bob and his wife, Sherrie, to move to Stockton. (At both Gilroy and Sacramento, Bob ably led the confrontations with Teamsters Union locals over concessionary contracts).

After a few years working together out of Suzy Bel headquarters in Stockton, and with Frank Piciullo retiring, I appointed Bob to become SFP's on-site President, a position he occupied until his retirement in 2003.

With Bob in place as SFP president, I began lobbying him about improving plant culture from the floor up. I believed we could do so in a positive way without initiating a turf war with the Teamsters' Modesto local. However, it turned out that the first person I had to convince was Bob Ilse! Having been around canneries for so long, Bob did not believe the "us-against-them" Teamster mindset could be positively changed.

I, on the other hand, was convinced it could be changed and was itching to try something that had worked very well at CFI. "Bob, we need to find a way to incent our workers to be more productive." Bob would look at me in disbelief. "Dino, you don't know these union people. I've been around them all my life and they can't be incented," he said flatly.

Since buying SFP, I had closely studied plant operations each year during the ten-week fresh-pack season required to supply sales requirements. In a cannery, "efficiency" is measured by how many cooker can pockets are filled and how many run empty, and SFP's efficiency rate was a long way from "filling every pocket" and our Union foremen were not motivated to improve it.

For instance, whenever a mechanical breakdown and line shut down occurred, the union mechanics (summoned by walkie-talkies), would take their sweet time walking to the breakdown and studying the problem before fixing it. In the meantime, fresh tomatoes backed up on halted conveyor belts as hourly workers stood around waiting for the shut down line to restart. Lack of productivity was exemplified by the leisurely pace of all personnel under the watchful eyes of union shop stewards enforcing contract work rules—an unfortunate mindset common in unionized plants throughout America.

Early in my farming career, I had found a way to deal with a similar mindset—*il pasito* (slow walking)—among Mexican crews working by the hour. In an effort to overcome il pasito, at the start of that season I selected a small group of full-time workers and explained CFI's cost/yield targets for each crop in Spanish.

In addition to incenting their own productivity, I believed the behavior of this selected group could positively influence the behavior of seasonal workers. Using basic arithmetic, I reviewed the per acre costs and yield of each crop needed to earn a reasonable profit—and most importantly to them, that a specified percentage of each crop's dollars would go into a figurative *Vaso* (in Spanish, a glass jar), and at the end of the season all monies accumulated in it would be equally divided amongst the *Grupo del Vaso* members. Keep in mind these were relatively uneducated *campesinos*, yet with careful explanation they caught on fast.

Almost immediately bi-monthly meetings to measure progress against CFI targets began motivating Vaso group productivity, and by their example started influencing seasonal worker behavior. At year-end when Vaso proceeds were distributed, the Grupo members were true believers. Obviously Vaso participants appreciated the bonus dollars, but the big "ah-ha" was they absolutely loved *being measured against goals*!

The following year CFI took the Vaso program a step further to solve a Workmen's Compensation insurance problem. From prior experience, Emiliano, Gene, and I knew that about a week before the end of tomato harvest, a rash of back sprains among some sorters on CFI tomato harvesters would lead to disability claims being filed. This was not stoop labor, but rather fourteen people, mostly women, on each harvester standing at sorting belts as the machine moved through the field at a slow pace. They did not have to walk or bend over and were protected from the sun under canvas shades, so being a tomato sorter was a desirable job. But the increasing number of late-season back sprains were leading to increasing Workmen's Compensation insurance rates. Of course, Workmen's Comp doctors had their own financial incentive to keep a "disabled worker" coming back for visits.

In its second year, the Vaso program added Worker's Comp Insurance rebates to the target list. At that time CFI was paying about $350,000 a year in Worker's Comp premiums, but would get back a 50 percent premium rebate minus any disability dollars paid out by the insurance company. The Vaso group was told CFI would put half of its Worker's Comp rebate into the Vaso. As I explained that could be as much as $50,000 to $60,000 *Vaso* dollars, everyone's eyes got very big! Sure enough, that year Vaso peer pressure resulted in seasonal Worker Comp claims dropping dramatically and remaining down in subsequent years.

As I described CFI's 20 years of Vaso success in modifying worker behavior to Bob, he remained skeptical. "Dino, it may have worked on the farm but you just don't understand Teamsters. Trust me, we need to talk to them nice, and if they like us they won't screw us too bad. But if we push them in any way, they will 'slow walk' us to death! I know what I'm talking about."

I had heard similar words from Frank Piciullo in earlier years. "Dino, don't mess with these guys in the back," Frank would say under his breath as we walked through the plant. "If they get the idea you're trying to push them, they'll screw you good."

Undeterred by all this conventional wisdom, I continued to lobby Bob that the program would work if it was fair, transparent, easy to understand, and if the financial incentives were *equally divided* among the selected participants.

"We should set up the program on a daily measurement basis," I explained, "so that each day is a fresh start with each canning line earning its own reward. That way if one line breaks down it doesn't affect rewards earned on others. The daily hurdle rate should be set at an achievable number of cases for each line. You, the president, the boss, have to be the guy who sets the rates for the following day, depending on what product each line will be running. I suggest we start with $300 into the pot for each line that meets its daily hurdle rate. Finally I suggest you be the one to personally post the prior results each day, including year-to-date dollar totals, on a big board in the plant for everyone to see."

"Bob, trust me that being measured against fair targets with generous awards for achievement will foster a team spirit because everyone named to the program will get the same share out of the pot! Finally, when the season ends, bring the group together and *you personally* hand out the bonus checks to each member *of the group*. Bob, believe me—I know it will work!"

Despite my patient eloquence, Bob remained unconvinced the plan would incent hardcore Teamsters. However to his credit he eventually relented. "Okay, I still think we're messing with fire and that it won't work, but I'm willing to give it a good try."

And that's how the Pushing Over The Top (POTT) program was born.

True to his own competitive nature, Bob went all-in on POTT. Before the season began he gathered together the 55 key plant personnel he had named as participants and explained the program.

"So, Bob, how did it go?" I asked afterward.

"Dino, their attitude was total cynicism, as in, 'I've heard company bullshit before and this is more company bullshit!'"

At the season's opening Bob rolled out the program even though he remained skeptical about the results. From day one he began setting daily hurdle rates for each line that were achievable, but not gimmes. If the hurdle rate for that line was met or surpassed, $300 went into the POTT. If ten lines met/surpassed their individual hurdle rates, $3,000 went into POTT for that day.

A large, white erasable board was secured to a wall near where everyone punched their time cards, and each morning at shift change Bob would post the prior day's results in line-by-line cases produced, dollars earned, and year-to-date POTT dollars. For the first several weeks crew members were indifferent. However, as year-to-date POTT dollars started adding up on the big white board, Bob began noticing a few people happening to sidle by when he posted daily numbers. As the season progressed, a few more sidlers appeared but the hard-core majority remained certain POTT was nothing more than company BS.

How did the union react as total POTT dollars built up? (Unions hate productivity programs!) A few weeks before the end of the season, the local Teamsters Business Agent put SFP on written notice we could not pay workers differentially because the union contract specified equal pay for each job classification. Therefore POTT was a contract violation.

Bob had anticipated this problem and had expressed that concern during our initial discussions about the program. When we received the business agent's warning, I encouraged Bob: "Let's test the size of his balls! What is he going to do about it after you give the POTT participants the extra money? Is he going to tell them they can't keep it?" By this time Bob owned the POTT program, and didn't like the union telling him we couldn't do it.

A few days later the business agent came to see Bob and blustered, "If you give those people extra money, then we're gonna make you pay everyone in those classifications the same amounts."

"No, I don't agree." Bob said. "This is a production bonus spread over people who directly affect line productivity." The business agent insisted. "It's in the contract—you can't pay over scale unless you pay that amount to everyone in that classification."

"Fine, if you want to tell our POTT participants the union contract doesn't let me pay them the money I feel they earned, go ahead. But I'm going to hand them their bonus checks anyway. If you want to tell them they can't take it, there's nothing I can do about that."

The last day of the season Bob gathered the POTT participants in the cafeteria, holding a stack of checks in his hand, calling out names one by one. Bob handed out the checks which were each $3,500. A number of the younger workers began to let out whoops and whistles. POTT wasn't a management scam after all! The hardcore union guys in the group were not cheering but they took their checks anyway. After we called the union's bluff, they apparently decided to fold their hand because nothing more was said and the POTT participants got to keep their money.

After that first year, worker interest in POTT went up dramatically, and was so motivational as to productivity that we had to put in quality parameters to only credit case production that met or exceeded SFP's strict quality specifications. The POTT program not only enhanced SFP's plant efficiencies, it also positively enhanced worker attitudes. Except for a couple of hard-core shop stewards, our workers reveled in the new team spirit, became pumped to excel, and the former we-they union attitude essentially disappeared.

Whenever Bob posted the prior day's results, a throng of workers going off shift would gather, and each time he posted a line result greater than its hurdle rate—which the crew came to call "redlining"—onlookers would hoot and clap. When all ten canning lines red-lined, high-fives would be flying as they celebrated a team victory.

As Bob's ownership of the POTT program grew, he went from skeptic to messianic convert. In later years, he came to claim POTT as his own invention, which was fine with me because he was the one who made it work. As the saying goes: "Success knows many fathers—only failure is an orphan."

Twenty-five years later, the POTT program is still going strong, and the SFP production team enjoys an esprit de corps absolutely unique in our industry. If we wanted to push the issue, I believe SFP workers would vote to decertify the Teamsters union. We haven't done that because the usual work-rule grievances and other issues that frustrate most employers have virtually disappeared.

Done fairly and properly, I have always believed anyone can be motivated to excel because competition is part of our human DNA. Just set up reasonable hurdle rates for people to achieve in order to earn a reward, measure performance honestly and accurately, and then get out of their way.

Today at SFP when a bell goes off signaling a line stoppage, foremen and mechanics *run* to the problem like firemen responding to a fire. Forewomen responsible for managing line flow rates constantly tweak for greater efficiency. In the off-season, mechanics make suggestions to management for equipment modifications to enhance line reliability and plant productivity. In short, SFP workers own their jobs.

Within a few years of POTT's beginnings, the plant was running as close to the fill-every-pocket maximum as mechanically possible. All the humming, clattering, plant racket was music to our ears, and we exchanged a few high-fives of our own. On the productivity side, the bar had been raised, but on the sales/marketing side, we had greater heights yet to scale.

A TIPPING POINT

Notwithstanding the mental stimulus of structuring Suzy Bel and acquiring SFP, back at CFI we were still farming on a large scale. Suzy Bel's shareholder Board of Directors was urging me to "stop screwing around with farming" and to focus full-time on increasing our food processing activities. Their rationale was that Bob Graham and I could make more money doing the latter than the former. I knew they were right, but farming had been my first love and was hard to give up.

By 1982 CFI was farming 2,500 row crop acres in the Stockton area—of which 1,500 acres were double-cropped—and 4,000 acres 100 miles south near Chowchilla—of which 2,000 acres were double-cropped—essentially 10,000 acres of crops including tomatoes, bell peppers, kidney beans, wheat, and sugar beets. Additionally, CFI owned and farmed 600 acres of wine grapes and 100 acres of cherries. Between a balanced mix of contracted crops and open market acreage, the 1982 season looked to be a bountiful year.

Then Mother Nature dropped the most devastating weather hammer on northern California that I had experienced in my entire farming career. Extremely heavy rains throughout the winter of 1981-82 caused severe damage to fall-planted crops and continued through April, severely delaying planting of spring crops in saturated fields. After the false promise of a normal summer, unseasonal heavy rains began again in the first week of September and continued through the end of November. Caused by the then unknown El Niño effect, multiple storm systems pounded northern and central California with high winds and torrential rains.

By spring 1982, CFI's 3,500 acres of winter wheat was drowned or diseased. Yields dropped from the three tons/acre norm to one ton/acre. Typically, sugar beets in Chowchilla were a profitable wintertime crop, and we had 600 acres under contract. After establishing a beautiful stand in the fall of 1981—thinned, weeded, fertilized, and growing vigorously—heavy winter rainfall kept us from applying herbicides, and by the following spring winter weeds were as tall as the radiator cap on a tractor! We had to roto-chop a jungle of weeds just to find the rows of puny sugar beets that had survived. After spending a great deal of atypical expenses, "crappy" is the only word to describe the resulting June beet harvest.

On the heels of the abysmal wheat harvest, we planted 3,500 acres of double-crop beans—wheat/bean double-cropping was one of CFI's economic foundations from its beginning. During 1982's short summer the beans grew fine, but soon after beginning the fall harvest, it began raining. Ultimately, we threshed about 70 percent of the bean acreage, which rain damage reduced to 50 percent of budgeted yield, and the rest of the acreage was abandoned. The 50 percent-yield beans were puffed up from all the rain and had to be artificially dried, which lowered their grade, bringing $17 per 100 pounds, compared to the $30 to $32 we had received in previous years. The weekly September rains prevented any harvest of our 600 acres of wine grapes and one hundred percent of our crop rotted on the vines!

The torrential spring weather created super-saturated ground conditions, which forced CFI to invent a new way of planting tomato seeds mixed in a peat soil medium. The technique worked and although the planting came late, it produced a very good stand of tomatoes. Just when it looked as if CFI might dodge a bullet, it started raining ten days after harvest began, and 80 percent of the tonnage rotted in the field.

Like many farming operations in 1982, the disastrous weather left CFI saddled with a heavy load of short-term bank debt. We were unable to pay off several million dollars of CFI's line of credit from crop revenues as we normally did each year. Not only was Bank of America pressing for immediate repayment of CFI's 1982 line, the bank refused to finance 1983 operations until they were made whole on the 1982 debt. In other words, our line of credit was maxed out and frozen at the unpaid multi-million dollar debt level. Other farmers, large and small operators alike, faced similar dilemmas. After the disastrous 1982 year, inability to secure crop financing for the following year was causing a rash of equipment auctions and farmland disposals at fire-sale prices.

During the fall of 1982 there were many cold-sweat nights when I would wake up in the wee hours. Twisting and turning to escape bad dreams, my mind would race and prevent getting back to sleep. I shared my "sweaty nights" problems with Fritz Grupe, a dear friend since college days and the Chowchilla Ranch equity investor. Fritz had become a very successful developer and had put up all the equity money to buy and develop the Chowchilla Ranch. Fritz said "sweaty nights" had happened to him during periods of high stress and he had discovered a remedy: "Keep a notepad by your bed, and when you wake up during the night, turn on the light and write down every single thing that's bothering you. Then lay down and you'll go to sleep."

Fritz's remedy worked for some sweaty nights, but not all—not that fall!

Fortunately, during times of high stress my daytime mind became focused and more able to evaluate alternatives objectively rather than emotionally. The times our businesses have faced the greatest danger have found me calmest and at my best. Bar none, 1982 represented a real body blow and the greatest financial hit I had ever experienced.

CFO and partner Bob Graham could not see how CFI could handle 1982's huge cash shortfall, and he was looking to me for leadership. Meanwhile, I was doing a lot of self-talk: "Okay, this is the biggest financial crunch of your life. Stay cool, don't weaken, and figure a way out of it."

CFI had valuable assets, including significant equity in farmland ownership accumulated over the preceding 15 years, and developed into 600 acres of productive vineyards and orchards. The problem wasn't net-worth—it was *finding the cash* to pay off operating debt. What CFI had to avoid at all costs was being forced into fire-sale liquidation of hard-earned assets to repay B of A.

In November 1982 Bob Graham and I had a summit meeting with B of A representatives in the CFI conference room. Present were two of our local loan officers, our regional credit officer, and a "suit" from the bank's Problem Loans department in San Francisco. This suit was demonstrably experienced at being an enforcer, figuratively putting on brass knuckles and beating up under-water borrowers until they folded and did whatever the bank dictated.

Bob and I had previously prepared a workout repayment plan, and told the foursome that given CFI's strong balance sheet and long record with B of A we deserved their trust and patience. Our two local bankers and the regional credit officer had faith in us and seemed willing to be flexible. However, the suit was playing hard-ball insisting on immediate asset disposals. His trump card was bringing up our personal guarantees and stated that the Problem

Loans department was prepared to immediately move on the personal guarantees to force asset liquidation and prompt repayment of CFI's multi-million line of credit.

At that point my temperature began rising and I took on the suit: "Don't try to threaten me, because I don't threaten worth a damn! If you want me to get up and leave this meeting, I will and then I'm going straight to CFI's attorney. You can call in your attorneys and we'll get it on! Worst case, we will keep you tied up in court for two to three years and buy time to sell CFI assets on an orderly basis. Best case, we'll prove that B of A's personal guarantee wasn't designed to force fire-sale liquidations and therefore isn't enforceable against me or anyone else who signed one. So here's what we're not going to do: *we are not going to sell CFI assets at fire sale prices.*"

The local bankers got real quiet, and Bob Graham turned white as a sheet. Earlier in the meeting Bob had presented CFI's workout plan in a professional manner, but this was nose-to-nose verbal combat and my nice-guy partner was rendered speechless.

"The way for the bank to get all its money back," I continued, "and you will get it all back, is to give us time for an orderly disposition of some CFI assets. If I let you do it the way you're threatening, CFI will have to sell most of its assets to repay the entire debt, and I will have thrown away 20 years of work building up CFI's equity value. So if you really want to pay hardball you can count on us fighting you in court every step of the way."

The suit knew it was not an empty threat. We could tie them up in court for years, delay repayment at least that long, and perhaps knock out their personal guarantee. He stared at me and I stared right back. It was a tipping point moment and time seemed to stand still.

Finally the suit spoke: "Mr. Cortopassi, I'm not authorized to agree, but what do you have in mind?"

At that moment I knew that if we didn't overplay this hand, B of A would go along with our workout plan and CFI would make it through the dark tunnel and into the sunshine again!

I then asked Bob to reiterate our proposal which included liq-
uidating specified land assets within a three-year time frame once
prices stabilized. Within that time frame CFI sold the 600 acres of
wine grapes to Suzy Bel Inc. and 500 acres of row crop land south
of Stockton to a land developer. In return for Bob and me devoting
virtually all our management time on Suzy Bel business, the board
was happy to buy CFI's vineyards, which CFI continued to farm
under lease, and which Suzy Bel resold to Joan and me four years
later at a substantial profit. As subsequent events demonstrated,
the aggregate value of CFI's fixed assets was very much greater than
the B of A hole, but it would take time to work all that out.

Meanwhile, back at the do or die, B of A meeting, I demanded
that as long as CFI met the workout plan pay-down dates, no further
interest would accrue on the remaining balance. The suit looked as
if I had asked him to toss his firstborn into the deal.

"Oh no, we have to accrue interest," he sputtered.

I looked at him coldly. "Don't give me that BS! CFI is on B of
A's problem–loan list and FDIC regulations don't let you count
accrued interest on problem loans. You're just trying to gild the
lily—the bank doesn't need the accrued interest, and piling on
interest will just make it tougher for CFI to pay back the principal.
Besides, your best assurance of being paid off is our diligence in
orderly asset liquidation. We are committing that you will collect
100 percent of the face value on your notes. But no more interest."

After some more sparring, the suit grudgingly agreed, but not
before asking for our Suzy Bel stock as added collateral.

"No, we're not going to do that either," I told him.

And that was the end of B of A negotiations for CFI's workout.

When crucial events in business pile up, they can seem insur-
mountable. The key to remember is the essence of a quote I framed
and hung on my office wall 40-plus years ago: "Life is a series of
opportunities cleverly disguised as insoluble problems."

Sure enough, while Bob Graham and I were still in the process of
finalizing the B of A paperwork, fellow founder of Suzy Bel, John
Kautz added an unexpected complication.

John came to see me saying he wanted to sell his Suzy Bel stock due to his Kautz Farms financing issues. John was farming less land than CFI, but the weather had also dealt him a severe blow, and his bank—Wells Fargo—was demanding immediate repayment of Kautz Farm's operating line of credit. I counseled John to hold onto his Suzy Bel stock and like CFI come up with a land-selling schedule that would satisfy Wells' demands.

"John, that's what I'm doing with B of A. You will make more money from Suzy Bel stock than you can owning the farmland, so hold onto your stock." It was truthful counsel, but I also didn't need another cash complication in my life at that particular moment.

"No, I've thought about it," John said, "and I want to sell my stock. Suzy Bel has always been your deal—you're the CEO and you've run it from the beginning. My deal is farming wine grapes. I've got three boys who want to farm so I don't want to sell any of my land."

I kept trying to talk John out of selling his Suzy Bel stock but his German mind was made up, and he wanted all cash!

Back at the time of Suzy Bel's formation, John and I had established a "Buy-Sell" agreement between us. In the event either of us wanted to sell our Suzy Bel stock, we had agreed to offer it to the other and negotiate in good faith and to come together on a price. If we couldn't agree on price, then the seller was free to shop the stock to an outside buyer, establish an acceptable price, and re-offer the stock at that price to the non-selling partner.

If John was going to sell his stock, I definitely wanted to be the one to buy it, although concurrent with the CFI debt workout, how that could be accomplished was indeed problematic?! John and I were long-time friends and had been partners in Cal-Gift from 1968 to 1978, so price negotiation wasn't easy for either of us. We went back and forth, with him wanting to sell for more and me wanting to buy for less.

Finally, I offered to throw in an 80-acre vineyard that I owned personally and John coveted—it was adjacent to vineyards he already owned. Throwing in the vineyard plus a Suzy Bel stock purchase price considerably higher than its book value allowed us to reach price agreement. Now the problem became where to find the cash to buy John out.

I had participated in the annual Harvard Agribusiness Seminar for the previous nine years, where I had recently met a banker who was hustling me for some Suzy Bel loan business. Based in New York City, Dave Sprague headed up the U.S. entry of a Dutch bank (Rabobank) that was new to the United States. I called Dave and explained the agreement worked out with John.

"So you need a loan to buy the stock?" he asked.

"That's right."

"When are you going to pay it back?"

"Five years or less."

"If I make you the stock loan, will Rabobank get a shot at SFP's line of credit loan?"

"You can have a shot at it, but I won't guarantee you'll get it."

"As long as you promise me a fair shot that's enough. I'll fly out to California and we can work out the stock loan details."

In our subsequent negotiation, Sprague insisted that Bob Graham and I pledge all the stock purchased from John, plus the Suzy Bel stock we already owned free and clear. I had arrived at the tipping point of my business career. As they say in Texas Hold-em, buying John's stock at that moment of CFI's crisis was an all-in bet. I had played plenty of poker in my life but this pot represented a *big part* of Joan's and my net worth.

Between the CFI workout deal signed with B of A and pledging all our Suzy Bel stock, what we had built up over the prior 22 years was in play. From that point forward our net worth could climb skyward—or swoon like a wounded duck!

If I had an ace in the hole, it was that I had always refused to accept failure. That didn't mean I hadn't failed in the past—far from it. But failing is separate and distinct from accepting failure. When things seem the darkest I always remember a vignette from Vince Lombardi's storied career.

Lombardi was being interviewed by a reporter after his first season with the Green Bay Packers. He told the reporter the Packers had "been undefeated" that year. The reporter pointed out they had lost five games. Lombardi replied, "No, that's not correct. There were five games that we happened to run out of time before we could win."

That anecdote explains the difference between failing and *accepting* failure. Like Vince Lombardi, failure has never been acceptable to me.

Through YPO I got to know a number of successful leaders who shared the common trait of refusing to accept failure. A key question I used to ask myself was why are these leaders able to turn problems into opportunity, while most cannot? Certainly anyone can be hit by unforeseeable misfortune. So does luck (good or bad) play a part in overcoming the misfortune? Sure! But I had long believed that success eventually gravitates towards those *who prepare themselves to get lucky*, and observing successful YPOers confirmed for me that Chance Favors the Prepared Mind.

After the high stress events of late 1982, CFI entered 1983 without an operating loan, but somehow we eked through. Fortunately, a lot of ground tillage had already been done in the fall of 1982 and it didn't take much cash to plant winter wheat and other low-intensity crops. Additionally, we sub-leased significant acreage to other farmers and reduced the scope of CFI row-crop operations.

Slowly CFI began working its way out of the 1982 weather disaster. It took four years, but CFI made good on every nickel of the B of A debt, and additionally paid off the Rabobank stock loan with cash proceeds from the 1986 LBO of Stanislaus. The 1982 tipping point had been weathered, and I vowed to avoid any more all-in repeats!

WORK OF ART

At The Real Italian Tomato Company, we learned from standing in the shoes of independent pizzeria and Italian restaurateurs that they desired *authenticity* in the presentation of their food. Our message to them was that Stanislaus delivered "Real Italian" by virtue of our superior quality and our family roots. End-users of Italian heritage reveled in our shared ethnicity, and those not of Italian descent believed our products help make their P & I food more authentic.

To better communicate our "Realness" in 1990 we began publishing a four-page newsletter, *La Trattoria*: *Idea Exchange for*

Independent Restaurateurs, and 24 years later we are still sending it out bi-monthly to a proprietary list of 80,000 independent P&I restaurateurs.

The cardinal *La Trattoria* (LT) rule we originally set remains unbroken: i.e., the newsletter has not/does not promote our products/our company. Instead, LT provides "idea exchange " (through stories, letters, advice, and recipes) between independent restaurateurs and ourselves. We solicit ideas that have improved their businesses, publish the best of them in each issue, and say *grazie* by sending each published contributor $100.

We have received thousands of cards and letters from readers over the years, some in Italian, which my mother, affectionately known at Stanislaus as "Mama Teresa," translated. Comments run the gamut of "We enjoy your stories;" "I love what your family stands for because it reminds me of my own;" "I'm not Italian but wish I was;" "Thanks for the great idea about . . ." "the pasticciata recipe is delicious;" and so on.

For years, I wrote *La Trattoria*'s front-page, "Sharing Success" column embodying strategies and tactics applicable to independent restaurants. (An example of sharing success follows:)

• • •

BEING "REAL" PAYS OFF!

"A well-tended field, a well-made shirt, a well-built car, a well-prepared meal, whatever the work, I enjoy seeing it done well! A commitment to excellence, attention to detail and caring about the outcome, these are the personal attributes I enjoy seeing in others. Similarly, I look upon my own work as an extension of my character; a personal signature that validates my competence.

What about you? Are you committed to excellence? To caring about the outcome? To providing your patrons with the very best you can do? As independent business people, our products/services provide us the canvas to display our individual competence. As entrepreneurs, we have the latitude of making a personal commitment to excellence and that is what differentiates us from the corporate types. Real products and services are how we attract the attention and respect of the kind of customers we want.

Said another way, if the product/service offered is truly Real, the business attracts local customers who value Realness and are willing to pay for it. If, on the other hand, the offered product/service is mediocre, it must be heavily promoted and attracts fickle customers unable to see the difference between true Realness and a thin veneer thereof. In both instances, the business ends up attracting the customers it deserves!

Because genuine Realness in a product/service does in fact attract knowledgeable customers, it also attracts competitors unwilling to pay the price for Realness and who therefore try to make themselves look like us with `veneer' (e.g., new ad campaigns built on copycat themes, copycat names, copycat colors, layered over their same old produce mediocrity and promoted by their same old discounting.) Are those kinds of copycat strategies a con job? Of course! If our success is built on Realness, could that kind of copycat veneer confuse some of our customers? Yes, but don't worry about it because customers who value Realness may be fooled once or twice, but they will catch on and come back. That's why, despite their copycat imitations, competitors relying on veneer end up with the kind of fickle customers they deserve!"

DINO CORTOPASSI

THE YEAR AFTER launching *La Trattoria*, Stanislaus participated in the first annual Pizza Expo trade show with hundreds of exhibitors pitching their products to pizzeria operators from around the country. Prior to the show I had a major disagreement with our then VP-Sales who wanted to use our booth space to pitch our products. SFP's Marketing VP Julie Ambrose and I were against that conventional approach, and instead wanted SFP to show up for a different reason: to say thank you to our customers. After all, how many opportunities do we have to thank end-users personally?

I described what I wanted the Stanislaus space to feel and look like: when you visit the home of an Italian family, the first thing you hear is "Come in, sit down, have something to eat." That is traditional Italian hospitality. I want people who are weary of wandering the show to feel like they walked into our home. I want them to sit down at tables with real tablecloths, real napkins, real silverware, real crockery, real glasses, and real food. We can serve them cold Italian appetizers, hot pasta dressed with our sauces, and pour them Italian wines. But just like *La Trattoria,* we will *not try to sell them anything.*

Despite the VP-Sales' reluctance, that's exactly what we did at that first show, with a friendly, inviting booth manned by family members and a dozen SFP office employees who volunteered to serve as wait staff. I wandered around, worked the tables, and greeted guests like *il padrone di casa*. At first, booth visitors looked at us kind of funny, as if waiting for the hammer to drop and the sales pitch to start. When that didn't happen everyone relaxed. People began coming back just to sit down or to have seconds on the pasta and wine!

In later years we added a restored old tractor or classic motorcycle inside the expanded booth with a photographer present for anyone who wanted their picture taken. In those pre-digital days we offered to mail the photo free, which is how we added restaurateur names to our expanding mailing list for *La Trattoria*, Christmas cards, etc. As Julie enthused: "It's all about relationship building with follow-up."

Over the years, the popularity of SFP's Pizza Expo booth became legendary and forced multiple expansions. Today, it's about five times the size of a large conference room, and like the best Italian restaurant in the neighborhood, is always packed with happy people. Seeing our success, other major exhibitors tried to create a similar ambiance with their booths, but failed the acid test of "no sales pitching."

The personal bond of SFP customer relationships arises from the personal way we communicate with them—not only face-to-face but on the phone and in writing. An example is how we handle customer complaints. SFP's 800-number is printed on every can label and all our written communications. The 800-line is always *answered by a real person during 8-to-5 business hours every business day of the year*. Anyone in the office may answer the 800-line, from the most junior employee to a department head, but it must be answered by a real person!

That in itself sets SFP apart from other companies, virtually all of which have automated answering systems, many of which require callers to leave their message without ever speaking to a human being. Nobody enjoys being taken for granted, especially a customer who has a problem. When a complaint is received, whether via the 800-line or an SFP person in the field, it is *immediately* relayed to a senior person who *immediately* calls the customer back.

Experience has taught us that nineteen times out of twenty, the reported problem isn't our responsibility, but we *never* say that. Most companies fall into the habit of saying, "It's not our fault." Even though that may be true, it's a guaranteed way to piss off a customer. SFP people are trained to always say: "Thank you for letting us know. We always strive for perfection and appreciate your help." Why? First, very occasionally the complaint helps us find a chink in our armor. Second, we want every end-user to be a raving fan of our company, and a brushed-off customer will never be a raving fan.

Printed, framed, and hung in the offices of all SFP representatives is the following: "Customer complaints are an opportunity to gain a customer for life!"

Another way we personalize end-user relationships is through the SFP "We Care" Department, which we formed after an accidental discovery some years back. While gathering information for a marketing campaign, we did a random telephone survey of one thousand existing end-users. Our discovery was how much they appreciated getting a call. It made us even more real. As a result, we promptly staffed-up the We Care department to ensure every single restaurateur using SFP products is telephoned at least once a year: "This is Stanislaus Foods calling to see how everything is going with you. How's business?"

The results have been phenomenal. Year in and year out, we continue to reinforce personalized communications with customers who realize that we care enough about them and their business to call to see how it's going.

Maintaining personal channels of communication with customers is more than just good public relations. It also provides us with up-to-date local information from every market in America. End-users were the source of early intelligence about one of the biggest challenges we faced in my three decades at SFP's helm. Before that long-running war was over, it had turned into an epic never seen before in the food-service industry.

DAVID vs GOLIATH

I n this version of the famous story, Stanislaus Food Products was cast as the slingshot-wielding shepherd boy, and
the nine-foot-tall Philistine none other than SYSCO, a $37 billion,
Fortune-100 food-service distributor—in SFP lexicon, a "Big-D."
SYSCO was founded by John Baugh, an entrepreneurial independent food source distributor from Texas who in 1970 persuaded
nine fellow food-service independents around the country to merge
into SYSCO and go public.

In seven years, thanks to more mergers, SYSCO had become the
largest food-service supplier in America. In 1988 an acquisition

of its next largest competitor gave SYSCO national coverage, with 180 locations and approximately 45,000 employees.

With its coast-to-coast network of warehouses and huge fleet of trucks, SYSCO currently sells products to 400,000 food-service customers. In the early years of SFP's footprint expansion into new regional markets we began selling products to SYSCO houses as we did to independent distributors. Collectively these new-market distributors sold and delivered SFP brands to restaurants attracted to us by our Real Italian marketing.

Given the Baugh strategy of letting each individual SYSCO house operate autonomously, many of those houses welcomed carrying Stanislaus products for their street cred influence with independent P&I restaurateurs—a segment SYSCO was trying to penetrate. Everything was going fine until the early 1990s when a new SYSCO CEO came along and changed the autonomous philosophy of the Baugh-era.

Under pressure to keep SYSCO earnings growing and a stock price that had gone from $3 to $30 a share climbing, the new CEO issued a corporate dictum that SYSCO houses increase their push of SYSCO private labels. Like other Big-Ds, SYSCO enjoyed fatter margins on the sale of its private labels versus selling manufacturer brands. Up to that point the relationship had been symbiotic since SYSCO benefited from carrying our brands and SFP benefitted from our brands being broadly available. Unfortunately as is often the case in corporate suites, it was a symbiosis the new president failed to appreciate.

At that time we were selling products to 35 SYSCO houses throughout the country. We first got wind that an old practice known as bait and switch was happening in the Phoenix area. SYSCO's "bait" came from winning the business of P&I restaurateurs using SFP products, and the "switch" came later when the SYSCO rep would say, "Hey, why don't you try our private label? I can save you two bucks a case." A few restaurateurs would go along with the switch, but most were loyal to SFP and declined. The rep would then up the pressure by claiming to be out of stock, and suggesting delivering a SYSCO label "until we get the next load of Stanislaus."

As a result of end-user calls to our 800 number, we promptly sent a letter to SYSCO-Phoenix: "It has come to our attention that your reps are attempting to convert users of our products to SYSCO brands. This is contrary to Stanislaus business interests. We ask you to ensure your reps do not do this again because if we continue to hear about it, we will discontinue selling you our products."

In those days, SYSCO was so powerful that the Phoenix house did not take us seriously and kept right on doing bait 'n' switch because SFP's phone kept ringing. The next letter we sent was shorter: "It is clear your business interests are not congruent with SFP's business interests, so effective immediately we will no longer sell you our goods."

At that time in food-service distribution, SYSCO was comparable to what Wal-Mart is today in the retail segment. Just as manufacturers today fall all over themselves to sell Wal-Mart, in those days every food-service manufacturer wanted to sell to SYSCO. I should point out that SYSCO—truly the 800 pound gorilla in the food-service industry—had become accustomed to negotiating inside deals from both private-label and branded manufacturers. An "inside deal" was a manufacturer's rebate paid at the corporate level which SYSCO "cost-plus" contract customers never saw. When SYSCO corporate had previously sought an inside deal, from SFP, we had politely declined citing our core value principle of "same price for everyone." They had been disbelieving. *How dare we?* But we held our ground.

Now the Phoenix house was trying to switch out our brands with SYSCO private label products on which they could earn a higher per-unit profit. Looking upon what they were doing as nothing less than a cannibalization of our hard-earned brand recognition, I saw this as a fight we could not avoid. Word spread throughout the industry about what the crazy guys at SFP had done in firing a SYSCO house. *No one did that to SYSCO!*

As it turned out, Phoenix was SYSCO's first shot across SFP's bow, and corporate's dictum that their houses replace manufacturer's brands with SYSCO labels spread to other regions. So whenever we found one of their houses engaged in bait and switch tactics, after one warning we would cut them off.

I remain convinced that in their arrogance, SYSCO thought they could crush SFP because they were big and we were little. In fact both then and now they had giant companies like Heinz, Sara Lee, and others kowtowing due to the huge volume of sales SYSCO represented. But because SFP's sales strategy was based on nurturing many relatively small distributors we had a loyal foundation to rely on without SYSCO. Thanks to the wise counsel of Frank Piciullo many years before, SFP's growth had been built on the strategic foundation of avoiding risk from really big accounts. I believe if SFP had not been so positioned, SYSCO could well have made us knuckle under.

At the beginning of the SYSCO saga I didn't have a lot of support from the Stanislaus Advisory Board (SAB) or around our SMC table. There were valid concerns that this was a war we could not win against such superior force. I kept saying, "We have no choice but to cut off any SYSCO house engaged in bait and switch. It isn't a fight we started or wanted, but in the face of this frontal assault on our brands, *we have to defend our turf*."

I heard comments like: "Geez, I don't know, Dino. SYSCO is the major force in the food distribution business. They've got the trucks."

"I know they have the trucks" I would respond, "but we've worked too hard building loyal restaurateur relationships to give them up without a fight. Look, I know we can't stop SYSCO from trying to push their private label, but we don't have to keep selling them the bullets to shoot back at us!"

Over a period of several years, SFP terminated 18 SYSCO houses we caught engaged in bait and switch. The other 17 SYSCO houses so needed SFP's street cred that they ignored the periodic dictums from SYSCO corporate, did not try bait and switch, and we continued to sell them our products throughout the war.

What was most satisfying to me was that in each market where SFP cut off a SYSCO House, other distributors lauded our courage and quickly picked up the slack. In each of those markets we maintained or grew sales volume, and on a national basis, SFP's sales kept blowing the doors off!

It took more than a decade—and a new president—before SFP was extended an olive branch. SYSCO invited SFP to meet with their senior people at their Houston headquarters. Both Bob Ilse and I decided not to go for fear that at some point in the conversation we would say, "Go screw yourself" and walk out. Instead we sent Bill Butler who is always cool as a cucumber.

Bill ended up making several trips and helped negotiate a peace treaty that we were able to get in writing. First, any SYSCO house that we put back on had to promise to not engage in bait and switch, stock at least eight of our products, and sell them at a reasonable margin rather than loss leaders to steal end-users from other distributors. Even with those huge concessions, to date SFP has not resumed selling to a number of SYSCO houses cut off during the war.

From his position on the Stanislaus Advisory Board, Gary Rogers, CEO of Dreyer's Ice Cream, had a front-row seat for the SYSCO saga. As he later explained, "When Dino takes someone on, it's a fight to the death and he beat SYSCO because they eventually figured out he was right. They got the point that Stanislaus brands were so valued in the P&I segment that for SYSCO to try attacking that brand dominance with their own private label was crazy. They were better off to use SFP brands as an entry into P&I restaurants and then try to sell those customers *other* private-label products. In the end, SYSCO needed Dino more than he needed them but it took a decade for them to get it!"

FLYING WITH EAGLES

For more than two decades we have been fortunate to have the sage counsel of Gary and the other SAB members. Immediately following the 1986 LBO, setting up that board was one of my first priorities. Before that the SFP board had been composed of other Suzy Bel shareholders who had good agribusiness instincts but didn't understand the value-added process.

To learn how to put together the kind of talented advisory board I envisioned, I went to see YPO friend John Lillie, then CEO of Leslie Salt. John was among a group of YPO heavyweights that we younger members looked up to. This influential group included Paul Foster of Foster Farms, Herb Dwight of Spectra-Physics, John Boreta of Buttes Gas & Oil, and several others. John Lillie had always been friendly toward me, and I had often heard him talk about his board service for other major companies. I explained to John that I was seeking his advice for assembling a strong board of advisors.

"Dino, there are three things to remember," John said. "First, eagles don't fly with turkeys."

I waited to see if he was making a joke, but he was dead serious.

"If you want eagles on your board, *you've got to get all eagles* because they have to respect and like each other," he explained. "If you get somebody on the board who is below par, it's not going to work."

"Okay John, I've got it. All eagles—no turkeys."

"Secondly," he went on, "you're an entrepreneur, SFP is an entrepreneurial company, so you want advisors who think entrepreneurially. You can't pay successful entrepreneurs enough money to keep them sitting on your board so you have to pay them in other ways. The best way is to pay close attention to their advice. That means sometimes acting on what they say. Not all the time because they shouldn't know as much about the business as you do, but when they do come up with something that could work give it a shot! Eagles get paid by feeling they made contributions the company followed through on."

John smiled. "Lastly, Dino, make sure they have fun."

"*Fun?* What are you talking about?"

"Sure, let me use the example of my last Saga board meeting."

I knew Saga as a giant in the institutional food service business that also owned several restaurant chains.

"We arrived in Saga's large conference room to find the big mahogany table covered with sod. *Real lawn.* This was the spring meeting so there was a centerpiece of colorful flowers planted in the sod. They provided us a self-serve picnic lunch with hot dogs, potato salad, pickles, and all this other great stuff. After lunch they handed out loaded water pistols. Dino, I want you to picture all these eagle-type CEO's squirting each other with water pistols across a conference table covered in sod! The point is Saga always makes sure there is some fun at our board meetings. Let me tell you, Dino, nobody misses a Saga board meeting. So if you want guys to stay on your board and participate, listen to their advice but make sure they're having fun."

Wow that was great advice, especially for the YPO eagles I wanted on my board! Fortunately they all agreed to join, and here is the cast in order of appearance.

After finishing his hitch as a Navy Officer following Holy Cross graduation, Art Ciocca had been in ascending positions in sales management, ending up as president of Franzia Wine Company, then owned by Coca-Cola Bottling of New York. In 1981 Art led a management buyout of Coke-NY's Franzia wine assets, and built it into The Wine Group, today the third largest wine company in the world. Art knew more about street selling and how it worked than anyone I knew. Moreover he was a devotee of trying out promising ideas in the real world rather than prolonged analysis.

At the time Gary Rogers was Dreyer's Ice Cream CEO and in the process of expanding the company's footprint. Gary was the best strategist I had ever met. A graduate of UC Berkeley and a Harvard MBA, he had the intuitive right stuff to evaluate and appropriately weigh conflicting issues relative to strategic choices. Early on I believed Gary would make a great success of Dreyers which is the subject of a separate chapter.

In my view, Larry Mindel was the smartest and most tastefully attuned Jewish/Italian restaurateur in America. Starting with Spectrum Foods back in the 1970s, which consisted of 18 Italian themed restaurants which he and financial partner Jerry Magnin built and then sold. In the mid-1980s Larry took over a small group of Italian bakeries which he expanded into the Il Fornaio restaurant chain; Larry *really* understood the restaurant business, and provided keen insight into how restaurateurs felt.

Michael Berolzheimer was one of two sons of a multi-generation pencil slat manufacturer based in Stockton. A Harvard MBA oriented to marketing, Michael had developed the Duraflame brand fire log business and was an old YPO friend. Unfortunately some watershed personal issues arose and Michael left SAB after a couple of years and was replaced by Bill Harlan.

Acting as Suzy Bel's financial advisor, Bill Jesse had outlined the SFP LBO on cocktail napkins flying home from Canada. He had a brilliant financial mind and was a great help in quickly quantifying qualitative board input. Regretfully, after a number of years on the board, Bill and another SAB member had a falling out over a business deal, and Bill chose to resign. (By then SAB had been functioning as a cohesive, knowledgeable unit for many years, so Bill was not replaced.)

A true outside-the-box thinker, Bill Harlan is a marketing genius and the most creative guy I knew in YPO. Bill was successful in a number of entrepreneurial endeavors, including real estate development, but eventually followed his long-held ambition to produce California equivalents of the Grand Cru Bordeaux wines. The result is the highest-rated Napa Valley wine under distinctive labels, the most renowned being Harlan Estate, which is currently selling its wine for $500 per bottle at the winery.

In the first couple of years some of these eagles beat me up pretty good at SAB meetings pointing out how retro some SFP policies were. For example, I caught lots of flak over SFP's policy of same price for everyone. Early on, SAB members didn't think that made sense, opining that high-volume distributors should get a price break. Another critique was SFP's focus on independent distributors, as well as certain other core beliefs. Those critiques notwithstanding, I heeded John Lillie's advice and continued to listen for other suggestions that SFP could implement, many of which were most helpful.

As they gained knowledge of SFP and the industry, SAB input became increasingly valuable and increasingly acted upon. Each board member personally contributed a great deal and has been most valuable to SFP's success over the past 25+ years. Additionally while I haven't yet handed out water pistols, we've had lots of fun along the way!

One year I took the board to Italy. As several SAB members later recalled: "For the purpose of understanding the philosophy of being Real Italian we were there a whole week. The trip mission was 'seeing

Italy through the eyes of an Italian.' It was classic Dino. We flew into Milano and boarded a luxurious Mercedes-Benz bus outfitted like an executive suite! Dino's cousin, Piero Viani, had chartered it from Germany and accompanied us throughout the trip. After taking in the Parma Food Festival with incredible displays of prosciutto, cheese, olive oil, etc., we toured a number of places off the tourist track including Lucca and visiting Cortopassi relatives."

LATE—1980 *Joan/Dino's "apartamento" in Lucca, Italy.*

"Apartamento" interior.

"Dino took us on walking tours of the city, and with his translations we had fascinating chats with people we met. Piero is a Luccan businessman and we learned what some of his issues were and how Italians think about things. At one point we got on motorbikes and lit out into the hills. We even visited an old cemetery where Dino's grandparents and a lot of other Cortopassis are buried. It was an incredibly rich experience."

"It was *fantastic*," said Julie Ambrose, who along with Bob Ilse went along on the SAB trip. "Dino not only knows Italian culture from his family heritage, he has studied Italy's long history. He gave us a tour of Italy that would have been impossible to get any other way."

Writing this book has caused me to look back and the progress SFP achieved, in all humility, was remarkable in our industry. When

ABOVE: *Mounting trusty steeds, the gang is ready for adventure.*

BELOW: *"On the road again!" with first stop at Zia Maria's house. Where's Bruno? (and Art?) While Piero goes back to find the Brunomobile, it's onward into the hills to Carignano cemetery and the tombs of Dino's grandparents.*

The Wild bunch ends up back in Lucca . . . and since the sun is setting, Ramadan ends with pizza and beer in the Apartment.

Suzy Bel bought SFP in 1978, it processed 150,000 tons of tomatoes and sold 2.5 million cases of products annually. Of that total, only 600,000 cases were SFP brands.

Today, SFP processes 750,000 tons of tomatoes and sells 15 million cases annually, of which 12 million cases are sold under our own brands. In a capital-intensive industry, our growth in branded products has been 20-fold!

In 1978, there were 18 California companies operating 36 fresh-pack tomato plants supplying the food-service market. Today, including SFP, there are four companies operating just four fresh-pack plants. SFP grew to be the largest fresh-pack tomato cannery in the world because we chose to invest all our energy and capital on independent P&I segment: restaurateurs. Those independents valued SFP's quality superiority, the values we stood for, and rewarded us with their fierce brand loyalty.

The 25 years it took to build SFP from a sleepy little company to a branded icon opened up a whole new world. From 1978 onward my business life became more challenging, more fulfilling, and stretched my envelope in innumerable ways.

I hope this doesn't sound presumptuous, but I have come to think of SFP as akin to a work of art. Like a painting or a sculpture, SFP is one of a kind, with uniqueness embedded in its very essence. Our values, our core beliefs, and our reverence for customers unify the work and in my view make the whole greater than the sum of its parts. And like other enduring works of art, SFP has appreciated in value and contributed to family wealth.

For me, however, the greatest payoff has been the exhilarating opportunity to play on all the strings of a beautiful guitar!

AN INSOLUBLE PROBLEM
TURNS INTO OPPORTUNITY

I n the spring of 1986, Congress passed the Tax Reform
Act of 1986 which President Reagan signed at mid-year.

Principal features of the Act decreased individual income tax rates,

increased corporate tax rates, and restricted real estate tax shelters.

Of significance for Suzy Bel shareholders was elimination of the

General Utilities Doctrine (GUD), which defined how acquisitions

could be structured for tax purposes.

Under GUD when an acquirer paid a purchase price higher than

the acquiree company's book value, that price premium could be

assigned to a "stepped-up" cost basis in depreciable assets (e.g.,

equipment), and therefore depreciated over future years. The elimination of GUD, in effect, *doubled* the after-tax cost of purchase-price
premiums above book value, and hence reduced the purchase price
an acquirer would be willing to pay. The GUD had been in place
since the 1930s, but after December 31, 1986 it would be gone.

GUD elimination meant that a company like Stanislaus whose
relatively low book value and growing branded business—a hefty
price premium candidate—would automatically be worth less on
January 1, 1987 than it was worth the day before. Equally important to a holding company like Suzy Bel Inc., the sale of a wholly-
owned subsidiary like Stanislaus after 12/31/86 would result in
paying capital gain taxes *twice*!

By January 1986, Bob Graham, Suzy Bel's CFO since its 1978
inception, was semi-retired so I had engaged a YPO friend, Bill
Jesse, as Suzy Bel's financial advisor. Because the 1986 Tax Reform
Act would become law in June and took effect January 1, 1987, the
three of us discussed the implications to Suzy Bel and Bill opined,
"This looks like the right time to sell Stanislaus." With one foot
out the Suzy Bel door, and the other soon to follow, Bob was very
much in favor of "a liquidity event."

After our four years of labor paying back the debt from CFI's
1982 hole while simultaneously packing the debt of buying John
Kautz's Suzy Bel stock, the idea of a liquidity event didn't sound
too bad to me either! So the agenda of the upcoming San Tomo
Board meeting included discussion of a possible sale of SFP. After
Suzy Bel had purchased two other processing companies its name
had been changed to San Tomo Inc. (STI).

At the STI board meeting Bill Jesse presented his analysis of the
pending 1986 Tax Reform Act, and directors immediately zoomed
in on what kind of price he thought SFP could bring. Going through
the valuation rationale a buyer would follow, Bill concluded: "Forty
million. Maybe a little more."

Suzy Bel had bought SFP in the fall of 1978 for $13 million.
In the subsequent seven years we had distributed significant cash

dividends, plus bought two more canneries from retained cash. Since the tax code changes meant SFP would be worth less to potential acquirers after 12/31/86, if we could get $40 million for what we bought for $13 million, the farmer-shareholder directors' consensus was "Hell yes, let's grab the cash!" Accordingly, the board voted unanimously to ask $45 million, hope for $42 million, but accept $40 million.

On one hand, I was torn about selling. SFP was growing sales nicely, but given the capital-intensity of fresh-pack canning, continuing sales growth meant continually reinvesting after-tax cash flow in expansion of plant and inventory. On the other hand, by downsizing row crop operations and selling some land, CFI was finally out of the hole with B of A. In terms of managerial time, I had honored my commitment to the board and was spending virtually all my time growing San Tomo, and they were pleased with our performance. As for Joan's and my personal finances, I still had to figure out how to pay down the Rabobank loan borrowed to buy John Kautz's Suzy Bel stock.

While our personal net worth at age 50 had grown to a significant sum, Joan and I didn't have much extra cash laying around. We had been married 28 years, had four grown kids, and still lived in the second house we ever owned—a gracious 1920s vintage home located on a 40-acre farm I had bought circa 1970. For several years we had talked about building our dream house on one of our farms, but I was reluctant. Although I would take on debt for business purposes at the drop of a hat, whenever we got around to building that dream home, I wanted to pay for it in cash!

Prior to the board meeting, I had run some figures on what the sale of SFP could mean to Joan and me personally. After paying off the remaining principal on the Rabobank stock loan, and after paying our share of capital gains taxes on a $40 million SFP sale, my calculations showed we should end up with significant cash. Having started out leveraged and continuing in that mode for 25 years, I had never even dreamed of having that much green in my life!

ABOVE: MID—1970s   *Christmas morning "Rip n' Tear."*

OPPOSITE TOP: CIRCA—1968   *Family portrait.*

OPPOSITE BOTTOM: MID—1970s   *Katie, Becky, David, and Gino with Governor Brown at Live Oak Road house (Fundraiser for John Garamendi.)*

LATE—1970s   *Traditional Christmas afternoon football at the Live Oak house.*

Even so, the thought of selling SFP was deeply troubling. By 1986 I had learned the business, greatly enjoyed the strategic and tactical challenges of brand-building, and loved our team, our customers, and our prospects. But after the dark 1982 tunnel we had crawled through, maybe it was time to take some chips off the table, have plenty of cash in the bank, and build that dream house? My mind went back and forth, but ended up in the same place as the board of directors: prudence said San Tomo should sell Stanislaus. So in June 1986, Bill Jesse and I made up a short list of prospects and set out to find a buyer.

Of course, many other business people had recognized the implications of the 1986 Tax Reform Act, and the race was on to close acquisition deals by year-end (12/31/86). Our first meeting was with a publicly-traded major food company that on two previous occasions had tried to engage me in selling them SFP. Bill and I met with their COO and CFO at their corporate headquarters in Pittsburg. The discussion was most cordial as they reconfirmed their keen desire to buy SFP. However, under direct questioning they admitted that the Tax Reform Act had caused some very big deals to pop onto their plate and they couldn't guarantee us a year-end closing. Recall that closing after year-end would have *doubled* our capital gains taxes. Rats! That eliminated the most likely buyer.

Next in line was the Merrill Lynch venture capital group represented by two guys we met with high above Wall Street. Both Bill and I found this duo to be totally arrogant, strictly oriented to financial structuring rather than real business, and dismissive of whether they could close by year-end: "Everybody is knocking on our door, offering us bigger deals than this one—blah-blah-blah!" Mainly they were MBA-type jerks who reflected a culture I would not have enjoyed working with going forward, so we crossed Merrill-Lynch off our short list and flew home without a backward glance.

Our number three candidate was a venture capital group we met with in Los Angeles whose fund was composed of private money. In contrast to the arrogant Merrill-Lynch MBAs, these were knowledgeable business guys I would have been happy to work with.

Moreover they had done their street homework and quickly grasped the business strategies of the SFP story. They genuinely liked our entrepreneurial culture and they understood our reason for selling was the impending tax changes. But being entrepreneurial guys they, too, had lots of impending deals and couldn't guarantee a 12/31/86 closing. Like our first candidate, they made it clear that if SFP was still available after 1/1/87, they very much wanted to do the deal.

Our short list was getting shorter, and the fourth candidate was a publicly-traded Canadian beer company whose CEO I had gotten to know through YPO. To diversify their beer business he had started them buying small food companies a couple years prior. So Bill and I flew to Toronto to meet with my CEO acquaintance and the president of their Foods Division, who was a former co-op president from Oregon that I had previously met through NFPA Board service (National Food Processors Association). The CEO's insightful questions demonstrated that he quickly grasped SFP's business concept and very much liked our food-service brand-building strategy. By contrast, the Foods Division president displayed his production-oriented co-op background, going on and on about how difficult the processing industry was (true!), and how relatively little branded value could be added to processed food (false!), etc.

As the discussion continued on through lunch it became evident this ex-co-op guy was in way over his head—he was sacked a year later—and that despite the CEO's obvious interest in getting an SFP deal done, the negative reaction of the Food Division president meant he would find ways to delay a pre-12/31/86 transaction. Boarding the Toronto to San Francisco flight, Bill and I settled into our first-class seats and ordered martinis on the rocks before the plane's wheels left the ground.

"Bill, I can't believe how hard it is to sell a great little business!"

"Dino, I have to admit it's pretty discouraging. I thought knowledgeable buyers would see SFP for the jewel it is and jump at the chance to buy it."

We had knocked down the first round and were halfway through our second when Bill turned to me and said, "Dino, maybe you should buy SFP yourself."

"Bill, what are you talking about?!"

"I'm talking about you buying Stanislaus yourself—doing an LBO."

Was this our financial guru or the gin talking?

"Bill, please, for the first time in my life I've anticipated getting out of debt and into some real spendable money! Now you're talking about me piling on more debt?! I'm tired of packing debt—I want some green in my jeans!"

"Relax, Dino. I think there may be a way for you to end up owning 100 percent of the company, plus coming out with some cash."

With that, Bill took out his calculator and started doing numbers. I knew that LBO stood for Leveraged Buy Out, but didn't know the ins and outs of how LBOs were structured so I mused while Bill cranked numbers.

As our third martini arrived, Bill began to educate me about senior debt (a.k.a primary security), junior debt (secondary security), mezzanine debt (unsecured), subordinated debt (*really* unsecured), and the end of the daisy chain—equity (what I would end up with). Bill then moved on to explain how he thought we could generate enough cash from the four debt levels to satisfy Suzy Bel's selling shareholders, pay off what I still owed Rabobank, end up with five million after-tax cash in the bank, and own 100 percent ownership of a multi-leveraged SFP.

While our third martinis undoubtedly influenced Bill's talking and my listening, after the four preceding short list whiffs, Bill's LBO idea was sounding more and more attractive. Joan and I would become sole owners of the company I loved; I could continue the brand-building strategies I found so stimulating; instead of having multi-millions in the bank, we would have $5 million, but that was still more than enough to build the dream house. What was *not* to like?!

Even though the LBO horse was a long shot, the more I thought about it, the more my debt-packing fatigue of the past four years began to fade. I had lived through every one of the previous 25 years with business risk and business debt, so once my brain got around the concept, it began to make sense. However, I wouldn't have considered doing it if I didn't believe every bit of that new debt would get paid. As always, family honor would be at stake.

I knew our shareholder directors possessed sound business instincts, and that springing the LBO concept might raise suspicions that Bill and I had baked a cake. Cautioning Bill that the first thing to do was see how the board felt about an LBO, I convened an emergency meeting. As the company's financial advisor, Bill went through each of our first four short-list whiffs in detail. Then I explained that on our way home from Toronto, Bill had brought up the LBO idea to me for the first time. To wit, that utilizing my existing 50 percent stock ownership, there was a reasonable chance an LBO of SFP could be financed.

Right away two of the directors asked, "At what price?"

Having anticipated their suspicion, my reply was, "I don't expect, nor would I ask for a discount from what we all previously agreed to. You all know that although we've controlled 55 percent of San Tomo stock since 1982 (Bob Graham owned 5 percent of that 55), I've never used that majority power and won't do so now. Since we all agreed on asking $45 million, with a $40 million floor, let's split the difference at $42 million."

Their suspicions mollified, the board agreed that was a fair price.

"We were willing to take that price from anyone else so we should do that with Dino," said one director. "But, Bill, do you really think you guys can finance this LBO?"

Bill explained he couldn't guarantee a successful outcome. "The deal will turn on being able to borrow enough senior debt, mezzanine debt, and you selling shareholders taking back some five-year junior subordinated debt."

The board then voted unanimously to sell SFP to me and since he too was selling, authorized Bob Graham to represent San Tomo sellers in the deal.

At that point, San Tomo owned SFP, Gilroy Canning, and Sierra Packers. If I succeeded in buying SFP, the other two canneries would continue to be owned by San Tomo and continue to be managed by me. Bob Graham had already announced full retirement by the end of 1986.

From that August board meeting forward, Bill Jesse and I worked with bankers and lawyers to negotiate the LBO financing, and it was a drawn-out, high-stress, five-month ordeal. After sorting through several bank candidates, we entered into definitive negotiations with two banks, advising each of them they were in the finals against one unnamed competitor, and that we would take the best offer package.

Since my days as a Pillsbury grain buyer I had always refused to "shop a bid"—telling a bidder what another bidder was offering. I had never shopped a bid and we didn't violate that credo in this, the biggest deal of my life. In the end, the competition of a two-horse race was what finally got the LBO done, although Wells Fargo dragged the financing details out to the last day of the year! The final papers were not signed until 2:00 p.m. on December 31, 1986. After four months of serious negotiations, we closed the deal only ten hours before the 1986 Tax Reform would become law and the LBO would have become impossible!

Wells Fargo was the lender for SFP's revolving line of credit and they wanted to hold on to that attractive piece of business. Although SFP was leveraged to the hilt with multiple levels of debt holders to pay off, Joan and I now owned 100 percent of the stock, subject to a 15 percent equity dilution which Wells Capital Markets held via seven-year stock warrants it received for providing the mezzanine financing.

Within four years the subsequent sale of San Tomo's two other canneries, plus SFP's stepped-up depreciation cash flow, funded paying off 100 percent of the selling shareholders' junior subordinated debt, 100 percent of Wells Capital's mezzanine debt, and moved SFP into Wells' "Conventional Borrowers" classification.

The end of 1990 marked my paying off the last all-in bet of my business career. From that point onward I avoided company debt that wasn't "plain vanilla"—within conventional borrower guide-lines. I also avoided investment debt that wasn't backed up by liquid assets greater than the sum of that debt, and I continued to completely avoid personal debt. My debt aversion included the then-popular tax shelters—deferrals that simply put off the day of tax reckoning. My tax mantra became: I pay taxes the same year I earn the cash, so I won't have to pay them later when I may not have the cash.

A word about that dream house Joan and I had long wanted to build. As Bill Jesse had initially calculated, we did end up with $5 million cash in the bank after the LBO financing closed. The first thing I did was put aside half of it and advised Joan we finally had the cash in hand to pay for our dream home. We built it and are still in residence there 25 years later!

ON THE ROAD TO BECOMING
REAL ITALIAN

During the building of SFP's powerhouse brands, many people contributed to my learning curve for which I am most grateful. Perhaps the single most powerful marketing concept I embraced early on came from a bright marketer named Dick Butler, a YPO member from Los Angeles. We had originally met several years before during chapter-to-chapter retreats. I liked Dick immediately and over subsequent YPO get-togethers came to see him as a real marketing pro. Later when I began immersing myself in the how of brand building, I called him.

"Dick, I need you to give me a crash course in Marketing 1A—can you do that?"

"Sure, Dino. Come on down."

I chartered a plane and flew to L.A. with Randy Pura, a Harvard MBA I had engaged to help me on marketing strategy. We spent an entire day with Dick.

Settling into his conference room equipped with note pads and pencils on the table and several erasable white boards and pens, I had the distinct feeling I was back in school, and boy was that right!

We began with Dick asking lots of questions about SFP's channels of distribution and what value our products delivered to the end user. My responses tended to focus on the products' superiority, and Dick's questions kept circling back to what did that superiority mean to the customer?

At one point Dick went up to a white board and in bold letters hand-printed an equation in capital letters:

$$\frac{DV + PV}{P} = S? \ NS?$$

"Dino, this little algebraic equation captures all parts of both the marketing/selling proposition of every product or service sold in this world," he said. "You need to understand it, embrace it, and practice it 100 percent of the time. If you do, sales growth will follow."

With that introduction, Dick began to explain the equation. "DV stands for *Demonstrable Value*. DV is what a target prospect can see, smell, touch, and feel of any product. Because DV is *objective*, it gets measured analytically by the brain's left hemisphere. PV stands for *Perceived Value* and represents the prospect's *feelings* about a product. PV is *subjective*, therefore not measured by the left brain, but rather is *intuited* by the brain's right hemisphere. And by the way, right brain feelings override left brain analysis more than the other way around."

I understood the DV concept, but was less clear about PV.

"Let me give you a PV example," Dick said. "You've got a pen in your shirt pocket. It has a white star on top of the cap. What does that star mean?"

"That it's a Mont Blanc," I said.

"Right. A famous Mont Blanc pen that sells for about $200?"

"That sounds about right."

"Have you ever used a Bic pen?" Dick asked.

"Sure."

"And a Bic sells for around ten bucks?"

"That also sounds right."

"Okay, does a Mont Blanc write any better than a Bic?"

I shrugged. "I haven't thought about it that way, but probably not."

"In that case," Dick explained, "the DV was virtually the same between the two pen brands. So the only way Mont Blanc could sell pens at $200 apiece in a marketplace with $10 Bics available was because of greater *perceived value*. That little white star communicated a positive perception—it showed the world its owner was a success. That's PV!"

Dick went on to say that the "P" in the equation's denominator stood for price.

"The price Mont Blanc can charge for a pen or any seller can charge for any product cannot be any greater than the combined value of DV and PV of that product *in the prospect's mind*. To get more 'S' (sales) versus 'NS' (no sale), the customer has to receive more aggregate 'V' than the 'P' (price) he/she is asked to pay."

Dick summed up by drawing a shorter equation:

$$\frac{V}{P} = S?\ NS?$$

"Value divided by price (V over P) is the fundamental selling proposition, Dino. It rules everything. The more V you provide the customer, the higher P you can charge. Since increasing DV over competition is usually quite costly and not easy to do, increasing PV is almost always a good strategy. A note of caution, though: increased PV cannot be sustained unless your DV is no worse, and preferably better, than competitors."

Thirty years later I still recall Dick's algebraic equation as the moment when my marketing light bulbs really began going on! After getting my head around the $DV + PV = V$ proposition, marketing ideas of where we needed to go with Stanislaus began to emerge.

Act One of the Stanislaus story had been the company's long-time focus on private-label business. The products had superior DV based on quality factors, but zero PV. Therefore, SFP selling prices were limited to a 50-cent per case premium relative to private-label competitor pricing.

Act Two began with Suzy Bel's purchase of SFP and my insistence on limiting private-label sales, and expanding into new geographic areas, but only with our own brands. We had indeed increased our branded footprint and some new-area brand awareness, but had only scratched the surface of communicating superior DV, and we had done nothing to create PV.

Act Three was about to unfold. It would involve understanding end users, creative PV messaging, and heightening DV awareness. My head was in a whirl! Per Dick's algebraic equation, increasing PV would provide us with two strategic alternatives: either raising price relative to competitors—thereby increasing margin dollars to invest in DV enhancement—or leaving price constant and ramping up sales. Either way, Dick had helped me understand the path to building a brand.

As our Cessna 210 flew home I knew the road ahead would take significant time and effort to traverse. I had a lot of marketing work—that would prove to be *fun*—ahead of me. I could hardly wait, but the first thing to do was to find a really good marketing professional to bring aboard the team.

That first key marketing hire took place in 1985. Up until then, over the course of more than 40 years in business, SFP had never employed anyone with any marketing or advertising background, nor had it ever engaged a marketing consultant. Ironically, the person I ended up choosing, Julie Ambrose, had shifted from production to marketing only a few years before, but I chose her over several more experienced candidates I had interviewed. It was one of the best hires I ever made. Julie was smart, organized and most importantly, mentally disciplined—a combination my instincts told me were crucial to the mission before us.

While Julie was going to college majoring to be a Home Ec teacher, she began working summers in a pet food plant. To her surprise, she enjoyed learning plant operations, and was soon overseeing production workers. Post-graduation from UC Davis, she went to work for Hills Brothers Coffee in San Francisco supervising production lines. After earning a night school MBA at UC Berkeley, Julie transferred from the production side to Hills Brothers marketing where she also won promotions. Sometime thereafter our San Francisco headhunter recruited her to look at a marketing position with a privately-owned food company from Stockton. We had our first interview a short time later.

Julie later revealed that she was impressed the company owner came to San Francisco for the interview. She recognized that "Dino had a passion for the business," and that SFP was an entrepreneurial company without layers of corporate hierarchy. Julie also liked that she would be part of a start-up marketing program. A big-city girl, her one hesitation was: "Why does it have to be in Stockton?" Fortunately she accepted the job I offered and relocated.

During her first six months I asked Julie to ignore marketing and instead get up to flank speed on our products and distribution system, and to travel with our sales people to call on distributors. Julie later confessed she hated the sales calls and it didn't help that Frank Piciullo frequently debunked the idea of marketing tomatoes to restaurateurs.

Meanwhile I was coaching Julie towards my belief that SFP's real customers were in fact restaurateurs, not distributors, and that our secret mission was to create marketing communications that would resonate with end users. To her credit, Julie was the first of our team members to accept the new, "End Users are the customer" paradigm and came to believe in it wholeheartedly.

As she and I began strategizing marketing ideas she strongly lobbied for hiring an ad agency "like all the big branded guys do." At first I went along and sat in when she began interviewing established Bay Area agencies invited to our offices.

I soon noticed that whenever Julie asked the agency reps to describe what they had done in the past, they would reel off impressive client names, and then proceed to describe in detail the "confidential" core of their clients' business strategies. As that happened in every interview, which made me increasingly concerned. I had adopted Frank's philosophy that everything SFP did, stayed within SFP—we did not want to educate competitors to our good ideas. Or as Warren Buffett puts it: "Good ideas are too rare to share!" By the time all the ad agency interviews were over, I had concluded that route was just too risky.

"Julie, do you realize every one of the agencies gave us rhyme and verse of their clients' business strategies?"

"Yes, I guess they did. But how is that relevant to us?"

"Okay, here's how. Are we going to hire one ad agency for life? Are they always going to work for us?"

"Probably not. They do change."

"Of course, and today nobody understands the food-service channel like we do. Our big-branded competitors still focus their marketing on the retail channel and are currently ignoring food service. But that won't always be the case. In the meantime, we will be teaching whatever agency we hire all we know about food service because it's obvious they don't understand it now. So what will happen if we fire them or they quit? Julie, who is going to be the first competitor they call on?"

Reluctantly, she named several food processing giants selling branded tomato products through the supermarket channel.

"I rest my case. That's why I don't think we should hire an agency."

Julie looked stricken. "Dino, I understand what you're saying— but my God—how are we going to do marketing without an ad agency?!"

I smiled. "You and I are going to do it with help from some task-specific consultants who we will find and hire just for just the selected tasks. You and I will be the only ones to know our business strategies."

And that's exactly how SFP's successful marketing campaign was put together over the next dozen years. We hired task-specific consultants, but none of them got to see "the playbook" of our hard-won secrets about food service.

In designing SFP's first ad, we were careful to keep it low key. We wanted to target restaurateurs, but needed to do so without upsetting important distributors who were private-label customers.

In Julie's un-minced words the result was: "Basically a beauty shot. It was so mild-mannered, I'm not sure readers even stopped long enough at the page to get our 'non-message.'" But it served the purpose of testing the marketing waters, and there was no distributor pushback from the first SFP ad they ever saw. It was a baby step.

Our next advertising effort was a series of full-page color ads built around the slogan: "We're Not For Everyone." The stated message being that SFP products were special and though costing a little more, they were worth it. Subliminally the ads assured *existing* end-users that they were "special." The We're Not For Everyone campaign featured four elegant graphics, and ran over the course of a year in two food-service magazines. Our name was finally out there, but we were a long way from building perceived value.

During the progression of the We're Not For Everyone campaign, Julie wanted to gather more information about independent P&I restaurateurs. To design the most effective marketing, she believed we needed to better understand the inner needs/wants of our target end-user segment.

With a bit of trepidation I went along with Julie's desire to use focus groups, where selected individuals answer questions about their reactions to specific products. In the early 1980s focus groups were a popular mechanism for gaining consumer feedback. A number of YPOers had cautioned me to not read too much into the outcomes: "It isn't a given that putting ten people in a room and asking them questions always results in straight answers." But thanks to Julie's persistence we stayed the course. Ultimately, focus groups provided us with valuable insights—in large part because we redesigned them in a new and unique way.

Shortly before this, Joan and I had gone through marriage counseling, which I came away from convinced of two verities. One was that despite the struggle of meshing two remarkably different family backgrounds, we loved each other and wanted to continue our marriage. The second verity was that feelings are a whole lot more powerful than thoughts.

Prior to counseling, my mind relied more on left-hemisphere thoughts than right-hemisphere feelings, and Joan was just the opposite, relying much more on feelings. The long and the short of it was that my pre-counseling left-brain behavior was not meeting Joan's needs. Parenthetically, I have continued to work on the deficiency and have gotten better at the feeling side, but old habits are hard to break.

One of the things I learned in counseling that seemed applicable to focus groups was that humans have four basic emotions—mad-sad-glad-scared. There are derivatives of each, but those four are the fundamental feelings underlying most human decision-making. I suggested to Julie that our focus groups strive to discover what made our target customers mad-sad-glad-scared. If we understood how they related to those four basic emotions, we could more effectively communicate with them. Julie immediately bought into the approach and set about designing a new focus group format.

As she interviewed several professional focus group firms, more than a few were puzzled by our feelings approach which required participants *not knowing* the company's name, the product line, or anything about who was behind the one-way mirror. In fact, we were not interested in the product feedback that focus groups were typically set up to collect!

To find the right facilitator to run our groups we tested several candidates. The first was a man, and although he was a pro, our instincts told us he wasn't sensitive enough to get other men to open up to their feelings. We tested another man, and he was also too alpha male.

Julie suggested we try out a female moderator; someone who could be both a leader and a calming influence in the room. Bingo! The second woman we tested, Dee Innoue, was wonderful at getting people to open up. If Dee got stuck with a guy dominating the discussion, she had a disarming, gentle manner of calming that down. Most importantly, she could get participants to feel safe and therefore more willing to share their feelings.

After the core script and Dee were tested and set, our focus group team went on the road, scheduling multiple groups in Los Angeles, Chicago, New York, and Boston. Julie and I were behind the one-way mirror for most of the sixteen individual sessions, all of which we videotaped. By the time the road trips were done, we had a much better sense of target customers and what made them mad-sad-glad-scared.

First and foremost was remarkably similar feelings about life/family/business regardless of where they lived and worked. They were generally down-to-earth types who came from modest beginnings and often had worked in independent restaurants before starting their own. Some were immigrants and many were first-generation Americans of Italian descent, along with a smattering of Greeks and other ethnicities. Almost invariably their restaurant was a family operation, with spouses, children, or parents involved. Often their start-up capital came from relatives' loans. Finally, they felt strongly about the importance of family values.

These operators' sense of self-worth tended to relate to the success of their restaurant, and their "scared" feelings centered around the business failing—thereby letting down their family and financial backers. Even though virtually all of them had successful restaurants, they still were concerned about losing customers. What if a regular was unhappy with his meal one night and didn't come back? Independent restaurateurs highly value regulars as indicators of customer satisfaction.

Often their "glad" feelings came from happy customers; from third-party praise about the quality of their food, as well as pride in having made it as independent businessmen and women.

Concurrent with the focus group activities, I was reading everything on marketing I could find, and came across a book whose concept I immediately embraced. Entitled *Positioning: The Battle for Your Mind*, it was written by Jack Trout and Al Ries, two former Madison Avenue guys who had established their own Trout and Ries consulting firm. Their book came to be considered the seminal work in the positioning discipline they were the first to describe.

Among other insights, the book explained how the human brain categorizes information, and the desirability of positioning a brand within a unique category. Filled with common-sense dos and don'ts, the book stimulated my second marketing epiphany right up there alongside Dick Butler's DV & PV equation! Julie and her then assistant Steve Rouse, who is now in charge of SFP's marketing, both read *Positioning* as enthusiastically as I had. We agreed that Trout and Ries were not only right on, but that we should consider engaging their consulting services.

Julie called and learned Trout and Reis no longer did traditional ad agency work and were all about positioning, for which they charged $20,000 a day! They were willing to sign a definitive confidentiality agreement we prepared that covered everything we would disclose about our business. We contracted for three days of their time, and after pre-mailing them lots of stuff, Julie, Steve, and I headed to New York.

During the first morning in their comfortable Westchester offices, Jack and Al launched a barrage of questions at us. Questions about the company, our products, our marketplace, and about me, my family, and so on.

Jack Trout took the lead and by afternoon he came to their bottom line: "Everyone already believes that Italians know more about tomato products than anyone in the world and it doesn't matter if that's really true. In positioning what counts is what people already believe. Your company was founded by Italians, uses Italian processing equipment, your family comes from Italy, you still make your own salami and wine, and your name is Italian. Everything about you reeks of Italian authenticity and trust me, people believe in *REAL*. The people you are trying to reach are in the Italian food business and will relate to doing business with a *real* Italian tomato company. Therefore, SFP's positioning should be 'The Real Italian Tomato Company'!"

I smiled. *Why we didn't think of that? These guys are good!*

Trout continued, "But there's one problem, and that's your company's name. Stanislaus is not an Italian name and doesn't sound Italian. It sounds Polish. It's tough to be 'Real Italian' with a name that sounds Polish, so you have to re-name the company."

Whoa Hoss! "Sorry Jack, we're not going to change the name," I said.

"Why not?" Trout asked.

"Listen, we're now doing close to two million cases a year under brands identified as from Stanislaus. We have lots of distributors who know us as Stanislaus. Our name has great quality credibility in the trade and we're not going to lose all that goodwill built up over the years."

For the rest of that afternoon, we went back and forth with Al Ries joining Trout in trying to persuade me to change the name. As we left for our hotel, I muttered to Julie, "At $20,000 per day, I hope we're not going to keep arguing about a name change tomorrow!"

Evidently Jack thought about it overnight because the next morning he started out: "Okay, if you're not going to change the name, then you've got to explain it."

I was relieved he had bowed to the inevitable. "Great Jack, but what do you mean—explain it?"

"Have you guys ever heard of a company called Smuckers?"

Julie, Steve, and I chorused, "Of course. 'With a name like Smuckers, it's got to be good.'"

Trout looked pleased. "Who do you think wrote that for them?"
"You guys did?"

Jack nodded. "Al and I had them as clients when they were a little jam-and-jelly maker on the Michigan-Ohio state line. They wanted to go national but didn't want to change their name. They were proud of their family name. We couldn't persuade them, either, which meant we had to explain it. So we turned their name into a selling proposition. As soon as you hear 'with a name like Smuckers it's got to be good,' the human brain says, 'Yeah, that makes sense.'

"So, here's the concept to explain why the 'Real Italian' tomato company has a Polish name. In a few lines of text you explain the history of Italian immigrants, including your own family, in California's Central Valley, and how the company took the name of your county."

They continued on with some other ideas, but the heavy lifting had been done—Stanislaus was going to be "The Real Italian Tomato company with the Polish Name."

The Trout and Ries day rate was expensive, but it was the best marketing money we ever spent. In all of our advertising thereafter we used derivatives of "The Real Italian Tomato Company" positioning, and continue to do so today.

The first ad which told the Polish name story began "In 1942, the Quartaroli family established the Italian-American roots of our company in Stanislaus County . . ." We avoided talking about the World War II years, but continued explaining where the company's Polish name came from.

Subsequent ads fleshed out the theme, including one that ran for two years that told its story under the headline: "Our name may seem Polish but our roots are Real Italian." In every graphic of every ad, like the ubiquitous Playboy bunny, there is a "Stanislaus County Line" road sign!

Over the years, restaurateurs' favorite ad was one that went right to the heart of their strong family values. The headline was "Every Sunday Our Tomatoes Face The Real Italian Taste Test." The two page graphic shows an Italian family at a long table enjoying Sunday dinner. The ad resonated on several levels. First because "everybody knows" that Italian families get together for Sunday dinner after church. Secondly, because the graphic shows four generations easily identified as grandparents, parents, adult children, and great-grandchildren. And finally because we didn't hire actors—the big Italian family pictured is the Cortopassi clan gathered for Sunday dinner at Joan and Dino's house!

My concern about ad agencies divulging proprietary information to competitors carried over to Trout and Ries. I had been willing to take the initial risk after they signed the confidentiality agreement. However, Julie wanted to continue using them as consultants, and I wanted longer term protection. For both reasons she negotiated an exclusive contract for ongoing consultancy, and we kept them on retainer until they retired!

BRAND BUILDING—BRICK BY BRICK

O ur desire to learn how P&I restaurateurs saw things continued on long after focus groups. Besides magazine advertising, we wanted to directly communicate with restaurateurs using our products. But in order to reach out to them, we needed their names and addresses. Getting that information was very difficult since our products were delivered to end users by a great many distributors, all of whom felt very proprietary about their customer lists.

To build the database of end-user names/addresses we used several creative tactics. One that worked well for years was putting a stamped, self-addressed postcard into every tenth case of our tomato products. The card promised we would send them a $5 bill for answering a few questions about the product, providing their name and address, and dropping the card in the mail. The targeting of this approach was highly effective because cases shipped from our plant were not opened by the distributors, but by the end users after they were delivered. As we received postcards back from restaurateurs and sent $5 in the return mail, we began building a list of real-time customers.

Trivial Pursuit was then a popular board game so we invented "La Triviata" and called it the Real Italian version. In every tenth case we put a card with a multiple-choice question related to Italian history or culture. People were invited to circle the right answer and send it back to enter a drawing for attractive Real Italian prizes. The questions were easy and we received many responses, further building the database.

Once known end users are added to the list, we never stop expressing our appreciation to them. For example, every year we send Christmas greetings and a little gift to every customer in the database. The card contains a short letter thanking them for their loyalty and sharing a few highlights of Joan and Dino's year. More importantly, it demonstrates that we truly value end-user restaurateurs as part of the extended Stanislaus family.

One of the more interesting "blind" surveys we repeatedly conducted asked independent P&I owners to rank five factors that most contributed to their restaurant's success. The factors they were asked to rank 1 through 5 were location, menu price, food quality, service, and ambiance. Out of thousands of responses an incredible four out of every five responses ranked food quality as the number one success factor of their restaurant, with service rated second. This was great news because if P&I independents believed food quality was the principal factor of their success, it meant they would be amenable to buying superior quality ingredients! As a comparative test, we sent the identical survey to many P&I *chain* franchisees and they generally ranked food quality third or fourth. This reinforced our belief that independents were Stanislaus-type customers and chains were not.

In the food-service channel the communication link between manufacturers and distributors has traditionally been independent brokers. The typical broker often started out as a manufacturer's rep before deciding to go into the brokerage business. In a medium-sized market area the average-size brokerage firm might represent eight to fifteen manufacturer's lines and earn commission on the distributors' purchase of their principals' products.

Traditionally, manufacturer and broker sales efforts were focused at the distributor level. Brokers spent most of their time and effort developing distributor relationships. Periodically their principal(s) would try to increase sales via promotional dollars paid to distributors. In a nutshell, the definition of the push strategy is manufacturers paying distributors to push the promoted product to restaurateurs.

Because we were operating on the new paradigm of restaurateurs being the real decision-makers who could pull our branded products through the distributor, we needed to re-focus and re-train Stanislaus brokers to spend their energy on the street rather than on distributor relationships. Our marketing efforts air mailed directly to end users gained us brand awareness, but along with that awareness we needed brokers doing belly-to-belly selling out on the street.

That meant that our Regional Sales Managers (RSMs) and our brokers all needed to buy into the new paradigm that end users were the real customer. In 1985 we set up SFP's first annual "Brokers Meeting" and brought all our brokers and their key broker sales reps to Modesto for an intense two-day seminar. Julie and her marketing team generated the teaching materials, the SFP sales team were the faculty, and my job was to scare them into changing behavior.

I began by reviewing what had happened to independent distributors and brokers who used to service the grocery-store channel during the 1960s/70s. They were gone! Disappeared! Vaporized by channel consolidation!

"Once supermarket chains got to sufficient scale they didn't need independent distributors," I told them, "and once the distributors were gone, manufacturers didn't need brokers! The same thing will happen in the food service channel. If you keep relying on distributor relationships, at some point, you too will be gone. The only way to have a long-term future as a broker firm is to get strong on the street. If your firm gets good at converting restaurateurs to buying your principals' products, then your principals will continue to need you."

"At SFP we are committed to building end-user loyalty to our brands and we will do that by maintaining product superiority and by rewarding brokers who are strong on the street! Your choice is to lean into the harness and get good at belly-to-belly selling or to get unhitched from our wagon!"

I stopped—the big room was silent.

A voice called out, "Are you saying we're gonna be out of business?"

"I'm saying the food service channel will change, SFP is ahead of that change, and those of you who won't change will sooner or later be gone."

Then I told them the story of the frog in the pot. Drop a frog into a pot of hot water and he will jump out. Put a frog into a cold-water pot and warm it slowly and he will sit there until he dies. "Which frog do you want to be?!"

It was a real wake-up call to guys—in those days there were no female brokers—who had always believed building distributor relationships was how to succeed in the brokerage business. I was turning their world upside down. These were successful men, and here I was telling them that their way of doing business was going the way of the dinosaurs.

While it took some time for our sales team to begin demanding "strong on the street" broker performance, from the get-go I knew we would have to weed out those who remained mired in the old paradigm of "Distributor Relationships." In the end, those who made it discovered that getting good at "belly-to-belly selling" helped them become more valuable to their other principals.

"They call it cold calling for a reason, "I continued. "It's about knocking on lots of doors, having some slammed in your face, and going on to the next one. It's like what we used to say about sex in my era: 'You've got to ask a lot to get a little.' And by the way, we are going to pay you to be strong on the street for us. We're implementing an end-user conversion program that will mean extra money to you and your sales reps."

Now they were *really* paying attention. Back then, there was not a single other food service manufacturer paying brokers to knock on doors and make end-user conversions. Today, 25 years later, a few companies have developed reliable systems to pay brokers for end-user conversions. What there is much more of are companies that reduced their brokerage expense by consolidating brokers on a regional basis. In other words, many frog-in-the-pot brokers were "consolidated" out of business!

I closed my remarks by showing them the "Four-Box Matrix" of prospect characteristics.

• • •

[FOUR BOX MATRIX]

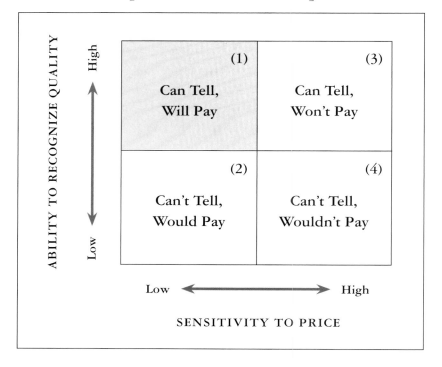

"Gentlemen, this is a handy way to decide which end-user prospects to invest your time in trying to convert to our products, and which ones to walk on by!

"On the left side of the matrix is the 'Quality Recognition' scale running vertically from low at the bottom, up to high. Across the bottom the matrix is the 'Price Sensitivity' scale running from low on the left to high on the right. Dividing the matrix into four boxes results in four sets of prospect characteristics.

"Box #1 should be your primary targets—these are restaurateurs *able to recognize superior quality and willing to pay for it*. If you can get in front of Box #1 prospects with SFP products, the odds are in your favor of making the sale! Box #2 prospects rank low on Quality Recognition, but fortunately also low on Price Sensitivity. In this case, you will need to do missionary work to teach them how to recognize superior quality in order to make the sale. *Once they know how to judge tomato quality, you can convert them.* Box #3 prospects are high on Quality Recognition, but unfortunately also high on Price Sensitivity. Even though they can recognize quality, they won't pay for it. *So walk on by these characters—they are a waste of your time!* The people in Box #4 are hopeless! They don't know quality when it hits them in the face and they wouldn't pay for it anyway! *Run right past these time-wasters!*"

It was a lot of information for the brokers to digest in that first year, and as our marketing and sales teams debriefed the seminar, we were sure many of them went home with heads spinning. However each year thereafter, the combination of our marketing efforts "air-mailed" to end-users and increased focus on End-User Conversions (EUCs), began showing significant results; proof that we were on the right track. What cheered me even more was how the whole SFP team rallied to the cause, internalizing and embracing the new paradigm that end users were the real customers.

Per Dick Butler's marketing equation, as we increased both the PV and DV of SFP products, sales growth increased. And because we only increased prices enough to cover cost increases, Dick's promise came true and SFP sales growth went ballistic!

EXPECTATIONS: UNREASONABLE
AND HEIGHTENED

E rnest Gallo stood at the podium before our YPO chapter members who had spent the day touring E & J Gallo-Modesto, the world's largest winery. I was in charge of chapter education that year and had persuaded Joe, a relatively new member, to host the monthly chapter meeting at Gallo, widely-known as a secretive company. Joe had chosen his father to finish the program.

Ernest began by acknowledging how the nation's top business schools taught the importance of one-year, five-year, and ten-year strategic plans. "If you are a graduate of Stanford, Harvard, or any other fine school," he said, "you have been trained to use a structured way of conducting your business. In other words, you know what you want and what you are going to do to achieve these goals and projections. I have read that this approach is the mark of successful business managers. Let me compare that to how our company operates."

At the time considered to be one of America's greatest marketers, Ernest explained that the company he and his brother founded in 1933 with $5,900.23—$5,000 of it borrowed from Ernest's mother-in-law—was "very unstructured and disorganized. We do not have a table of organization; we do not have rigid job descriptions; we do not have formal budgets. Over the last fifty years, I have read about the importance of long-term planning. Several times we have wondered whether perhaps we should try this. But as quickly as the idea came to us, we dropped it."

By now, Ernest's comments had riveted the attention of every B-school graduate in the room!

He then explained why he and Julio had come to that decision. "It was impractical to "to make meaningful projections for any given period when we cannot know what wine consumption will be—or the pricing policies of our competitors—or the amount of money we would have to spend in advertising—or what the foreign exchange rate will be."

"I am often asked what I think the consumption of wine will be in this country next year or five years or ten years from now. My honest reply is, 'Your guess is as good as mine.'"

Ernest went on to describe the advantages of a privately-held company over a public one. "At Gallo, our immediate actions are influenced by what is best for our company long-range. If a better piece of equipment comes on the market, we buy it immediately. If competition increases and more salesmen or more advertising or more competitive prices are indicated, we do what is required immediately. We do not give a thought as to what our profit will be for the quarter or for that year as compared to the past. Whatever we feel is best for the company long-range, *we do now*."

"The principal advantage of a private company is speed of decision and speed of action. Because our own money is involved, an error is stopped the moment it is discovered. We don't waste time arguing over whose fault it was or trying to cover it up. In some public companies, before a change can be made, a scapegoat must first be found. This can be costly, both in money and in market share."

"In privately-held companies there is no short-term pressure to do something at the expense of what is best for the long haul—quite the opposite. Privately-owned companies are invariably focused on *terminal value*—making investments in the business that cost some earnings in the near-term but generate more company value in the long-term."

Shooting a gimlet-eyed look at his rapt audience, Ernest counseled, "If you have a private firm, stay private and if you are public, try to buy it back."

In summary, the key factors to which he attributed Gallo's success, were:

"We have a *high sense of urgency*. We want things done right away. No waiting, no dawdling—as soon as we make a decision, we do it before our competitor gets it done.

"We have a *constant drive for perfection*. Whether it's in the product, the advertising, the selling, our relationship with the wholesaler, or with the retailer, or the consumer's perception of our wine.

"We are *continually unhappy*. About a lack of fine wine grapes; about the speed with which we improve our winemaking technology; about the effectiveness of our advertising and our sales force; that our relationship with our wholesalers is not better; that our relationship with our retailers is not better; that our wines do not have the image with the consumer that they deserve. *We are unhappy that we are not selling all the wine in the country*."

As Ernest was saying those words, E & J Gallo sold 40 percent of the wine in the United States!

"The reason we are unhappy is simple. We are never complacent and never satisfied. We continually strive for perfection. We know we will never achieve perfection, but the effort keeps us ahead of our competition."

I sat there, certain that I had just heard one of the great business talks of all time. *That speech should be taught in every business school in the land, as there was more in it than any MBA course*!

I very much related to what Ernest said about never being satisfied. I had long been known as a hard-driving guy always pushing for better performance despite past success. I had long equated feeling satisfied as the equivalent of losing the competitive edge.

Later that evening I asked Joe for a copy of his father's speech which he sent to me after my promising to use it solely for my own reference. I still have that copy, which is now dog-eared from the number of times I pulled it out to re-read.

Ernest Gallo and Vince Lombardi were cast in the same unsatisfied mold. I don't know if Lombardi could have built the world's largest winery, but I'll bet Ernest could have coached winning football. Both of their personalities were about drive, discipline, and winning results. They shared the characteristic of setting unreasonable expectations, toward which they drove everyone—themselves included. Like Ernest, I believed leadership wasn't about attaining perfection, but about striving for it all along the way.

RAISING THE QUALITY BAR

Year in and year out, we continued to raise the bar at SFP. When we bought the company in 1978, I knew SFP's products were somewhat better than the competition. Our production mission every year was to widen the quality gap as measured in fresh flavor and case-to-case consistency against our competitors. This required continually investing dollars in state-of-the-art equipment and better personnel, which we did annually.

I have always believed "What Gets Measured Gets Done," and through constant reinforcement that became our senior management mantra. For example, we began measuring quality *during* production, rather than after the fact in a Quality Control lab. (Classic Edward Deming philosophy.)That's why SFP came to have three times as many quality measurement personnel as comparable plants.

Sporting distinctive red hardhats, our army of inspectors are stationed throughout the plant and each one has the authority to stop a production line at any time. As Bob Ilse was fond of saying, "I've been in a lot of canneries in my day, but never have I seen so many Q C people running around, any one of which can turn a line off!"

At SFP, when a production line is stopped, bells and whistles go off for everyone. And that line doesn't restart until whatever caused the product to fall outside our specs is corrected. Rather than being criticized for halting production, Q C people who shut down a line are complimented for their vigilance.

Ingraining a quality consciousness in our production personnel caused something extraordinary to happen. By authorizing the stopping of any line that fell even slightly outside SFP's high specs, operating people took greater pride in staying within the quality standards. As a result, the consistency of our products—as measured can-to-can, case-to-case—trended steadily upward over the years.

These systemic and cultural changes did not happen overnight. In fact, in the beginning Bob Ilse and I did not always see eye-to-eye. He came from a production efficiency experience base, and sometimes had resisted when I suggested something outside conventional cannery wisdom. I'd say, "Bob, what if we did this?" He'd reply, "Let me think about it, Dino." And then never bring it up again. I soon learned "let me think about it" meant he had tossed the idea in a corner and left it there.

After a while, Bob became bolder. He'd look cockeyed at me and say, "Dino, you don't understand production. Here's why we can't do that." He would take me through the established way of doing things, and end with, "See why that's crazy?" More often than not, I had to agree he was right.

The important thing was how Bob and I approached problem-solving and turf division. After navigating some early rough waters

(Bob later admitted he almost quit a half dozen times), we agreed that when I made a production suggestion, Bob would carefully consider it before responding why it wouldn't work.

While I accepted that many of my production suggestions were impractical, over time Bob began accepting those that merited trying. He later acknowledged I caused him "to think about things a lot differently than strictly a production guy." Bob also credited me with "Bringing Italian-ness to our flavor profiles." He later ribbed me: "I had to listen to quite a few dumb ideas to get to your off-the-chart good ones!" I accepted the ribbing and we grew comfortable enough to talk to each other like that. Between the two of us a number of significant breakthroughs over the years came from challenging conventional production wisdom.

As Bob absorbed a more entrepreneurial mindset and the constant "pushing the outside of the envelope" that I apply to business, I came to consider him not just our production chief but a strong right arm and partner in all aspects of SFP's business. That's not to say we agreed on everything over the years, but despite different backgrounds, styles and capabilities, we enjoyed a mutually beneficial, long-term partnership.

Starting in the mid-1980s and early 1990s, SFP's growth rate accelerated including the development of new products/new brands. Most food manufacturers develop new products in R & D labs. Our "skunk-works" of product development was housed in kitchens. In the early years, in Joan's and my kitchen, and later in a new SFP test kitchen that we built. Like many Italians, I am a big believer in "taste test" recipe development! In our new SFP kitchen, Bob Ilse, Mark Kimmel, and I would add a dash of this and a pinch of that, and often at my insistence more olive oil to various tomato combinations until the flavor profile was unique. Our standing rule was that I had to love the new product before we took it to market.

The impetus for one of our new brands came from the annual trips I took to tomato Mecca to visit with distributors and end-users in the five boroughs of New York. I also traveled to other SFP markets, but New York was a yearly event. Not only is the Big Apple our largest market, but New Yorkers are very knowledgeable consumers of Italian food, as are the knowledgeable restaurateurs who serve them. On each of these trips I would interrogate distributors of imported Italian tomatoes, and it was increasingly irritating.

Over the years SFP had canned a few whole-peeled tomatoes, but mostly we chopped or ground them fresh into one of our sauces. While our New York business was growing, all those imported tomatoes made me wonder if we were missing an opportunity.

"Why do you buy your whole-peeled tomatoes from Italy?" I would ask the distributors.

Generally their response was: "Because Italian tomatoes are really good . . . because restaurateurs want them . . . etc., etc. Dino, SFP is very good at making sauces for pizza and pasta, but whole-peeled San Marzano tomatoes from Italy are the real thing."

I knew the San Marzano were no longer grown in Italy because no one could afford its hand-harvest costs and that San Marzano labeling was fraudulent. So on one trip I started challenging distributors: "Well, with all due respect, I don't think Italian tomatoes are that good, so show me."

The owner would open a can, pour out the contents, and hand me a spoon. Evaluated with my eyes and my palate, the Italian tomatoes were unattractive to the eye and tasted metallic! The owner would mumble "it must be a bad lot." and I would go on my way.

On that trip I sampled Italian whole-peeled tomatoes at several NYC distributors. Most had that same metallic taste. However, I did find some that looked as plump as fresh-picked. How did that packer do that?

Before I got on the plane for home I called Bob Ilse. "Brace yourself, we're gonna take on the Italians! I know we can make better tasting whole-peeled tomatoes than they do, and there's a big market here in New York. When I come home we're going to sit down and figure out how to beat them."

"I know how to make whole-peeled tomatoes," Bob said.

"Wait a minute, Bob. You know how to make American-style whole-peeled tomatoes. *Not Italian-style.*"

I brought home some Italian canned tomatoes, and we set out to see how we could do better. For starters, all of our products were packed in enamel-lined cans, so we wouldn't have the metallic-tasting issue. However, in the U.S. calcium is added to whole tomatoes to firm them up and reduce breakage during canning.

Instead of using calcium (which did affect flavor) the best Italian processing evidently handled them more gently without breakage. I came to the conclusion that we couldn't use calcium for taste reasons, so until we figured out how to solve the breakage issue, we were not ready to challenge Italian tomatoes in New York.

As luck would have it, that fall Bob and I took a trip to Italy to see a new type of puree finisher—Italians are very creative in designing and building specialized food-processing equipment. We were visiting canneries with the puree finisher company representative, when out of the corner of my eye I spotted a small, odd-looking machine that neither Bob nor I had ever seen before. It was off in one corner, humming along like The Little Engine that Could, and as it turned out was cooking and cooling whole-peeled tomatoes.

We watched as cans were gently moved from one level to the next through the cooking and cooling stages.

Quietly I said, "Bob, this could be our no-calcium breakthrough." He whispered back, "Could be, but at this slow pace we would need a fleet of them."

I called the plant manager over and in Italian asked him about the machine.

He said, "*Questa e una macchina vecchia che si usa soltano per pomodori senza calcime—la produzione e molto bassa pero non rompe I pomodori.*" (This is an old-style machine that we only use for whole tomatoes without calcium—the production rate of this machine is very low but it doesn't break the tomatoes.)

Bingo!

I asked where it was manufactured, and the manager said somewhere in Parma by two older partners named Delargine and Ghiretti (D & G). A couple of days later we visited D & G and were disappointed to learn they had no machines available; in fact, no inventory at all. They only built their machines to order. We talked with the partners, who only spoke Italian, about some specifications, including bigger size machines, and also about prices. I then asked them if they could build two large machines for us in time for our next tomato season.

They looked stunned, then explained, *"No signore, per una fabbrica piccola come la nostra sarebbe impossibile di fare due machine alla volta."* (Their small factory could only build one smaller machine in that period of time.)

After more persuasion, I named a bonus amount we would pay if they could build two machines for us by next season. The bonus was so big it got their attention, and that's how we acquired our first two Little Machines That Could! In fact, we had D & G build them to double the capacity of the first one we had spotted—and the following season (despite installing the machines shortly before the season) we started producing "Real Italian" whole-peeled tomatoes! When Bob asked how many cases of no-calcium whole-peeled tomatoes we should make our first year, I paraphrased a line borrowed from Ernest and Julio Gallo: "You try to make more cases than I can sell, and I will try to sell more cases than you can make!"

Julie and I worked hard on developing a high-end brand name, Alta Cucina, and a unique positioning for the new product. To drive end-user trials we introduced the Altas at a price point below Italian imports, which meant selling at a loss. That didn't bother me because Alta Cucina quality was demonstrably superior to the Italian imports, and DV + PV would eventually win the day.

Although old habits die hard and it took longer than I had anticipated, eventually that's exactly what happened. Over time the lush, red-ripe appearance and sweet taste of Alta Cucinas grew to be a huge success. Today, SFP sells more Italian-style whole-peeled tomatoes in the U.S. than total tomato imports from all Italian processors combined! And we do so at selling prices $3-$4 higher than the Italian imports because, like every SFP product, we continued to increase Altas' quality superiority every year.

An excellent exemplar of the power of positioning comes from the first big brand we created out of an existing product—select chopped tomatoes originally sold under SFP's Full Red brand with the description: All-Purpose Chopped Tomatoes. An "All-Purpose" descriptor is non-differentiating, and the *antithesis* of positioning. While it was a very good product—developed and named by Frank Piciullo—SFP was only selling about 40,000 cases per year. The hidden message that needed to be brought out was its extraordinary end-user value compared to whole-peeled tomatoes.

In the standard, one-gallon can sold to restaurants, after chopping up whole-peeled tomatoes, an end-user ended up with approximately 40 ounces of tomato pulp and 60 ounces of liquid juice—a total of 100 ounces. By contrast, the All-Purpose product contained about 75 ounces of tomato pulp and only 25 ounces of tomato juice—a total of 100 ounces. So for end-users looking for *pulp yield*, the value of All-Purpose was almost double the value of whole-peeled tomatoes!

Studying how to reposition this product, Julie and I racked our minds for a new brand name that reflected the inherent pulp advantage, and also a new descriptor that transferred the idea of superior quality. The process went on for weeks and weeks as we batted around various ideas. Eventually we hit upon the word "filet" because everybody knows the best steak is a *filet* mignon—and the "Tomato Filets" descriptor was born.

The next stop was production. I explained the problem to Bob Ilse: "We've got to find a way to slice these tomatoes into strips like a tomato 'filet.' I'm thinking long and thin, rather than short and chunky." Bob was not at all into Julie's and my marketing bent, and often thought we were off on snipe hunts. However, as was his style, he said, "Let me work on that—there may be a way to get there." Sure enough, after a number of attempts, Bob produced tomato strips we could reasonably call tomato filets.

With the new descriptor in hand, we searched for a brand name that memorably drove the value proposition: our tomato filets delivered 75 ounces of meaty pulp compared to the 40 ounces of pulp resulting from chopping up whole-peeled tomatoes. After many non-starters......Bingo! Since alliteration is more memorable, the best name to drive the value-added message was—descriptively alliterative – – – ta-da!—74-40! (Label side panels explained the 74 ounce/40 ounce difference.)

So essentially the same product, albeit in larger shape and dressed in the new 74-40 Tomato Filets positioning, hit the market with mailers and trade advertising. We had already started building an end-user database, and were able to mail announcements directly to restaurateurs. E-mail didn't exist yet!

On the street, comparative demos against whole-peeled were slam-dunks. In addition to nearly twice the pulp, 74-40 filets' appearance was more delicate than the chopped version. Our 74-40 positioning worked like a charm, but the real kicker was that while our sales volume was dramatically growing, competitors sat on their hands. They were not into marketing and thought we were nuts using up all those hand-sorted whole tomatoes to pack 75 cases of tomato filets that could have made 100 cases of whole-peeled. Private-label competitors always thought in terms of case yields/case costs, whereas our secret weapon was to think in terms of *added value to the customer.*

To forestall labeling copycats, we had been able to trademark Tomato Filets. Still I worried about competitors coming out with knock-off products. To my surprise, it didn't happen for three years, and competitors' quantitative mindsets allowed us a following wind and open sea. By the time competitors' private-label customers forced them to start making 74-40 knock-offs, our 74-40 ship had already sailed. Eventually, 74-40 case sales grew to 35 times greater than the original "All-Purpose" predecessor!

A vital factor in sustaining SFP's sales over the years was our continual striving to enhance product superiority. We didn't sit on our quality laurels, particularly because our marketing was so effective! Why? Because effective marketing results in raising prospects' expectations which leads them to give your product a try; if prospects' expectations are not raised they don't bother to try your product. When the prospect tries your product against those raised expectations, the product must meet the expectations for the prospect to become a customer. Conversely, when effective marketing succeeds in raising the prospects' expectations, but the product doesn't meet the raised expectations the prospect feels cheated and will never try that product again.

Utilizing the personalized messaging that independents appreciated and trusted, we gradually built SFP's product line into a family of have-to-have brands that met both demonstrable and perceived needs of the customer segment we most valued—independent restaurateurs oriented to pizza and Italian food.

P & I restaurateurs throughout the U.S. and Canada developed a fierce loyalty to Stanislaus brands, and woe to the distributor who tried switching them away to their own private-labels. Our customers' brand loyalty was, and remains, incredibly deep, while competitors relying on conventional push strategies went out of business one-by-one. My early-on belief in pull marketing proved justified, and is the source of our company's strong position today.

CHOOSING THE NEXT LEADER

As the time for retirement approached, I thought a lot about the next chapter—whether we continued to own the company or sold it to eager buyers, could the unique culture that made it a work of art be preserved? In addition, would the next leader have the right instincts to defend SFP against the periodic challenges all market leaders inevitably face, and the requisite grit to make gutsy calls? I had witnessed many other entrepreneurial company founders wrestle with the thorny issue of succession and knew it wasn't easy.

Bob Ilse had planned on retiring at the same time I did, so over the preceding two-year period, he and I began quietly evaluating SFP's management team for possible internal candidates. At the same time we secretly met with three outside candidates who had impressive credentials. Despite their talents my recurring concern was that outsiders wouldn't "get" SFP's unique culture before inadvertently destroying it! As this parallel process continued, one candidate emerged from the management team—Tom Cortopassi, my nephew.

Tom's connection with SFP began many years before when as a freshman at Santa Clara University he started working summers during SFP's tomato packing season. A business and finance major, Tom also worked part-time for a Silicon Valley manufacturer in San Jose during his last two years at Santa Clara. With graduation approaching, Tom was offered a full-time job by the Silicon Valley company, but before accepting it came to ask me about going to work full-time at SFP.

"Tom, I'm sorry to say I don't think that's a good idea." My words caused his face to fall.

"Look, Tom, you've always done a good job at everything we asked of you here. But if we hire you now, you wouldn't have the opportunity to experience working for anyone else. I think it's better for you to go to another company and see how they do things. You'll learn the strong and not-so-strong points of their strategy/ tactics. Both categories are important to your career development Tom, so go get some experience elsewhere. Work for another company for at least two years, then let's talk."

I know Tom left my office disappointed, but as I suggested he accepted the Silicon Valley company offer. A couple of years later, Tom wrote me a letter. In it he talked about not having a passion for the high-tech sector and how he really got the canning business. He explained he wanted a career in an industry he understood and appreciated.

So I met with Tom, then had him talk with Bob and a few other senior managers before we hired him. Because we wanted him to learn all aspects of the business, he started with staff work in the office, and then was shifted to the cannery floor during tomato season. Before he headed off to production I said, "Tom, I'm going to tell those guys if you screw up it's okay to fire you." And he knew I meant it.

For a number of years we moved Tom around a lot, and he gained wide experience in the business. For a while he reported to Charles Ross in warehousing, shipping, and distribution; then to Bill Butler in finance and administration; then to Bob Ilse for a solid backgrounding in production. Eventually Tom began working more closely with me on sales issues and reported to Rick Serpa, our Senior VP-Sales.

One thing was clear: wherever we put Tom he excelled. Any SFP employee who initially might have thought he was being fast-tracked because we shared a last name soon saw that was not the case. He worked hard, and over time earned respect throughout the company.

Several years later as I wrestled with the succession question, Bob Ilse urged me to consider Tom as the best candidate to lead the company in the future. "Dino, we could go on and on looking, but Tom's the best shot."

"Bob I agree, my only concern is, will he have the inner steel when gut-check times arrive?"

"I think he will, and besides he is totally committed to the SFP culture."

There was another person I wanted to bring in on the final decision: Bill Butler, my first hire after we bought SFP back in 1978.

"Bill, this is an important decision for the company's future, and I'm not making it unilaterally," I told him. After listing the reasons Bob and I thought Tom should have the position, I added, "I'm counting on you to give me your honest opinion if you think Tom is the right guy or if you don't think so."

Bill didn't answer immediately. " Dino, You don't know how much I wish I was the right guy," he finally said. "But I'm not. Tom is the right guy, and that's the way we should go."

Bill's comment once again demonstrated his unwavering integrity and loyalty, and confirmed that Tom was our best choice. I had one more question. "Will some of our people feel Tom got the job because of nepotism?"

"No," Bill said. "Throughout the company people know Tom has earned his spurs. I can't think of anybody who would believe he got the job because his last name is Cortopassi. And everyone will be delighted you didn't go outside for our new leader."

Today, Tom owns 11 percent of SFP stock and runs SFP. Both internally and with our customers it's clear to everyone that in all respects Tom is "The Man" at SFP.

As for the future of SFP, I believe from Tom on down the right people are in senior positions and they love what they do enough to maintain what they see as "their company." All senior managers own SFP stock. At some point will the company be sold? I really don't know, but I'm confident our four offspring, who like Tom each own 11 percent of the stock, will stick with Tom until he wants to call it a day.

ADDED VALUE AND ARBITRAGE

P rior to business schools' invention of the term "value-added"—or added-value—most entrepreneurs intuitively understood the concept. Buy something at X (commodity pricing), enhance its intrinsic utility to the end-user, and sell it at Y. The spread between X and Y (minus enhancement cost) is the value-added profit.

By contrast, the term "arbitrage" does not add value. It generates profit by buying and selling a product with the same intrinsic utility at price differentials that exist between seller and buyer. Arbitrage relies on enhanced price knowledge, rather than enhanced product utility. The most significant added-value profit in my career came from memorable brands marketed to end-users willing to pay more for an advantage in consistently greater utility. That decades-long saga was personally and professionally very satisfying.

Other combinations of value-added and arbitrage on behalf of Suzy Bel holding company included buying the processing facilities of bankrupt competitors, building profitable businesses from the skeletons, and subsequently reselling those entities at higher values. These turnarounds required a combination of skills including: buying at the right price, disciplined management, sensing when to exit, and finding the right buyer. Two were outright "pick-up the broken pieces" (Gilroy Canning and Sierra Packers); one was an organic products "scratch-start" (Muir Glen Brand); and one was entering the can-making business.

As the reader might expect, turnarounds are not easy, take an enormous amount of energy, and ultimately are not as personally rewarding as building a branded business. The scratch-start was personally rewarding—the Muir Glen brand is still prominent—however, its retail channel nature was not! Those realities not-withstanding, I learned much through these experiences and each caused brain-stretching in new and different directions.

One of the more memorable Suzy Bel gambits came to be known internally as "The Great Peach Bluff," but first some back-ground. By the mid-1980s, consumption of canned peaches had been trending downward for a long time as consumers gravitated from canned to fresh fruit. As a result, the number of companies canning peaches in California had shrunk to five: One branded company (Del Monte), a large farmers' cooperative (TVG), a smaller cooperative; (PCP), and two small independents. (Harter Packing in Yuba City and Bercut-Richards in Sacramento). The only *cash* buyers left for farmers' peaches were Del Monte and the two independents; whereas the two co-ops processed the farmers' peaches, sold the canned fruit in the private-label mar-ketplace, and distributed the cash remaining after expenses to the farmer-members.

Bercut-Richards, an old-line Sacramento company, had been a longstanding family operation, located on 50 acres of metro land on Richards Boulevard with lots of buildings, canning equipment, and cold-storage facilities. Fifteen years after the family company had been sold to a dairy multi-national by Tom Richards II, his high-flying son, known as "T-3," re-purchased it and after four years of mismanagement, drove the new entity into a $37 million bankruptcy.

One of T-3's largest peach growers, Sanner Brothers of Yuba City, petitioned the Sacramento bankruptcy court to lease them the plant as they and other Yuba County peach farmers needed an outlet for their peaches. To help finance the deal, California Peach Growers Association (CPGA) sided with Sanner to take over the cannery. In the hopes of preserving cannery jobs, the Teamsters Union also supported Sanner's petition.

But the bankruptcy court had another option to consider. Two warehousing tycoons had joined forces to buy the plant site, auction off the machinery, and convert the buildings to leased warehousing. In the end, the bankruptcy judge split the baby, allowing the tycoons to buy the property providing they gave Sanner a ten-year lease on the plant site with an option to purchase. With backing from CPGA and an inexperienced Canadian bank, the newly-formed Sanner Packing Inc. struggled through their first year. Unfortunately the managing brother, Jerry Sanner, didn't have a clue about either production or sales, and CPGA had a very difficult time recouping their money.

Unwilling to continue financing Sanner, CPGA was desperate to find a processor with financial strength and industry presence to buy its members' peaches. During the winter, CPGA leadership came to Suzy Bel in the hopes of persuading us to enter the peach canning business. Armed with credible data that showed canned peach consumption declines had ended, and given the reduced number of peach canneries, CPGA made a good case why Suzy Bel should enter that segment, and offered to contract all the peaches processed the prior year by Sanner Packing.

TVG (the large farmer co-op) was a tomato competitor to Suzy Bel's Gilroy Canning Company (GCC), producing and selling both tomatoes and peaches into the private-label market. Bob Ilse, then-president of GCC, and GCC's sales managers were keen on the idea of having canned peaches in their sales mix to better compete with TVG in the private-label segment. However, Sanner Packing wasn't ready to toss in the towel, so Bob Graham, Bob Ilse, and I agreed to present the gambit to the Suzy Bel Board at the upcoming February meeting.

At the meeting, I laid out the background and presented the following scenario: "CPGA controls the entire 450,000-ton California peach crop, of which 200,000 tons goes to Del Monte who packs for the branded segment. The only other cash buyer, Harter Packing, buys 20,000 tons which goes to the private-label segment, as does the 18,000 tons Sanner processed last year. The two co-ops (TVG and PCP) collectively process 220,000 tons and would take over the Sanner tonnage in a heartbeat to eliminate a private-label competitor. But as a price-bargaining association, CPGA management prefers the Sanner peaches to go to a *cash buyer* to justify CPGA's continued price-bargaining existence.

"Gilroy believes they could better sell private-label tomatoes if they also had private-label peaches to sell with them. We could make a play here by contracting the 18,000 tons of CPGA's peaches now, leaving Sanner without any peaches to can. Simultaneously, we would announce we're going to can the 18,000 tons at Gilroy."

In those early days—and true to his prior co-op experience—Bob Ilse was always politically cautious in front of the Suzy Bel Board and he hedged. "Dino, it's true Sanner won't have any peaches to pack, but we won't have any cannery to pack 'em! There's no way we could get Gilroy ready to can peaches in five months!"

"Bob, that's right, but in this situation we need to think like poker players, not like production guys. You and I know that packing peaches at Gilroy is a bluff, but nobody else knows that—least of all Jerry Sanner! In this instance, we either play 'em like we've got 'em, or we fold the hand on peaches."

For the benefit of the Board, I further explained the strategy. "Look, once we have the peaches contracted, Sanner should be the one to blink first, and along with some "cash chum" let us take over the Sacramento plant lease. If for some reason Sanner won't turn the plant over to us, our eleventh-hour fallback plan will be to assign our 18,000 tons of peaches to TVG, who is dying to get their hands on that tonnage."

Neither the Board or the two Bobs were used to that kind of entrepreneurial thinking. "Look guys, to run a bluff we have to put something substantial in the pot! We can't get Sanner to believe we don't need the leased Sacramento plant unless we've committed to buy the 18,000 tons, and appear to be moving forward to pack them at Gilroy!"

The more adventurous board members were ready to approve the gambit, but a couple more risk-averse directors remained dubious.

"How are you gonna do that?" they chorused.

"Well, first we need to advertise. Everyone in the canning industry knows Bob Ilse is an experienced peach guy so we need to get him started shopping for peach equipment—far, wide, and loudly. Bob, you can solicit bids for peach pitters and get somebody started designing plans to build a peach sizer. With your gift of gab, you'll have the whole industry conned in short order."

The board did approve Suzy Bel contracting with CPGA for the 18,000 tons and word quickly spread that Suzy Bel was going into peach canning. TVG Board members were angry at CPGA and at their own management for letting another competitor into the business. Against that backdrop, Bob Ilse began shopping for equipment to add peach processing capability to GCC. He also hired two retired peach guys as highly-visible consultants for our phantom Gilroy peach operation. Keep in mind this was all occurring just five months before the contracted peaches would be ready for delivery.

Meanwhile, Sanner Packing was being pressured by the Canadian bank to sell the remaining canned peaches in inventory from the previous season. By mid-February, I met with Sanner and let him know he could turn over the plant lease to us and that he and other growers would have a home to sell their peaches. Unbeknownst to me, Sanner Brothers were also in financial difficulties at the farming level and Jerry Sanner needed to keep Sanner Packing going to have a job. He countered with an offer to co-pack the peaches for us. In order to do that, Suzy Bel would need to loan Sanner Packing some repair and maintenance money to get the plant ready.

"How much R & M money?" I asked.

"A million should do it."

Seeing this as the opportunity to get our foot in the door at the Sacramento plant, we negotiated an agreement contingent on Sanner getting financing for the co-pack; and in the absence of financing, Sanner's agreement to turn the lease over to us. Thereupon Suzy Bel loaned Sanner Packing one million dollars to get the plant ready for peach canning season. Up to that point it looked like the plan was working, but soon the first fly in the ointment appeared. In April, Sanner came back for more money!

I explained that we had a signed contract; that we had loaned him the million against Sanner Packing co-packing Suzy Bel's peaches; and that he was obligated to do so, or turn over the plant lease.

"Yeah, but if I can't raise more R&M money from you," he said, "Sanner Packing's only alternative is to file bankruptcy. If we go into bankruptcy court, we will lose the lease to the plant and your money will be gone."

By that time TVG management was really kicking itself for letting the tonnage go to us, so our fallback plan of turning over the assignable CPGA contract to TVG remained intact. On the other hand, I felt we would eventually end up with the Sacramento plant and wanted to see another card before folding our hand.

Bob Graham and I had consulted with Suzy Bel's law firm and learned that if Sanner did file bankruptcy, our co-packing contract wouldn't be enforceable. We could show up in bankruptcy court and ask the judge to let us take over the plant lease, but it was impossible to gauge what might happen. Decision time!

After discussing it with the two Bobs, we opted to see another card, so Suzy Bel loaned Sanner Packing another million to continue the plant R & M process. Despite our meting out the money, Sanner and his cannery staff went through the loan at a faster rate than projected and by June, Sanner was back for third loan. During that spring I had many sweaty nights kicking myself for getting us involved with a bankrupt business where contracts depend on the whim of the bankruptcy court. Lesson learned, I promised myself to never again rely on contracts with potential bankrupts.

With peach season just around the corner, the Canadian bank informed Sanner Packing they wouldn't loan any money to operate the plant the upcoming season. Sanner Packing owed us $2.5 million! It was game over for Jerry Sanner, but the question was what would he want in exchange for Sanner Inc. honoring the plant lease turnover as defined in our contract?

In the end, it turned out to be not much more than what we had already put in. Using the mediating services of a retired Sacramento judge, Suzy Bel agreed to pay Sanner's outstanding legal bill, which made his lawyer happy, and we hired Sanner as a consultant for one year at $150,000. In return, Sanner Packing assigned the plant lease to us. We got the keys to the cannery on July 5th, and started packing peaches on July 10th.

Bob Ilse did his "Red Adair thing," jumping right in to coach the plant personnel through the season and got that first year's peaches canned. After the season began, Bob was on familiar ground, which to a seasoned production guy was less stressful to him. During the springtime uncertainty, Bob was on unfamiliar ground and often confessed to "having feathers in my belly."

From the beginning of the play, I knew there was no way we could can those peaches without the Sacramento plant! But as an experienced risk-taker I was pretty sure we had "the edge" and I could see the play's possibilities more clearly than my colleagues, although the road turned out to be bumpier than I anticipated! Later, Bob Graham named the whole episode "The Great Peach Bluff." It was only after we succeeded that I shared with the two Bobs my own sleepless nights that spring.

Over the next nine years, peach canning proved to be a profitable proposition for Suzy Bel, but it took a lot of hard work to create added value.

At the outset, we challenged the Teamsters Sacramento local for a contract we could live with. After a hard-fought campaign, the workers decided a disciplined, financially sound employer was better than the two previous bankrupts. The Union hierarchy was forced to obey the vote of their members but continued to harass Sierra over work rules and we ultimately fought—and won—a second campaign with them four years later.

We formed a wholly owned subsidiary, Sierra Packers, to operate the plant and named Phil Banan, formerly a CPA who was working for Suzy Bel in finance, to run it. With Bob's coaching, and the production team he helped put together, Phil got the peach business organized, and Sierra began increasing peach tonnage processed every year. Additionally, the GCC sales team was able to sell peaches with GCC tomatoes and the Sierra sales team was able to sell tomatoes with Sierra peaches. Both companies began taking private-label market share from TVG—a growing thorn in their side which ultimately resulted in a big Suzy Bel payday when they bought us out.

Within three years Phil Banan began lobbying for Sierra to get into tomatoes. "How about we go into private-label tomatoes? We have all that shelf-size tomato equipment sitting unused in the plant."

"Phil, why do you think the previous owners went bankrupt? The private-label tomato, shelf-size business continues to be squeezed by bigger, meaner supermarket buyers. Gilroy is packing all the private-label tomatoes we can sell, and Sierra isn't going there!"

"Okay, how about organic tomatoes then?"

Before I go any further, note that this exchange took place more than 25 years ago, long before the advent of the many organic products now on the market.

"Phil, nobody knows yet if organic is a fad or a long-term trend; what's clear right now is there's not enough organic business to wad a shotgun. If it does turn into a trend, organic could be a worthwhile business, but if it's a fad we are going to end up going through a lot of start-up pain for no gain."

If nothing else, Phil was enthusiastic and persisted pushing getting into tomato canning. Eventually, the idea of starting an organic brand got hashed out in our Suzy Bel SMC meetings, during which all hands weighed in from the production, sales, and financial perspectives. SMC regulars at that point included Bob Graham, Bob Ilse, Bill Butler, Phil Banan, Julie Ambrose, and me. Even after he had retired, Frank Piciullo would often join us, sharing his common sense as a senior mentor.

Every two weeks SMC met in San Tomo's conference room at 9:00 a.m., worked through lunch, and usually wrapped up by 4:00 or 5:00 p.m. Everyone present got to put items onto the agenda which we would spend the day hashing out. No matter what was being discussed, I insisted on everyone participating and stating their yea-nay opinion, challenging participants to brainstorm aloud.

If anyone tried to shortcut to the chase saying, "Well, Dino, if you think this is a good idea . . . ," I would block off the shortcut at the pass. I didn't want me-tooers or yes people on the SMC, but instead wanted a team willing to disagree with each other in intense examination of the subjects and bouncing ideas around the table. I often characterized SMC's role as the crucible, just like a crucible that turns iron into steel.

Figuratively speaking, our competitors were content with making iron, but to create added value I believed we had to convert iron into steel. For example, it would drive me up the wall if someone tried to float an "I know what we can do" idea before we had identified where we wanted to go. A fellow YPOer had characterized this ass-backwards habit as "trips to Abilene"—going someplace you didn't want to go, just because you had figured out a way to get there!

During the discussions about whether or not to get into organic tomatoes, someone asked, "Who knows if we could even grow organic tomatoes?"

With that, I waved my hands like an NFL referee signaling time out. "That's not the issue," I said. "I *know* we can teach farmers to grow organic tomatoes because as a teenager working for my father and his partners, they essentially grew their tomatoes organically. They just didn't call it organic then."

How, I was asked, could we convince growers to jump through the hoops required to grow certified organic tomatoes?

I shrugged. "That's easy. We just pay them more for organic."

Even after SMC made the decision to go into organic canned tomatoes I wasn't convinced there was much money to be made, although I willingly joined in the decision to give it a try. Why? Because I was thoroughly brand-oriented and if organic became a trend we could be on the ground floor with a have-to-have brand, the epitome of value added. If the organic phenomenon was a passing fad, we could probably get out without too much cost. With that pragmatic mindset, we started packing organic tomatoes at Sierra Packers in 1990.

For months Julie and I struggled to create a distinctive name for the new organic brand, which would be sold in the natural food stores popping up around the country. We wanted a name that would resonate with environmentally-oriented shoppers. I made long lists and went through them with Julie, which she kept rejecting one by one.

"No. Not right. Nope."

Julie was like that; she wouldn't agree with something unless it really clicked for her, and it was why she and I were an effective team for so many years.

Finally we hit upon Muir Glen. The name paid homage to John Muir, a Scot photographer who became a naturalist, author, Sierra Club founder, and patron saint of the environmental movement in America.

The Muir Glen organic brand was positioned in the high-end, environmentally-friendly category, notwithstanding that those expensive products didn't represent much volume. They were only found in natural food stores which tended to be small operators.

There was a saying that you could tell natural food shoppers because they wore Birkenstocks and drove Saabs.

Owner-operators of natural food stores were hungry for environmental validation from their Birkenstocked customers, which made them very receptive to truly organic products. Muir Glen easily lined up distribution through the specialized wholesalers who serviced the natural food retail stores and easily won shelf placement in those outlets. Soon, Muir Glen was in distribution coast to coast, and within three years there wasn't a single natural food store in the United States that didn't have Muir Glen on its shelves! Unfortunately, 100 percent distribution still didn't amount to much volume because the environmentally-friendly market remained so small.

When it came to organic foods, economics was and is part of the problem, although more so back then. What Muir Glen sold for $1.00, the distributor sold for $1.50 to a natural food store. Natural food distribution costs are high because of low volume. What the store bought for $1.50, they would mark up to $2.50, so $1.00 of Muir Glen sales cost the consumer two and a half times as much! At the same time, non-organic canned tomatoes were selling in grocery stores for $1.25 a can because supermarket distribution involved much less markup, and private-label tomatoes cost much less than organic tomatoes. Consumers willing to pay the higher amount did so because they believed in supporting the environmentally-friendly concept, but they were decidedly in the minority.

As natural foods stores became more visible, conventional supermarkets began to notice. Hoping to attract natural food shoppers into their conventional stores, supermarkets began creating dedicated natural food sections. Because Muir Glen was a well-known national organic brand, we had no problem getting into select supermarkets with natural sections. I say "select" because natural foods' volume was still so small across a given chain that Muir Glen couldn't get into the internal warehouse system where distribution costs are much lower.

Within a given chain, only those stores situated in affluent neighborhoods or near universities (i.e., Birkenstockers driving Saabs!)

established natural food sections. As a result Muir Glen had to find its own way to get product delivered to supermarkets with natural food sections. That could only be done by "Direct Store Distributors" (DSDs) but at very high distribution cost.

In spite of these formidable economic hurdles, the Muir Glen team built the most successful organic brand of that era in the United States—but unfortunately a grand total of only $20 million a year in sales. In order to achieve even that relatively low level of sales, Muir Glen had to develop many different items including soups, ketchups, tomatoes, and pasta sauces.

Eventually, Muir Glen faced a major strategic decision. We couldn't solve the ugly math of high distribution costs without greater dollar volume of each supermarket drop. Muir Glen CEO Bill McGaughey, an old friend from YPO days, who had done an excellent job overseeing the company and owned stock, estimated we needed to reach $100 million in annual sales to materially reduce distribution costs. To get to $100 million in sales, we would have to go out and buy two or three other organic brands to combine with Muir Glen.

Bill opined, "We've either got to become acquirers or sellers. There are other companies in the same place as Muir Glen who would acquire us."

"What do you want to do, Bill?" I asked.

"At my age, I'd rather be a seller than a buyer."

"That's fine with me, go find a buyer."

Bill got Muir Glen sold in 1998, and as a brand it's going stronger than ever today. The natural foods industry matured from its early years into an estimated $25-30 billion in 2011 sales. While consolidation occurred and overall sales continued to grow, prices for natural food products at the supermarket level have continued to decline and frankly, I don't believe organic packers are any more profitable today than 20 years ago.

The Muir Glen experience was an innovative product success, a marketing success, but not a value-added success because we only earned a modest return on invested capital at the time of its sale.

Contemporaneous with the Muir Glen saga, our Sacramento peach canning business, Sierra Packers, kept gaining a bigger slice (pun intended!) of the total California peach pack every year. This growth in market share was also providing comparatively better returns for Sierra growers than TVG co-op was providing for its growers. As a result, in the peach grower community TVG was annually embarrassed by our comparatively better performance. Which is why as years went on, TVG management wanted Sierra out of the peach business in the worst way, and in the end were eventually willing to pay a lot of money to make that happen.

In and of itself, the lead-in, deal construction, deal consummation, is an interesting saga! However, this book is already too long, so that story will have to wait for its telling at a different time.

In addition to the moderate but steady profits Sierra earned during nine years of peach canning, Suzy Bel sold the Sierra Packers enterprise and the equipment in the Sacramento plant to TVG for $32 million in cash. We retained ownership of the plant real estate which we leased to TVG for five years at a good rent.

After TVG moved out, Suzy Bel sold the 52-acre Richards Boulevard property for $9 million and its cannery sewage rights for the equivalent of $11 million. In summary, from both added value and arbitrage, Suzy Bel earned $35-plus millions of exit profits all of which arose from The Great Peach Bluff!

Another added-value gambit that turned into quite an adventure involved Suzy Bel becoming a self-manufacturer of tin cans—it falls under the heading of "hedging the future."

Simply put, our three canneries were in the business of filling a great number of metal cans. When Stanislaus was acquired in 1978 and for a number of years thereafter, it bought its cans from National Can Company, the second largest manufacturer in the U.S., and we enjoyed excellent personal relationships with the company's senior management. All that changed in the mid-1980s when a series of consolidations shook up the canning industry, and threatened the cost structure of our canneries.

It was the heyday of financier Michael Milken's high-yield junk bonds, and still a few years removed from Milken's subsequent indictment for racketeering and securities fraud. In 1985, with his junk-bond machinery going full tilt, Milken provided financing to two unknowns from Brooklyn, Nelson Peltz and Peter May, to tender for and take over publicly-traded National Can Company. The National Can buyout for $460 million was big news, and it got bigger the following year when with similar junk-bond financing from Milken, Peltz and May bought American Can Company for $570 million! They then merged the two companies into American National Can—a can-making behemoth that became a quasi-monopoly in California.

A number of decades prior, the can industry was an *actual* oligopoly of about six manufacturers who manipulated can prices until a group of canners filed a lawsuit. The U.S. Justice Department intervened, and forced all the can manufacturers to sign a consent decree, in which they agreed to not exercise their power to control the limited market or collude to set can prices. Notwithstanding the consent decree, the manufacturers had been able to hold can prices high enough that Contadina, which was owned by Carnation Company, Del Monte, and all three big California co-ops had found it profitable to self-manufacture their own cans.

With the 1986 merger of the number one and number two can manufacturers the California landscape dramatically shifted. This new, more powerful consolidation had me very concerned about future prices for the huge quantity of containers our canneries purchased. The management of American Can had a well-deserved reputation as hard-asses, while the National Can guys were much easier to work with. They were all now under the same roof, but unfortunately for us, Peltz and May had awarded almost all the senior management slots to the hard-asses. Without competition, can prices were bound to escalate and I knew we needed a defensive strategy.

I had previously met a senior guy at the number three manufacturer, Continental Can Company, at the Harvard Agribusiness Seminar, so I approached him for a chat. Continental had a relatively small market share in California and wanted to exit the can assembly business, but remain in the tin coating of metal plate used in the making of cans. In fact, they had a can-making assembly plant in Modesto that they were interested in selling. So after a briefing from Bob Ilse, who understood can-making from his prior life at Cal-Can co-op, I set up a meeting with the Container Division President at Continental's Omaha headquarters.

After some discussion, he offered to sell us their Modesto can assembly plant and supply us the coated tin-plate we needed on a favorable long-term contract. The purchase price for the Modesto can-making plant was fair and we shook hands on the deal which closed shortly thereafter. The long-term, coated-plate contract remained to be worked out.

While I was hustling to put together the deal with Continental, the anticipated price increase from the new American National behemoth came in the form of a brusque phone call from an unpleasant guy we had run into before at American Can who I will refer to as "Steve Smith." Sans any attempt to justify the price increase, Smith had announced to Bob Ilse that our can prices for the coming year would be dramatically higher and if we wanted cans Bob needed to sign the contract.

As the ink dried on Suzy Bel's purchase of the Modesto can assembly plant from Continental, I allowed myself the luxury of a message back to Smith to the effect that he should become intimate with himself and the horse he rode in on!

Thereafter, we took on the steel workers union that had been entrenched at Continental's Modesto assembly plant by terminating the old contract, something a new buyer could do, by reestablishing a new seniority structure, and by restructuring wages, pension benefits, and contract work rules. The union was of course livid. But once again the workers wanted to keep working, voted to accept our proposals, and we began making cans with coated plate purchased from Continental.

Within 18 months of the American-National merger, Pechiney S.A., a state-owned French conglomerate, acquired the company from Peltz and May enabling these two smart guys from Brooklyn to pay off Milken's junk bonds and walk away with a major-league bundle of cash. Pechiney promptly sent Jean-Pierre Ergas from Paris to Chicago to take over running the company as CEO. One of the first things Monsieur Ergas did was to study American-National's sales books, and when he got to the #10-size cans, he noticed that a large, long-time California account—Suzy Bel—was no longer a customer. He asked Mike Hehman, our friend from the old National Can days, what had happened and Mike told his new French boss the truth: that shortly after the merger, American-National had tried to jack up Suzy Bel's can prices, and as a result Suzy Bel had gone into self-manufacture.

As Hehman later related to me, Ergaz asked, "Is there any chance we can get them back?"

"I don't know," Mike responded. "But if you want, I can call Dino and find out."

"By all means, see if Mr. Cortopassi would like to come to Chicago."

When Mike called me, he said, "The big boy from France would like to talk to you. How would you feel about responding to his invitation to come to Chicago for a meeting?"

We weren't saving any money by making our own cans versus what we had previously paid for them, but we were saving money compared to what Steve Smith had tried to charge us. All along however, I had considered the main value of having our own can plant was as a "scare card." In blackjack, when the dealer turns up an ace or a face card, it's called a scare card because of its probability of forming a winning hand. From the beginning my strategy had been to use our self-manufacturing capability to negotiate a beneficial, long-term deal with a can manufacturer, so although the invitation to reopen discussions was welcome, I didn't want to appear overly eager.

"Well, Mike, I don't know," I said. "Do you think it's worth my coming?"

"Yeah, I do," Mike said. "If nothing else, you can tell off that jerk Steve Smith."

"Will the French guy be in the meeting?"

"Yes."

"How about you, Mike? I would want you there."

"I can set it up to be at the meeting, but in that case so will Steve."

"Okay, you can tell Ergas I will accept the invitation on that basis."

"Do you want to bring anybody?"

"No," I said. "I'll come alone."

I was received in Chicago very graciously by Jean-Pierre Ergas and along with Mike Hehman and Steve Smith was shown into his private executive dining room high above Michigan Avenue where we were served lunch and engaged in general talk.

After lunch Ergas said, "It's time to talk business." Looking at me he said, "Would you care to tell me why we lost Suzy Bel's can business?"

"I could tell you but he won't like it," I said, pointing at Smith.

"Oh?" Ergas said. "Well, please go on."

"You lost our business because Mr. Smith is an arrogant jerk who tried to muscle us on pricing."

Smith reddened, but obviously was under orders to remain silent.

When Ergas asked me to expand on that statement, I said okay but not in the presence of Mr. Smith. I had said what I wanted to say to Smith's face, and I didn't want him to sit in on any new discussions.

Ergas said, "Well if you prefer that Steve leaves, then Mike probably should, too."

After the two of them left, I continued. "I knew the American-National merger could lead to some pricing pressure. But instead of trying to work with their biggest California customer, the merged company put arrogant jerks like Steve Smith in charge. Suzy Bel decided we weren't going to be held hostage to that and that we would make our own cans."

Unflappably polite, Ergas responded: "I understand your feeling that way but things are different now, Mr. Cortopassi. Pechiney has a different philosophy regarding our important customers. What if we could develop a long-term contract that you could be comfortable with?"

It was obvious that Mike Hehman had prepared him for this meeting!

"Well, Mr. Ergas, we are in the business of filling cans, not making them," I said. "However, we are not afraid to continue as we did this year, and are happy to continue doing so in the future."

Without missing a beat Ergas said, "I understand completely. However could I send a team to California to see if something acceptable to you can be worked out? We need your business. We have a plant in Modesto that is operating at less than half capacity since we lost your business."

Actually, I already knew that because their can manufacturing plant was right across the street from one of Stanislaus' warehouses.

"Well I suppose that can't hurt, but we're not interested in talking with Steve Smith."

"Oh, no, it's clear Mr. Smith should not be involved. It seems you have a good relationship with Mr. Hehman?"

"Yes, we got along fine for years when it was National Can."

"Good, then I'll have Mike lead the team. Thank you very much for coming to Chicago. I assure you we will put our best foot forward so that I can welcome you back as our most important California customer."

By the time Mike and two other guys from their Chicago headquarters arrived at our offices in California, Bob Ilse and I had made out a laundry list of everything we could hope for in a contract using a cost-driven formula to set the maximum price they could charge us for cans. Included would be a clause that if they sold cans to another canner for lower than our formula price, we would be given that lower price on all our cans. Finally, we had full audit rights of their internal books, allowing us to send in our CPA for a confidential audit every year. We negotiated the final contract containing virtually all of our laundry list, plus selling them our Modesto can-making plant at a modest profit!

Those 18 months of self-manufacturing cans allowed us to negotiate a very beneficial can contract that Stanislaus is still using 25 years later. Pechiney subsequently sold American-National to another can manufacturer, Silgan, who accepted and renewed the original long-term contract.

The decisive move into can self-manufacturing to gain negotiating strength continued to pay significant dividends because we had successfully hedged our future.

BULLS, BEARS, AND HOGS

Over the years, I've been asked many times for stock-market guidance. I always respond: "My advice is worth what it costs you, and since it's free you will probably not value it." That's not meant as a commentary on the person doing the asking; it's just human nature that we don't pay much attention to free advice. With that disclaimer, here's how I look at passive investments, e.g., financial securities.

For starters, owning gold is per se not a "good" investment. Gold doesn't earn interest; it doesn't build factories; it doesn't do anything. It just sits there. Aside from personal adornment, gold's only purpose is to protect its owner from the buying power erosion of "fiat money"—printed currency not backed by precious metal. Other than fiat money protection, owning gold reflects the "greater fool" investment theory: you do not make money owning gold unless you sell it to someone else at a price greater than you bought it for. Ergo, were you a fool to buy it, or is the guy who buys it from you the greater fool?

From time to time I have held gold ownership via the futures markets. On the other hand, buying fire insurance is also not a "good investment," unless of course your house burns down! However, I did so/do so only as a hedge (insurance policy) against cash Joan and I hold in the bank; i.e., I do believe it is national policy for the value of cash to erode over time relative to things we will buy. Cash held in the bank is exposed to erosion of our purchasing power, and yes, printing money to fund federal deficits does cause that erosion. The process is misnamed "inflation" as if the price of everything is going up when in fact nothing is going up; fiat money is going down!

With respect to stock ownership, I believe the most important element to successful stock investment is fundamental conviction. There have been times I bought stocks that subsequently increased in price but I wasn't there for the big celebration. Why? Because I didn't have a fundamental belief in that company. As Ben Graham succinctly phrased in *The Intelligent Investor*, stock prices are subject to the moods of "Mr. Market." In the absence of deep conviction about the underlying fundamentals of a company, most of us end up being short-term investors. Unless one is a Wall Street pro, short-term investing is a losing strategy. On the other hand, holding a positive fundamental belief tends to immunize us from Mr. Market moods and makes us become long-term investors. As Ben Graham's more famous disciple, Warren Buffet says, "Our holding time is forever."

As for bonds—corporate, government or any other type—the only time they are a good deal is when there is asset deflation and correspondingly declining interest rates. It was a great idea to own bonds in 1929 because the value of most other assets went down after the Stock Market Crash, and the value of money (cash) went up. Since bonds are essentially a cash basis asset, owning them in deflationary times is good, providing their issuer doesn't go broke! During times of persistent Buying Power Erosion (BPE) however, owning bonds is a mistaken way to "feel safe."

Let me explain why the term BPE is more accurate than the misnomer "inflation." Assume you have $1,000 cash in your pocket, and that $1,000 will buy a nice suit today that you could get utility from for five years. But if instead of purchasing the suit, you buy a $1,000 bond maturing in five years with a yield of 4 percent interest, you will receive $40 per year plus $1,000 five years later. Now assuming a 4 percent annual increase in the cost of suits (not compounded), today's $1,000 suit will cost you $1,200 to buy when you get your $1,000 back. Which means that including the $200 of interest you collected, your five years of bond ownership earned *zero* measured in comparative buying power. Moreover, if you paid income taxes—and spent the balance—of the $200 interest collected, when you go to buy that suit five years from now, you'll have to settle for one that's 20 percent cheaper than what you could buy today. That's not a good deal! Which is why I have always believed owning bonds is a bad idea except for rare instances like the recent five years (2007-2012) of asset deflation. "Inflation" is the political alias substituted for *depreciation* of fiat money that has been going on since the time of the Romans!

When it comes to stocks in general, I have three don't-forget rules:

RULE #1: *The trend is your friend. Don't fight it.* When the general market trend is slanted downward, being long any stock means you are fighting Mr. Market and vice-versa. Note: If your fundamental belief in a company remains intact, you can ignore Mr. Market moods since like Warren Buffett your contemplated holding time is forever. In and of itself, I do not believe Mr. Market's mood is a good enough reason to own stocks.

RULE #2: *Markets go up (or down) until they don't!* Mr. Market does change his mind. When your investments are consonant with Mr.

Market's long-term mood, remain alert for that trend reversing. Don't be mulish in fighting a definitive long-term trend reversal. Lots of investors do get stubborn, which leads to my final rule.

RULE #3: *Sometimes the bulls win and sometimes the bears win, but hogs never win.* What is a "hog" in stock-market terms? A hog is only happy when he/she sells at the top of the market, or when he/she buys at the bottom. Trying to pick tops or bottoms is a sure recipe to lose money over time. Several years ago, one of my duck club friends bought a high-tech stock for $10 a share that soon began going up. Each week he would tell me it had gone up two points or whatever. "You should get in it, Dino."

By the way, I have never owned stock in high-tech companies only because I don't understand their business and therefore *do not have a fundamental belief in them.*

By the latter part of the hunting season my friend's high-tech stock had hit $120 a share, but then Mr. Market had a techie mood swing and the stock quickly dropped and stabilized at $90. I asked him why he didn't sell at $90/share and capture an $80 capital gain on his $10 investment? My friend admitted that an eight-fold gain was terrific but he was going to wait for it to go back up to $120 and then he would sell.

In other words he couldn't accept selling at less than the stock's high, even though that sale would have captured an 800 percent profit in four months! So what happened? My friend rode the stock all the way down to the $10 share he had bought it for because all along the way he couldn't accept less than what it could have been. Now my friend is a really nice guy who would give me the shirt off his back, but in this case he demonstrated the stock market axiom of *why hogs never make money.*

STOCK MARKET CONVICTION

My most profitable stock-market investment in a single company could be a book titled, "Surfing the Dreyer's Wave," but it's really about deeply-held convictions. This story began for me when Gary Rogers joined YPO and we got to know each other. An engineering graduate of UC Berkeley and an MBA graduate of Harvard Business School, from the beginning Gary impressed me as a real strategist. He and a restaurant partner bought Dreyer's Grand Ice Cream in 1975 with venture-capital financing. How Gary had ended up at the helm of Dreyer's is a fascinating story, and since I've heard him recount it publicly I am not telling tales out of school by repeating it here.

After receiving his MBA, Gary went to work for a high-profile consulting company in San Francisco, during which time he went into the restaurant business with a UC Berkeley friend, Rick Cronk, with venture capital backing. Their first restaurant in the San Francisco Bay Area seemed fairly successful so they opened another, and then a third. Unfortunately, their fine-wine theme was a little ahead of its time, their restaurants were losing money, and the company was having difficulty paying its bills, so Gary went to see Dreyer's president about the large ice cream bill the restaurants owed. Gary's plan was to explain why it would take some time to pay down their account.

Shown into Bill Dreyer's office, Gary had no sooner sat down when the phone rang and Dreyer took the call.

Groaning "Oh, no, no," Dreyer hung up and placed his head in his hands.

Embarrassed, Gary offered to come back another time, but Dreyer demurred, and went on to explain that Dreyer's bank had just turned down his loan request to build a new ice cream factory. "I don't know what we're going to do," said Dreyer, who had run the Oakland-based business on College Avenue for many years. "We can't make enough ice cream in this facility to meet our sales growth. I am so tired of fighting it."

Gary listened with increasing interest, and as he walked out of the office he was already thinking of where he could borrow the money to buy the company. For a guy who went in to explain why he couldn't pay his ice cream bill, this was a bold idea.

Gary subsequently acknowledged he was in the right spot at the right time that day in Bill Dreyer's office. But while that's true, the difference between winners and also-rans is the ability to see hidden opportunity, the risk-appetite to reach for it, and the ability to manage the risk. As it later turned out, Gary and Rick tripled the company's ice cream volume in the same ice cream plant Bill Dreyer bemoaned as being too small.

Some time after Dreyer's went public I started buying the stock because I had a fundamental belief it would be a good investment, based on a sturdy tripod of reasons.

First and foremost, Dreyer's had their own truck fleet servicing stores directly, and didn't rely on supermarkets' internal distribution systems to deliver and stock their ice cream. Direct store delivery (DSD) was a *huge* advantage! No other ice cream company had DSD; in fact at that time the only other food manufacturer delivering with their own trucks was snack-food giant Frito-Lay.

Secondly, I had abiding faith that Gary's entrepreneurial and managerial ability combined with DSD capability would grow Dreyer's from a small regional player to industry prominence. I didn't know how far or how fast but I was confident that Gary was a very good jockey and Dreyer's a very good horse.

Thirdly, at that time the U.S. ice-cream industry was highly fragmented, with some 400 ice cream manufacturers across the country. I reasoned that a well-managed company with a big vision could gain significant market share by becoming an industry consolidator of small companies.

So the combination of these three sturdy legs led me to a deeply-held fundamental belief that Dreyer's had the potential to be a real winner. And as had been my practice in poker, business, and life, when confident of having the edge, I'm willing to make a significant bet.

However, because of the thin "float" (stock availability) it wasn't easy to accumulate a significant stake in Dreyer's stock. As a result, an order to buy a few hundred shares would automatically push up the stock price because daily trading volume was very light. I directed our family financial officer, Don Lenz, to begin chipping away at buying Dreyer's stock with price limit orders to avoid pushing up per-share price.

In December 1992, participants in the Dreyer's play included Joan and me personally, Cortopassi Farms Inc., the Cortopassi Foundation, our kids' trust, and Suzy Bel Inc. Eventually a coterie of colleagues, relatives, and friends would also personally invest in

Dreyer's based on my deeply held conviction. The family and companies I managed owned 20,000 shares at an average cost of $10/share. That month, the market value per share was $12.25, which meant that on $200,000 invested, we had $45,000 in unrealized profit. In subsequent years Dreyer's continued to grow, and as the market permitted, we kept buying.

During 1996, our group crossed the 5 percent ownership threshold which required filing public notice with the SEC, and by the end of 1997, we had an unrealized multi-million dollar profit on a significant Dreyer's position.

Then, in 1998, two bad things happened to Dreyer's. The first bad thing was Ben and Jerry's Inc. canceling Dreyer's profitable distribution contract to distribute Ben and Jerry's Ice Cream (via Dreyer's trucks) to grocery stores. The second bad thing was the price of butter fat futures (the pricing mechanism for the cream Dreyer's bought), started going up significantly as a result of futures manipulation by a large Midwestern farmer co-op.

As other shareholders began selling, the price of Dreyer's stock started to slip downward allowing us to buy more stock on each down-tick. From January to September of 1998, our multi-million dollar unrealized profit swung to a multi-million dollar unrealized loss. Ouch! So why didn't I start selling Dreyer's stock on the negative news like many other shareholders?

First, because I never wavered in my fundamental belief in the Dreyer's tripod. Fundamental belief in a company arms you to stay calm when Mr. Market starts to panic. Secondly, the stock decline was making stock available for us to buy. During those nine months, I recall Don Lenz periodically reporting we had picked up another block of shares.

"Yeah, Don, that's good," I would say. "As long as at some point it stops going down. *But keep buying.*"

And so we did, pretty much investing all our available cash, and then near the lowest price point, buying on margin. While Mr. Market was seeing nothing but stormy weather ahead for Dreyer's, the manipulated price of butter-fat started to fall back down to where it should have been, and Dreyer's reported slightly increased earnings.

Between September and December 1998, our very significant unrealized loss had shrunk back to about break-even. Whew! That was a relief! Within a few more months, break-even had turned into a gain and after that, Dreyer's stock price and our unrealized profits just kept truckin' upwards.

At the high-water mark, our group was the third largest holder of Dreyer's stock at 10.3 percent ownership. Only Nestle at 20 percent and GE Capital at 20 percent owned more than our group. During early 1999 we took down some unrealized profits in a series of sales circa $70/share. When our ownership stake was down to 6 percent we stopped selling and remained there until the next big Dreyer's event.

In 2002, Gary closed a sale of Dreyer's to Nestle for $2 billion! Dreyer's stock was valued at $83 a share, and all Dreyer's share-holders—us included—were bought out at that price.

Not counting personal investments by colleagues, relatives, and friends, when I got around to adding it up, all the combined entities in our group made a pre-tax profit that was like hitting a home run in the 9th inning of the 7th game of the World Series! After the public announcement because of ongoing FTC negotiations Dreyer's and Nestle were engaged in, I didn't communicate with Gary. However, when he and the rest of the Stanislaus Advisory Board came to San Tomo for our regular quarterly meeting, I had a special gift for him.

Back in the 1970s, after one of Cortopassi Farms' good years, we had ended up the year with a sum of disposable cash. I put two-thirds of it in Joan's and my personal savings account, and used one-third to buy one 100-ounce pure gold bar to put in our safe-deposit box. Showing Joan the bar, I said reassuringly, "Honey we're never going to be poor again no matter what happens because this gold bar will be sitting in our safe-deposit box!"

Twenty-five years later I removed that gold bar from the safe-deposit box and had it mounted on a special plaque to present to Gary when he walked into San Tomo's boardroom. The inscription read: "To Gary Rogers, who redefined what rich means. From Dino and Joan."

BONANZA AND BORASCA

After 50-plus years in a diversity of business enterprises, in retirement I am still a farmer at heart. I've traded a dusty pickup for a dusty SUV, but daily attire often includes work shoes, Levis, and a favorite John Deere cap as I make the rounds of farmland we own and lease to younger farmers I helped get started in business. Today, between four ranches held under various family entities, we own 7,000 acres of San Joaquin County farmland producing annual crops of rice, tomatoes, alfalfa, and corn, and perennial crops of apples, cherries, olives, walnuts, and wine grapes.

On a recent morning the young manager-partner of a lessee company was riding with me on a windshield tour of the farm. As we passed a field, I said, "Jose, it looks to me like you're putting on a little too much water here." As we passed another field, I made another observation about something I spotted that needed attention.

"Dino, you see more going by on the road at 25 miles an hour than I see standing in the field," Jose said.

"Yeah, but I didn't always. Don't worry if you really want it, you will learn to do that, too."

"How do you catch those little things so fast?"

"Jose, it comes from developing a critical eye, and looking for what's wrong with the picture. When I was in your shoes many years ago, I didn't have enough time to admire what was going right and got in the habit of looking for anything wrong."

The habit of always looking for what wasn't right came from my dear mother. From the time Teresa became the cook and housekeeper for the Lucky Ranch crew, she had to work sun to sun. If she stopped to admire what was right she would run out of time for what needed attention. Well, in my early business years that's me to a T. While this approach is time efficient, it could be a real pain in the butt to those I worked with.

As a management style my ability to see what was wrong and an impatience to get it right was irritating to others. Even when something was going pretty well, if it wasn't perfect I would point out improvements that could be made. As a result, I came off as hypercritical.

Over the years I worked hard to moderate that irritating management style. YPO colleagues helped me understand the importance of giving out attaboys to employees. I was counseled, "Catch your people doing something right and then give them a positive stroke: 'Gee, you're doing a nice job!'" It was excellent advice which I strived to follow, although I ruefully came to learn that ten attaboys could be wiped out by a single criticism, often delivered with blue language.

I grew up not receiving many attaboys myself—in our family "compliments" were the absence of criticism, which meant you must be doing okay. To overcome that negative reinforcement, I worked hard to praise employees. Some bosses gave out attaboys/attagirls for work or results that were at best average, which was something I just couldn't bring myself to do. Those bosses were wisely following another management verity: "Give your employees a reputation to live up to!"

The biggest regret in my business life was being too hard on those I had high expectations of. Don't get me wrong: I don't regret telling off jerks I encountered and letting them know our paths should never cross again. Rather, it was the people to whom I was closest and who I cared the most about that I could have been kinder to both at work and at home instead of letting innate intensity get the better of me.

In later years that occurred less frequently but even today I recall some incidents with embarrassment and regret. I wish I could go back and change that behavior, and very much appreciate everyone who loved me despite my behavioral flaws.

I was lucky to have been born in the late 1930s. I often say to my contemporaries that we had the best of it. Our generation was too young to face death in World War II or Korea, and too old for Vietnam. Additionally, getting out of school in the late 1950s were opportune times for young people starting out. America was starting on a long run of good times, while other countries—Asia and much of Europe—were working on recovery from the devastation of war.

Not unlike a century earlier during the 1950s and 1960s America was still a nation of relatively smaller communities. Those were awfully good years; during which the barriers to entry in business were much lower. Whether you were a tradesman, shopkeeper or farmer, the hurdles to getting started in "owning a piece of the rock" were not as high. It troubles me that the barriers to entry are so much higher today for young people starting out, and I fear for the impact that is having on our free-enterprise system.

Today, everything is so much bigger because of the consolidation in every sector of the American economy. Whether it's goods or services, fewer suppliers are providing a greater amount of productivity. Free-market capitalists argue that consolidation has made for more efficiency and is better for consumers which is true. However, the flip-side of that consumer benefit is a reduced number of entrepreneurial entry points for someone trying to become a producer/supplier.

Take retail, for example. In any town in America back in the '50s and '60s, there were independent drugstores, grocery stores, hardware stores, clothing stores, etc. An employee in one of those stores could save some money for a down payment, take a note back from the owner when he retired, and go into business. They had a real shot at getting started. What does the retail sector look like today? Big Box chain stores in every sector. And the barriers to entry? Other than high-tech, they are higher than almost anyone can jump!

As for farming, my brother and I began by renting small acreages of bad dirt. There was no guarantee that we would succeed, but at least we were able to surmount the barrier to entry. Smaller rental parcels like that no longer exist. And the capital requirements of farm equipment are exponentially higher. Multiply by a factor of at least ten the initial $25,000 loan we got to buy used equipment and grow crops. For young men and women who want to get into farming today the ladders of opportunity are so far apart you have to either inherit or marry a farm!

Getting Ahead was the mission of my father's generation and it became mine as well. That's why immigrants came to America, what they worked so hard here to achieve, and what became my model. With sky-high barriers to entry in so many industries, I'm afraid the American Dream will remain that—just a dream and beyond reach.

Recently I was asked what I would say to my father if I had the opportunity to speak to him one more time. My answer was I would say the same thing to both my parents: *"Grazie! Mille Grazie!"*

There are many things for which I would thank my father, but his volatile temper and the boyhood whippings are not among them. Thankfully I got past that and forgave him for that flaw. As I'm reminded every morning when I look in the mirror, nobody's perfect!

I would thank my mother for her insatiable curiosity to know the why of things, and despite her abrupt demeanor, for her loving, compassionate heart. She held me to high performance standards but was proud of what I became.

I would thank both Amerigo and Teresa for their personal qualities and bedrock values which became part of who I am. They lived with honor and integrity, and modeled the value of having a good name. By example they showed if you work hard and are not afraid to take a risk, you can Get Ahead!

1984—WATERLOO   *Amerigo/Teresa 50 Golden Years.*

Celebrating the Life of
Amerigo Giovanni Cortopassi
January 2, 1904 - July 8, 1998

On July 8, 1998, after 90 years of productive, happy life, and four years of Alzheimer's deterioration, Amerigo Cortopassi died at home in the presence of his loving family.

Amerigo was born near Lucca, Italy on January 2, 1904, the seventh of ten children born to Alberto Cortopassi and Artemesia Rugani Cortopassi. At the age of seventeen, Amerigo emigrated to California under the sponsorship of his cousins Luigi and Giorgio Rugani, and subsequently became a proud citizen of this country which he loved.

Amerigo was a farmer. In partnership with other Italian-Americans he developed, owned and operated farms in the Linden and Delta areas near Stockton.

Amerigo was a family man. In 1934 he married Teresa Avansino of Linden. Their sixty-four year union resulted in a proud legacy of three children, nine grandchildren, and thirteen great-grandchildren.

Amerigo loved life. In addition to his passion for his work, Amerigo enjoyed hunting, fishing, mushrooming, playing cards, making salami, making wine, and the company of family and friends. He was an active member of the Italian Gardeners Society and Waterloo Gun & Bocci Club.

Memorial services are 9:00 a.m. Saturday, July 11th at St. Michael's Church in the Morada area. A "Celebration of Life" reception and dinner will follow the services. The family requests that in lieu of flowers, Memorial gifts be made to: Alzheimer's Aid Society of Northern California, 105 S. Washington Street, Lodi, CA 95240.

CIRCA 1999 *"Big Nonna" Teresa with 10 of her 15 great-grandchildren!*

Most importantly, they demonstrated that Getting Ahead did not rule out having a close family and good friends.

Early on I saw that life could be a banquet, yet many people starved to death. I resolved that my life would be a fulfilling and challenging banquet. Now well into my seventh decade, I bear witness to having experienced a wonderful life crammed with interesting people and fascinating work. Along the way, I realized that learning how to handle failure was as important as learning how to handle success. Entrepreneurs must learn to get back up after being knocked down. We all make mistakes and we all can have bad luck; in other words we all have ups and downs. Those who learn how to handle the downers and get back up are still in the game when uppers arrive.

In gold-mining terms, I've known Bonanza and Borasca. I've discovered mines rich in ore and gotten stuck with unproductive dry holes. After you've experienced both, you can never luxuriate in Bonanza because Borasca could be around the next bend in the road.

More important than the banquet of a fulfilling business career, has been the banquet of 55 years with my loyal, loving, life partner Joan, our four loving children, Gino, Katie, Becky, Dave, and our ten loving grandchildren, Sofia, Caitlin, Julia, Tucker, Jackson, Madeline, Trevor, Carli, Cort, and Natalie. I am so grateful for each of you and for all of you!

Joan and I were raised in very dissimilar family environments, but fortunately with similar family values. As a result, we had to struggle through the dissimilarities to build a life-long marriage on the bedrock of shared values. My heart is full of gratitude for Joan's enduring love and for her working on my sharp-edged shortcomings. She has been a wonderful lover, partner, mother, and grandmother. Honey, *Mille Grazie*, for the banquet we have shared—it's been a great life!

CIRCA 1998   *Family (plus "Friends") cruise of Maine coast via chartered yacht.*

ABOVE: *Horatio Alger Board meeting in Montana.*

OPPOSITE: CHRISTMAS—2010   *All ten grandchildren, two happy Nonni, and Tank!*

NONNO'S BIG FIVE
FOR THE GRANDKIDS

1.

Above all, always keep your word! Your word is your most valuable possession—*never* compromise it—regardless of the temptations to do so. Said another way, don't make promises you can't keep—and keep every promise you make!

2.

Take personal responsibility for your actions. The world does not owe you a living or the absence of tough breaks. Most of us get our share of good luck and bad. In both cases, give it your best shot, deal with the outcome, and be ready when it turns.

3.

Always be curious of the "why" of things. Relentlessly seeking the why of things is the pathway to lifelong growth in your knowledge base. When someone answers your question, it's amazing how much more you can learn by using "The Rolling Why!"

4.

All along the way, look for mentors in life. Seek advice from champions in their fields. There is always good reason(s) why someone becomes a champion, and those are the mentors you want. All along the way I was blessed with knowledgeable mentors whose counsel helped me succeed.

5.

Don't let thoughts overrule your feelings. Treasure a keen and active mind but listen to your feelings. Unfortunately, I learned this later than I should have. Fortunately, your Nonna helped me understand that feelings trump thoughts.